AQA GCSE

SPANISH
Foundation

COMPLETE REVISION AND PRACTICE

José Antonio García Sánchez
Tony Weston

Contents

 Shade in each level of the circle as you feel more confident and ready for your exam.

How to use this book — iv

Basics — 6
- Knowledge
- Retrieval

Theme 1 People and lifestyle — 22–56

1.1 Identity and relationships with others — 22
- Knowledge
- Retrieval

1.2 Healthy living and lifestyle — 32
- Knowledge
- Retrieval

1.3 Education and work — 39
- Knowledge
- Retrieval

Theme 1 Exam practice — 49
- Practice

Theme 2 Popular culture — 57–80

2.1 Free-time activities — 57
- Knowledge
- Retrieval

2.2 Customs, festivals and celebrations — 65
- Knowledge
- Retrieval

2.3 Celebrity culture — 69
- Knowledge
- Retrieval

Theme 2 Exam practice — 73
- Practice

Theme 3 Communication and the world around us — 81–115

3.1 Travel and tourism, including places of interest — 81
- Knowledge
- Retrieval

3.2 Media and technology — 88
- Knowledge
- Retrieval

3.3 The environment and where people live — 96
- Knowledge
- Retrieval

Theme 3 Exam practice — 108
- Practice

Grammar — 116–161

Nouns and articles — 116
- Knowledge
- Retrieval

Adjectives — 119
- Knowledge
- Retrieval

Adverbs — 126
- Knowledge
- Retrieval

Pronouns	129
⚙ Knowledge ⊖	
⤺ Retrieval ⊖	

The present indicative	133
⚙ Knowledge ⊖	
⤺ Retrieval ⊖	

The present continuous and reflexive verbs	137
⚙ Knowledge ⊖	
⤺ Retrieval ⊖	

Modal and impersonal verbs	140
⚙ Knowledge ⊖	
⤺ Retrieval ⊖	

The preterite tense	143
⚙ Knowledge ⊖	
⤺ Retrieval ⊖	

The imperfect tenses	146
⚙ Knowledge ⊖	
⤺ Retrieval ⊖	

The present perfect tense	148
⚙ Knowledge ⊖	
⤺ Retrieval ⊖	

The future tenses and the conditional	150
⚙ Knowledge ⊖	
⤺ Retrieval ⊖	

The imperative; Using *ser*, *estar* and *tener*	153
⚙ Knowledge ⊖	

Negatives and prepositions	157
⚙ Knowledge ⊖	

Word formation	161
⚙ Knowledge ⊖	

Exam practice	162–196

Paper 1 Listening	162
⚙ Knowledge ⊖	
⤺ Retrieval ⊖	
✎ Practice ⊖	

Paper 2 Speaking	170
⚙ Knowledge ⊖	
⤺ Retrieval ⊖	
✎ Practice ⊖	

Paper 3 Reading	179
⚙ Knowledge ⊖	
⤺ Retrieval ⊖	
✎ Practice ⊖	

Paper 4 Writing	188
⚙ Knowledge ⊖	
⤺ Retrieval ⊖	
✎ Practice ⊖	

Sound-spelling links	197
⚙ Knowledge ⊖	

How to use this book

This book uses a three-step approach to revision: **Knowledge**, **Retrieval** and **Practice**.
It is important that you do all three; they work together to make your revision effective.

 Knowledge

Knowledge comes first. Each chapter starts with a **Knowledge Organiser**. These are clear, easy-to-understand, concise summaries of the content that you need to know for your exam. The vocabulary, grammar and sound-spelling links content is organised to cover all the themes in the specification in a logical order so you can see how everything fits together.

Sample answers and guidance on tackling different questions are also provided where appropriate to help you understand what makes a good answer.

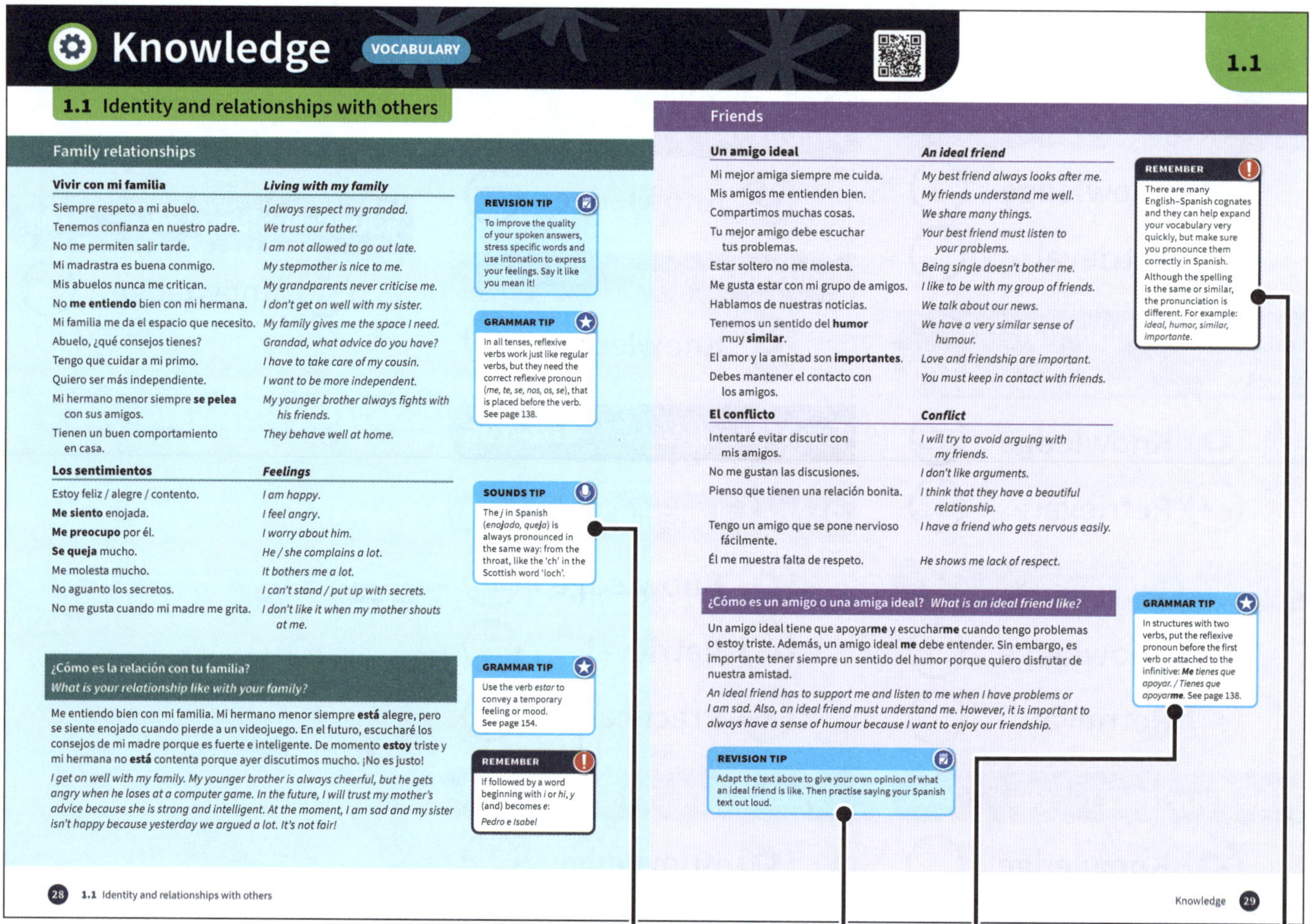

Additional feature

LINK

The **Link** box directs you to relevant pages to help you make connections between topics.

SOUNDS TIP

Sounds tips support your understanding of how to pronounce different words and sounds in the target language.

REVISION TIP

Revision tips offer you useful advice and guidance to aid your revision. They help with preparing for each of the four exam papers and with memorising key content.

REMEMBER

The **Remember** box offers helpful reminders and highlights things to watch out for.

GRAMMAR TIP

Grammar tips remind you of key grammatical knowledge and provide a page reference to the grammar section for more details.

Retrieval

The **Retrieval questions** help you learn and quickly recall the information you've acquired. These are short questions and answers about the content in the Knowledge Organiser you have just reviewed. Cover up the answers with some paper and write down as many answers as you can from memory. Refer back to the Knowledge Organiser for any you got wrong, then cover the answers and attempt all the questions again until you can answer *all* the questions correctly.

Make sure you revisit the Retrieval questions on different days to help them stick in your memory. You need to write down the answers each time, or say them out loud, otherwise it won't work.

Previous questions

Most Retrieval pages also have some **Retrieval questions** from **previous topics**. Answer these to see if you can remember the content from the earlier sections. If you get the answers wrong, go back and do the Retrieval questions for the earlier topics again.

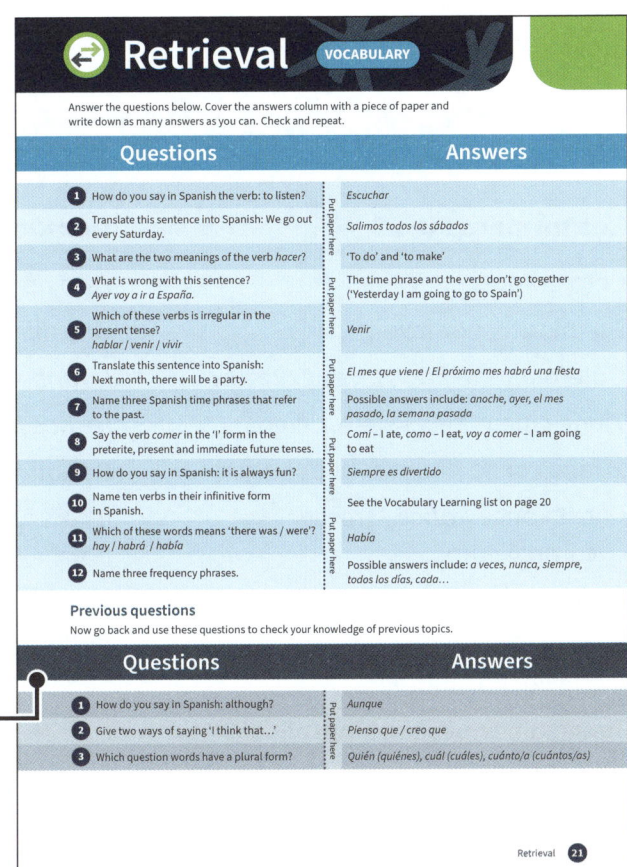

Practice

Once you are confident with the Knowledge Organisers and Retrieval questions, you can move on to the final stage: **Practice**.

Each chapter has **exam-style questions** to help you apply all the knowledge you have learned.

EXAM TIP

Exam tips help you understand different question types, provide guidance on how to answer them, and give advice on how to secure as many marks as possible.

Audio

You can scan the audio QR codes to access the audio for listening and speaking exam-style questions.

Answers and Glossary

You can scan the QR codes to access sample answers and mark schemes, a vocabulary glossary, and further revision support. You can also go to go.oup.com/OR/GCSE/A/MFL/Spanish/F

Knowledge  VOCABULARY

Basics

Numbers

Los números 0–29 | *Numbers 0–29*

Cero grados.	Zero degrees.
Un minuto, por favor.	One minute, please.
Quiero uno(a) / dos / tres / cuatro.	I want one / two / three / four.
Tiene cinco / seis / siete amigos.	He has five / six / seven friends.
¿Tienes ocho / nueve / diez euros?	Do you have eight / nine / ten euros?
Cuesta once / doce / trece / catorce euros.	It costs 11 / 12 / 13 / 14 euros.
Tengo quince minutos.	I have 15 minutes.
Hay dieciséis / diecisiete / dieciocho alumnos.	There are 16 / 17 / 18 students.
Tengo diecinueve / veinte años.	I am 19 / 20 years old.
(Él / Ella) Tiene veintiocho años.	He / she is 28 years old.

Los números 30–99 | *Numbers 30–99*

Hay treinta / treinta y un días este mes.	There are 30 / 31 days this month.
En Sevilla hay cuarenta grados.	In Seville it is 40 degrees.
El bebé tiene cincuenta y dos días.	The baby is 52 days old.
El libro tiene sesenta y cinco páginas.	The book has 65 pages.
Tenemos setenta y dos horas en Madrid.	We have 72 hours in Madrid.
Cuestan ochenta euros.	They cost 80 euros.
El autobús número noventa y nueve.	The number 99 bus.

¿Cuántos hay? *How many are there?*

En mi clase hay veintinueve alumnos. **Tengo** tres amigos: Tom, Paula y David. Tom y Paula tienen catorce años y David tiene quince años.

Tengo veintisiete libros. Mi libro favorito tiene noventa y dos páginas y **cuesta** treinta euros. **Es** un libro popular.

In my class, there are 29 pupils. I have three friends: Tom, Paula and David. Tom and Paula are 14 and David is 15 years old.

I have 27 books. My favourite book has 92 pages and it costs 30 euros. It is a popular book.

SOUNDS TIP

In Spanish, when the letter *c* is followed by *a*, *o* or *u*, it sounds just like the hard English c (as in cat).

When it is followed by an *e* or *i*, it sounds like an English *th* (as in *thin*). In some parts of Spain and Latin America, it sounds like an s (as in *salt*).

REMEMBER

Uno becomes *un* before masculine nouns.

REMEMBER

The numbers 20–29 are often misspelled in Spanish. Remember, the *e* is before the *i* in v**ei**nte (20). To form numbers 21–29, use veint**i**- (21 – veint**i**uno). Also note that there are accents on veintid**ós**, veintitr**és** and veintis**éis**.

GRAMMAR TIP

In Spanish, subject pronouns (I, you, he, she, it, we, they) are not used in front of verbs, unless they are needed for clarity or emphasis. For example, *tengo* on its own means 'I have' and *cuesta* means 'it costs'. See page 129.

More numbers

Los números 100–1.000.000 | **Numbers 100–1,000,000**

cien alumnos	100 pupils
ciento dos / ciento cincuenta kilómetros	102 / 150 kilometres
doscientas horas	200 hours
doscientos cuarenta minutos	240 minutes
quinientos euros	500 euros
setecientas páginas	700 pages
mil / seis mil / cien mil años	1000 / 6000 / 100,000 years
el año mil cuatrocientos noventa y dos	the year 1492
en mil novecientos ochenta y uno	in 1981
en dos mil cincuenta y cinco	in 2055
un millón de euros	a million euros
un millón y medio de bebés	one-and-a-half million babies
dos millones de libros	two million books

Los números ordinales | **Ordinal numbers**

el primer autobús	the first bus
la segunda clase del día	the second class of the day
la tercera página	the third page
el tercer mes del año	the third month of the year

REMEMBER

Cien is 100, but for 101–199, use *ciento* followed by the rest of the number (108 – *ciento ocho*). Do **not** use *y* after *ciento*.

To form 200, 300, etc., take the first number (*dos, tres,* etc.) and add *cientos* (300 – *trescientos*). The exceptions to this rule are 500, 700 and 900 – learn these carefully.

REMEMBER

Millón is followed by *de* before a noun.

REMEMBER

Primero and *tercero* become *primer* and *tercer* before a masculine singular noun.

En un día... *In one day...*

En un día, hay **veinticuatro** horas, **mil cuatrocientos cuarenta** minutos y **ochenta y seis mil cuatrocientos** segundos. En un año, hay **doce** meses, **cincuenta y dos** semanas, **trescientos sesenta y cinco** días y **ocho mil setecientas sesenta** horas.

In a day, there are 24 hours, 1440 minutes and 86,400 seconds. In a year, there are 12 months, 52 weeks, 365 days and 8760 hours.

GRAMMAR TIP

Numbers in the hundreds and the ordinal numbers change to agree with the noun that follows:

doscientas semanas – two hundred weeks

primera clase – first class

SOUNDS TIP

When *cu* is followed by another vowel in Spanish, the sound is more like an English *kw*. Try reading the text above aloud.

Knowledge

Basics

Vocabulary learning

Learn this vocabulary and then use the 'look, cover, write, check' technique to make sure you really know it. Cover the English first and then the Spanish.

Numbers 0–99

Spanish	✓	English	✓
catorce		fourteen	
cero		zero	
cinco		five	
cincuenta		fifty	
cuarenta		forty	
cuatro		four	
diecinueve		nineteen	
dieciocho		eighteen	
dieciséis		sixteen	
diecisiete		seventeen	
diez		ten	
doce		twelve	
dos		two	
noventa		ninety	
nueve		nine	
el número		number	
ochenta		eighty	
ocho		eight	
once		eleven	
quince		fifteen	
seis		six	
sesenta		sixty	
setenta		seventy	
siete		seven	
trece		thirteen	
treinta y uno/a		thirty-one	
tres		three	
uno/a		one	
veinte		twenty	
veintiuno/a		twenty-one	

Larger numbers and other basic vocabulary

Spanish	✓	English	✓
ciento veinte		one hundred and twenty	
mil		one thousand	
(un) millón		(one) million	
novecientos/as		nine hundred	
primero/a		first	
quinientos/as		five hundred	
segundo/a		second	
setecientos/as		seven hundred	
tercero/a		third	
el / la alumno/a		student, pupil	
el / la amigo/a		friend	
el año		year	
el autobús		bus	
el bebé		baby	
la clase		class, classroom, lesson	
costar		to cost	
el día		day	
el euro		euro	
el grado		degree (temperature)	
hay		there is / there are	
la hora		hour	
el kilómetro		kilometre	
el libro		book	
medio/a		half	
el mes		month	
el minuto		minute	
la página		page	
querer		to want	
la semana		week	
tener		to have	

Retrieval

VOCABULARY

Answer the questions below. Cover the answers column with a piece of paper and write down as many answers as you can. Check and repeat.

Questions | Answers

#	Question	Answer
1	What is the next number in the sequence: *cincuenta y cuatro, cincuenta y seis, cincuenta y ocho…*?	*Sesenta*
2	What is wrong with this number: *veintitres*?	There should be an accent on the final *e*: *veintitrés*
3	Which hundreds are *not* formed by adding *-cientos* to the numbers 2–9?	*Quinientos* (500), *setecientos* (700), *novecientos* (900)
4	Write the number 956 in Spanish.	*Novecientos cincuenta y seis*
5	Complete the sentence with the missing word: *Tienen un millón _____ libros.*	*Tiene un millón de libros*
6	Say the answer to the following sum in Spanish: *catorce + quince =*	*Veintinueve*
7	How do you say in Spanish: 30 degrees?	*Treinta grados*
8	How do you say in Spanish: 600 pages?	*Seiscientas páginas*
9	Translate these into English: *primero, segundo, tercero*.	First, second, third
10	Say the year 1994 in Spanish.	*Mil novecientos noventa y cuatro*
11	Translate this sentence into Spanish: It costs 120 euros.	*Cuesta ciento veinte euros*
12	How do you say in Spanish: I am sixteen years old?	*Tengo dieciséis años*

> **REVISION TIP**
>
> After testing yourself using retrieval questions, think about which questions you found easy or difficult and why. Make sure you revisit anything you need to learn more thoroughly.

> **REVISION TIP**
>
> To know 1–100 in Spanish, you only need to learn 37 numbers: 1–20, 21–29, then 30, 40, 50, 60, 70, 80, 90, 100. All the numbers in-between follow the same pattern, using **y** (and) as a link word. For example: *cincuenta **y** tres* – 53.

Knowledge  VOCABULARY

Basics

Days, months and seasons

Los días de la semana	Days of the week
Hoy es lunes / martes / miércoles.	Today is Monday / Tuesday / Wednesday.
El jueves tengo clases.	On Thursday I have classes.
Los viernes no salgo.	On Fridays I don't go out.
Quiero salir el sábado.	I want to go out on Saturday.
Me gustan los domingos.	I like Sundays.
El fin de semana salgo con amigos.	At the weekend I go out with friends.

Los meses del año	Months of the year
¿Qué fecha es hoy?	What is the date today?
Hoy es el dos de enero.	Today is 2 January.
Mi **cumpleaños** es el primero de febrero.	My birthday is 1 February.
Su **cumpleaños** es en marzo / abril / mayo.	His / Her birthday is in March / April / May.
Voy a Barcelona en junio.	I am going to Barcelona in June.
No hay clases en julio y agosto.	There aren't any classes in July and August.
¿Vas a **España** en septiembre / octubre / noviembre?	Are you going to Spain in September / October / November?
Salgo el martes catorce de diciembre.	I leave on Tuesday 14 December.
Hay cuatro estaciones en un año.	There are four seasons in a year.
Me gusta la primavera / el verano / el **otoño** / el invierno.	I like spring / summer / autumn / winter.
¿Hay clases en verano?	Are there classes in summer?

El verano   *The summer*

Me gusta el verano. **Los sábados** juego al fútbol y **los domingos** salgo con amigos. Mi cumpleaños es el cinco de julio. Este año, quiero una fiesta con veinte amigos. El **lunes**, primero de agosto, voy a la costa.

I like the summer. On Saturdays I play football and on Sundays I go out with friends. My birthday is on 5 July. This year, I want a party with 20 friends. On Monday 1 August, I am going to the coast.

REMEMBER
Days and months in Spanish never start with a capital letter.

REMEMBER
Use **cardinal numbers** to say the date in Spanish (*el siete de abril*). However, for the first of the month, you can also use the **ordinal number** *primero* (*el primero de octubre*).

SOUNDS TIP
The *ñ* is a distinct letter of the Spanish alphabet that is pronounced differently to the *n*. It sounds like the *ny* in 'canyon'.

GRAMMAR TIP
Months and days of the week are masculine. To say 'on' a day of the week, use *el*. For example:
el lunes – on Monday.

Use *los* before a day of the week to mean 'on' when talking about a habit. For example:
los martes – on Tuesday**s**.

Times and greetings

La hora	The time
¿Tienes la hora?	Do you have the time?
¿Qué hora es?	What time is it?
Es la una.	It is one o'clock.
Son las dos.	It is two o'clock.
Son las tres y cinco.	It is five past three.
Son las cuatro y cuarto.	It is quarter past four.
Son las cinco y media.	It is half past five.
¿A qué hora?	At what time?
A la una de la mañana.	At one in the morning (1am).
A las siete de la tarde.	At seven in the afternoon (7pm)
Hay una fiesta a las ocho.	There is a party at eight (o'clock).
Salgo a las diez menos veinticinco.	I leave at twenty-five to ten.
Hay clases hasta las dos.	There are classes until two.
Juego desde las siete hasta las **ocho**.	I am playing from seven until eight.
Voy por la mañana / por la **noche**.	I go in the morning / at night.
Salgo por la tarde.	I go out in the afternoon / evening.
Los saludos	*Greetings*
¡**Hola**!	Hello! / Hi!
¡Buenos días!	Hello! / Good morning!
¡Buenas tardes!	Good afternoon / evening!
¡Adiós!	Goodbye!
¡**Hasta** luego!	See you later!

GRAMMAR TIP

To say what time it is in Spanish, use *son las* followed by the hour, *y* for 'past' or *menos* for 'to', and then add the minutes. For example:
Son las seis y veinte.
It is twenty past six.

For 'one o'clock', use *es la*.
For example:
Es la una menos cinco.
It is five to one.

SOUNDS TIP

Practise the Spanish *ch* sound by saying *ocho* and *noche* aloud.

SOUNDS TIP

The Spanish *h* is nearly always a silent letter. Be sure to avoid using an English *h* when you come across it in Spanish!

Mi horario *My timetable*

Esta mañana tengo dos clases. Hay una clase **a las** nueve y cinco, y luego una clase **a las** diez y cuarto. Esta tarde **a la una**, no tengo clase. Juego al fútbol. Esta noche hay una fiesta desde las ocho y media hasta las once.

This morning, I have two classes. There is a class at five past nine, and then a class at quarter past ten. This afternoon at one o'clock, I don't have a class. I am playing football. Tonight, there is a party from half past eight until eleven.

GRAMMAR TIP

The Spanish preposition *a* is used to express 'at' with times and is followed by *la* or *las*.

Knowledge

Knowledge

VOCABULARY

Basics

Vocabulary learning

Learn this vocabulary and then use the 'look, cover, write, check' technique to make sure you really know it. Cover the English first and then the Spanish.

Days, dates and times

Spanish	✓	English	✓
a		at, to	
abril		April	
adiós		goodbye	
agosto		August	
buenos días		good morning	
con		with	
cuarto		quarter	
el cumpleaños		birthday	
de		of, from	
desde		from, since	
diciembre		December	
domingo		Sunday	
enero		January	
la estación		season, station	
febrero		February	
la fecha		date (in calendar), day	
el fin de semana		weekend	
hasta		until, up to, as far as	
¡Hasta luego!		See you later!	
hola		hello, hi	
la hora		time (specific)	
el horario		timetable, schedule	
hoy		today	
el invierno		winter	
jueves		Thursday	
julio		July	
junio		June	
luego		then, later	
lunes		Monday	

Spanish	✓	English	✓
la mañana		morning	
martes		Tuesday	
marzo		March	
mayo		May	
menos		to (the hour), less, fewer	
miércoles		Wednesday	
la noche; esta noche		night, evening; tonight	
noviembre		November	
octubre		October	
el otoño		autumn	
la primavera		spring	
¿qué?		what?	
sábado		Saturday	
septiembre		September	
la tarde		afternoon, evening	
el verano		summer	
viernes		Friday	
y		past (the hour), and	

Useful nouns and verbs

Spanish	✓	English	✓
la costa		coast	
España		Spain	
la fiesta		party, festival	
el fútbol		football	
ir		to go	
jugar		to play	
me gusta		I like	
salir		to go out, leave	
ser		to be	

Retrieval — VOCABULARY

Answer the questions below. Cover the answers column with a piece of paper and write down as many answers as you can. Check and repeat.

Questions / Answers

#	Question	Answer
1	How do you say in Spanish: it is one o' clock?	*Es la una*
2	Say all four seasons in Spanish.	*Primavera, verano, otoño, invierno*
3	How do you say in Spanish: at quarter past two?	*A las dos y cuarto*
4	Choose the correct meaning of *hasta*: since / until / soon	Until
5	Say the date of your birthday in Spanish.	*Mi cumpleaños es el… de…*
6	Name all the days of the week in Spanish.	*Lunes, martes, miércoles, jueves, viernes, sábado, domingo*
7	Find the error in this sentence: *Mi cumpleaños es el veinte de Marzo.*	The month should not have a capital letter (*marzo*), unless at the start of a sentence
8	What is the difference in meaning between *el lunes* and *los lunes*?	*El lunes* means 'on Monday' and *los lunes* means 'on Mondays'
9	How do you say in Spanish: from morning until night?	*Desde la mañana hasta la noche*
10	Which is the only month of the year in Spanish that starts with a different letter to its equivalent month in English?	*Enero*
11	Which letter is almost always silent in Spanish?	The letter '*h*'
12	Answer this question in Spanish: *¿Qué hora es?*	*Es la… / Son las…*

Previous questions

Now go back and use these questions to check your knowledge of previous topics.

#	Question	Answer
1	Say the year 1994 in Spanish.	*Mil novecientos noventa y cuatro*
2	Translate this sentence into Spanish: It costs 120 euros.	*Cuesta ciento veinte euros*
3	How do you say in Spanish: I am sixteen years old?	*Tengo dieciséis años*

Knowledge   VOCABULARY

Basics

Asking questions

Preguntas abiertas	Open-ended questions
¿Cómo estás?	How are you?
¿Cómo es?	What is it like?
¿Cuándo es tu cumpleaños?	When is your birthday?
¿(A)dónde vas?	Where are you going (to)?
¿De dónde eres?	Where are you from?
¿Qué es?	What is it?
¿A qué quieres jugar?	What do you want to play?
¿Qué tal (tu amigo)?	How are you? / How is (your friend)?
¿Por qué (no)?	Why (not)?
¿Quién es?	Who is it?
¿Quiénes son?	Who are they?
¿Cuánto cuesta?	How much does it cost?
¿Cuántas clases tienes?	How many lessons do you have?
¿Cuál es tu favorito?	Which is your favourite?
¿Cuáles son tus deportes favoritos?	Which are your favourite sports?
Preguntas sí/no	**Yes/no questions**
¿Juegan al fútbol?	Do they play football?
¿Hay muchos alumnos?	Are there a lot of students?
¿Está en clase María?	Is María in class?
¿Te gusta el verano?	Do you like summer?

SOUNDS TIP

The Spanish *qu* sounds like the English *k*. It is never pronounced like the English *qu*. Practise saying *qué* and *quieres*.

REMEMBER

You form yes / no questions in Spanish simply by using rising intonation in your voice. For example:

Juegas al tenis.
You play tennis.

¿Juegas al tenis?
Do you play tennis?

¿Quién eres? Who are you?

Hola, ¿**cómo** estás? Soy Ana y tengo algunas preguntas. ¿**De dónde** eres? Yo soy de México. ¿**Cuántos** animales tienes? Yo tengo dos perros. ¿Te gusta el fútbol? Yo prefiero el tenis. ¿**Cuáles** son tus deportes favoritos?

Hello, how are you? I am Ana and I have some questions. Where are you from? I am from Mexico. How many animals do you have? I have two dogs. Do you like football? I prefer tennis. Which are your favourite sports?

GRAMMAR TIP

In Spanish, the upside-down question mark indicates when a question is about to be asked. It can be used at the start of a sentence or even inside a sentence, at the point where the question begins.

GRAMMAR TIP

All question words in Spanish have an accent but only ¿cuál?, ¿quién? and ¿cuánto? have plural forms: ¿cuáles?, ¿quiénes? and ¿cuántos?

¿Cuánto? also has a feminine singular and plural form: ¿cuánta?, ¿cuántas? See page 130.

14 Basics

Giving opinions and extended answers

En mi opinión	In my opinion
Odio los lunes. Son aburridos.	I hate Mondays. They are boring.
Prefiero los sábados. Son divertidos.	I prefer Saturdays. They are fun.
Creo que es bastante malo.	I think that it is quite bad.
Pienso que es muy bueno.	I think that it is very good.
Parece interesante.	It seems interesting.
Para mí es genial.	For me, it's great.
Me gusta la música clásica.	I like classical music.
No me **gustan** los animales.	I don't like animals.
Me encanta la paella. ¡Es estupenda!	I love paella. It's wonderful!
Me encanta leer.	I love reading.
Me interesa la historia.	I am interested in history.
Me preocupan los exámenes. ¡Son horribles!	I'm worried about exams. They are horrible!
No **me importan** las fiestas.	Parties are not important to me.

Respuestas largas / Long answers

Me gustan Málaga **y** Sevilla, **pero** no me gusta Madrid.	I like Málaga and Seville, but I don't like Madrid.
Salgo mucho **porque** es verano.	I go out a lot because it's summer.
Me encanta mi perro, **aunque** es demasiado activo.	I love my dog, although he is too active.
Leo un poco **mientras** ella juega.	I read a little while she plays.
No sé **si** saldré **o** no.	I don't know if I will go out or not.

Mis opiniones personales / My personal opinions

Me gustan mucho los deportes porque son **divertidos**, pero mi favorito es el fútbol. ¡Es **genial**! Me interesan la historia y la música, aunque la música **clásica** parece un poco **aburrida**. Me encantan los animales. ¡Los perros son **estupendos**!

I really like sports because they're fun, but my favourite is football. It is great! I am interested in history and music, although classical music seems a little boring. I love animals. Dogs are brilliant!

REVISION TIP

Learn the verb *ser* for all persons. Remember: we use *es* for 'it is' and *son* for 'they are' when describing the characteristics of something.

GRAMMAR TIP

Me gusta literally means 'it is pleasing to me'. For verbs that work in this way, *-n* is added when the noun that follows is plural:
Me gustan mis amigos.
I like my friends.
Me encantan los domingos.
I love Sundays.
See page 133.

REMEMBER

Use a variety of conjunctions to extend your sentences.

Don't mix up *porque* (because) with *¿por qué?* (why?)

GRAMMAR TIP

Always check that the adjectives you use agree with the nouns they describe, whether masculine, feminine, singular or plural.
See page 119.

Knowledge

Knowledge

VOCABULARY

Basics

Vocabulary learning

Learn this vocabulary and then use the 'look, cover, write, check' technique to make sure you really know it. Cover the English first and then the Spanish.

Asking questions and giving opinions

Spanish	✓	English	✓
aunque		although, even though	
¿cómo?		how?	
¿Cómo es?		What is it like?	
creer (que)		to think, believe (that)	
¿cuál(es)?		which?	
¿cuándo?		when?	
¿cuánto(s) / cuánta(s)?		how much?, how many?	
¿dónde?		where?	
me encanta(n)		I love	
me gusta(n)		I like	
me importa(n)		it matters / is important to me	
me interesa(n)		I am interested (in)	
me preocupa(n)		I am worried (about)	
mientras		while, whilst	
o		or	
odiar		to hate	
para (mí)		for (me)	
parecer		to seem	
pensar (que)		to think (that)	
pero		but	
¿por qué?		why?	
porque		because	
preferir		to prefer	
¿qué?		what?	
¿Qué tal?		How are you? / How is…?	
¿quién(es)?		who?	
si		if, whether	
y		and	

Useful vocabulary for this topic

Spanish	✓	English	✓
aburrido/a		boring, bored	
activo/a		active	
algunos/as		some	
el animal		animal	
bastante		quite, enough	
bueno/a		good	
clásico/a		classical, classic	
demasiado/a		too	
el deporte		sport	
divertido/a		fun, enjoyable	
estar		to be	
estupendo/a		brilliant, great	
el examen		exam	
favorito/a		favourite	
genial		great	
la historia		history, story	
horrible		horrible	
interesante		interesting	
leer		to read	
malo/a		bad	
mucho/a		a lot	
la música		music	
muy		very, really	
la opinión		opinion, view	
la paella		paella (dish, usually of rice and seafood)	
el perro		dog	
poco		little, not much	
la pregunta		question	
saber		to know (how to)	

Basics

Retrieval — VOCABULARY

Answer the questions below. Cover the answers column with a piece of paper and write down as many answers as you can. Check and repeat.

Questions | Answers

#	Question	Answer
1	What is the Spanish question word for 'where'?	¿Dónde?
2	Which question words have a plural form?	Quién (quiénes), cuál (cuáles), cuánto/a (cuántos/as)
3	How do you say in Spanish: if?	Si
4	Give two ways of asking 'How are you?' in Spanish.	¿Cómo estás? / ¿Qué tal?
5	Translate this sentence into Spanish: I don't like dogs.	No me gustan los perros
6	Give two ways of saying 'I think that…'	Pienso que… / creo que…
7	Choose a synonym for *estupendo* from these options: genial / activo / aburrido	Genial
8	What is the difference between *porque* and *por qué*?	*Porque* means 'because', whereas *por qué* means 'why'
9	Translate this sentence into English: *Me encanta leer libros interesantes.*	I love reading / to read interesting books
10	How do you say in Spanish: although?	Aunque
11	Choose the correct option to complete the question and then translate into English: ¿Cuándo / Cuál / Cuánto es tu animal favorito?	¿<u>Cuál</u> es tu animal favorito? Which is your favourite animal?
12	How do you say in Spanish the verb: to seem?	Parecer

Previous questions

Now go back and use these questions to check your knowledge of previous topics.

Questions | Answers

#	Question	Answer
1	Say all four seasons in Spanish.	Primavera, verano, otoño, invierno
2	How do you say in Spanish: at quarter past two?	A las dos y cuarto
3	What is the difference in meaning between *el lunes* and *los lunes*?	*El lunes* means 'on Monday' and *los lunes* means 'on Mondays'

Knowledge  VOCABULARY

Basics

Using the present tense

¿Cuántas veces? — *How many times?*

A veces voy al cine con mis amigos.	*Sometimes I go to the cinema with my friends.*
Escucho música todos los días.	*I listen to music every day.*
Siempre hago mis deberes.	*I always do my homework.*
No como carne nunca.	*I never eat meat.*
Cada domingo, hay un mercado.	*Every Sunday, there is a market.*
Casi nunca voy a Barcelona.	*I almost never go to Barcelona.*

REMEMBER
Negatives are often placed before the verb in Spanish, but some, such as *nunca*, can also go after. See page 157.

En el presente — *In the present*

Hablo mucho.	*I talk a lot.*
Hoy visito a mis amigos.	*Today I am visiting my friends.*
Cada día tomo notas en clase.	*Every day I take notes in class.*
Juego en el parque.	*I play in the park.*
Paso mucho tiempo con mi perro.	*I spend a lot of time with my dog.*
No voy a la fiesta esta tarde.	*I am not going to the party this afternoon.*
No puedo salir ahora.	*I can't go out now.*
Pienso que mi trabajo actual es interesante.	*I think that my current job is interesting.*
Estudio mucho.	*I study a lot.*
Vivimos en un pueblo.	*We live in a village.*
Llegan a las seis.	*They arrive at six o'clock.*
¿Puedes ir también?	*Can you go too?*

GRAMMAR TIP
Regular verbs in Spanish can be divided into three groups: **-ar** verbs (*hablar*), **-er** verbs (*comer*) and **-ir** verbs (*vivir*). See page 133.

GRAMMAR TIP
Some verbs, such as *jugar, pensar* and *poder*, have regular endings, but they have spelling changes in their stem. See page 134.

El fin de semana — *The weekend*

Los sábados trabajo en un café por la mañana y luego **salgo** con mi amiga, Julia. Por la tarde siempre **salimos** con otros amigos. Nunca veo a Julia los domingos porque siempre **hago** mucho deporte y ella **hace** sus deberes.

On Saturdays, I work in a café in the morning and then I go out with my friend, Julia. In the evening, we always go out with other friends. I never see Julia on Sundays because I always do a lot of sport and she does her homework.

GRAMMAR TIP
Irregular verbs, such as *ir, ser, tener* and *venir*, don't follow a pattern. Some verbs, such as *salir, hacer, saber, dar* and *ver*, are irregular only in the first person in the present tense. See page 135.

Using past and future time frames

En el pasado — *In the past*

El mes pasado fui a Madrid.	Last month, I went to Madrid.
Dije que no comí la pizza.	I said that I didn't eat the pizza.
Anoche la película fue genial.	Last night the film was great.
Tuve clases ayer.	I had classes yesterday.
No hice deporte el fin de semana pasado.	I didn't do sport last weekend.
Mi pueblo era aburrido.	My town used to be boring.
Estaban aburridos.	They were bored.
Había treinta mil personas en el estadio.	There were 30,000 people in the stadium.
Nos vimos al día siguiente.	We saw each other the following day.
¿Saliste tarde?	Did you go out late?

GRAMMAR TIP

The preterite and imperfect tenses are used to talk about the past in Spanish. See pages 143–144 and pages 146–147.

En el futuro — *In the future*

Mañana la fiesta será divertida.	Tomorrow the party will be fun.
Voy a dar un libro a Camila.	I am going to give Camila a book.
Va a ser estupendo.	It is going to be brilliant.
La próxima semana visitaré a mi abuela.	Next week I will visit my grandma.
El año que viene iré a Sudamérica.	Next year I will go to South America.
¡Sería interesante!	It would be interesting!
Compraría un coche.	I would buy a car.
Me gustaría verlo.	I would like to see it.
¿Vas a salir esta tarde?	Are you going out this afternoon?

REMEMBER

In Spanish, *mañana* means both 'morning' and 'tomorrow'. So 'tomorrow morning' is *mañana por la mañana*.

GRAMMAR TIP

There are different ways to talk about the future in Spanish. See page 150.

Una semana interesante *An interesting week*

Anoche fui a una fiesta y fue genial. **Había** muchos alumnos de mi clase. Hoy es aburrido porque **hay** un examen de música a las dos. El fin de semana, **habrá** otra fiesta en la casa de Luis. ¡Va a ser divertido!

Last night, I went to a party and it was great. There were a lot of students from my class. Today is boring because there is a Music exam at two o'clock. At the weekend, there will be another party in Luis' house. It is going to be fun!

GRAMMAR TIP

The verb *haber* has one impersonal form in each tense:
hay – there is / are
había – there was / were
habrá – there will be
habría – there would be

Knowledge  VOCABULARY

Basics

Vocabulary learning

Learn this vocabulary and then use the 'look, cover, write, check' technique to make sure you really know it. Cover the English first and then the Spanish.

Time and frequency

Spanish	✓	English	✓
a veces		sometimes	
actual		current	
ahora		now, these days	
anoche		last night	
el año que viene		next year	
ayer		yesterday	
cada		every, each	
casi		almost	
el futuro		future	
hoy		today, nowadays	
mañana		tomorrow	
nunca		never	
otro/a(s)		other, another	
pasado		last	
el pasado		past	
próximo/a		next	
siempre		always, forever	
siguiente		following, next	
tarde		late	
el tiempo		time (general)	
todos los días		every day	

REVISION TIP

Practise making a full sentence with some of the verbs on this page. Make the sentences about you and your life so the words become easier to remember in context.

Verbs

Spanish	✓	English	✓
comer		to eat	
comprar		to buy, purchase	
dar		to give	
decir		to say, tell	
escuchar		to listen (to)	
había		there was, there were	
hablar		to speak, talk	
hacer		to do, make	
pasar		to spend (time), pass, happen	
poder		to be able to, can	
tomar		to take	
trabajar		to work	
venir		to come	
ver		to see, watch	
visitar		to visit	
vivir		to live	

Nouns

Spanish	✓	English	✓
la carne		meat	
la casa		house	
el cine		cinema	
el coche		car	
los deberes		homework	
el estadio		stadium	
el mercado		market	
la nota		note	
el parque		park	
la película		film, movie	
el pueblo		small town, village	

Retrieval — VOCABULARY

Answer the questions below. Cover the answers column with a piece of paper and write down as many answers as you can. Check and repeat.

Questions / Answers

#	Questions	Answers
1	How do you say in Spanish the verb: to listen?	*Escuchar*
2	Translate this sentence into Spanish: We go out every Saturday.	*Salimos todos los sábados*
3	What are the two meanings of the verb *hacer*?	'To do' and 'to make'
4	What is wrong with this sentence? *Ayer voy a ir a España.*	The time phrase and the verb don't go together ('Yesterday I am going to go to Spain')
5	Which of these verbs is irregular in the present tense? *hablar / venir / vivir*	*Venir*
6	Translate this sentence into Spanish: Next month, there will be a party.	*El mes que viene / El próximo mes habrá una fiesta*
7	Name three Spanish time phrases that refer to the past.	Possible answers include: *anoche, ayer, el mes pasado, la semana pasada*
8	Say the verb *comer* in the 'I' form in the preterite, present and immediate future tenses.	*Comí* – I ate, *como* – I eat, *voy a comer* – I am going to eat
9	How do you say in Spanish: it is always fun?	*Siempre es divertido*
10	Name ten verbs in their infinitive form in Spanish.	See the Vocabulary Learning list on page 20
11	Which of these words means 'there was / were'? *hay / habrá / había*	*Había*
12	Name three frequency phrases.	Possible answers include: *a veces, nunca, siempre, todos los días, cada…*

Previous questions

Now go back and use these questions to check your knowledge of previous topics.

#	Questions	Answers
1	How do you say in Spanish: although?	*Aunque*
2	Give two ways of saying 'I think that…'	*Pienso que / creo que*
3	Which question words have a plural form?	*Quién (quiénes), cuál (cuáles), cuánto/a (cuántos/as)*

Knowledge — VOCABULARY

1.1 Identity and relationships with others

Introducing family members

Mi gente	*My people*
Mi abuelo es argentino.	My grandfather is Argentinian.
Mi madrastra es chilena.	My stepmother is Chilean.
Mi mujer es **musulmana**.	My wife is Muslim.
El hombre es **alemán**.	The man is German.
Mi padre se llama Simón y mi madre se llama Carolina.	My father is called Simón and my mother is called Carolina.
¿Cómo se llaman las hermanas de Pilar?	What are Pilar's sisters called?
Nuestros padres no tienen un gato.	Our parents do not have a cat.
Marisa tenía cinco hijos y David era el menor.	Marisa had five children and David was the youngest.
Nuestro hijo es transgénero.	Our son is transgender.
¿Son religiosos vuestros primos?	Are your cousins religious?
¡Qué pena! Su perro está muerto.	What a pity! Their dog is dead.
Conozco a una chica **francesa**.	I know a French girl.
Antonio y Carmen son nombres muy comunes en España.	Antonio and Carmen are very common names in Spain.
Los cumpleaños	*Birthdays*
¿Cuándo es el cumpleaños de tu tía?	When is your aunt's birthday?
¿Cuál es la fecha de tu cumpleaños?	What is your birthday date?
¿Cuántos años tiene tu hermana mayor?	How old is your older sister?
Mi hermano menor nació en dos mil veinte.	My younger brother was born in 2020.

REMEMBER

When in their feminine or plural form, many adjectives lose the accent on the last syllable:

musulmán (m.) – *musulmana* (f.)

alemán (m.) – *alemana* (f.)

GRAMMAR TIP

Nationality adjectives can also be used as nouns:

Me gusta el alemán. I like German.

los franceses – the French

GRAMMAR TIP

Mayor and *menor* are irregular comparative adjectives. For example:

el hijo mayor – the older son;

Soy menor que mi hermano. I'm younger than my brother.

See page 121.

Te voy a presentar a mi familia — *I'm going to introduce you to my family*

Soy Alejandro y vivo con **mi** madre, mi padrastro y mi hermano. Mi hermano se llama Lorenzo y tiene diecisiete años. **Nuestra** familia es bastante pequeña. Tengo solo un tío que me gusta porque es divertido. Vive en México y **su** hermano es mi padre. **Mis** padres están divorciados. ¿Cómo es **tu** familia?

I am Alejandro and I live with my mother, my stepfather and my brother. My brother is called Lorenzo and he is 17 years old. Our family is quite small. I have only one uncle who I like because he is fun. He lives in Mexico and his brother is my father. My parents are divorced. What is your family like?

GRAMMAR TIP

Possessive adjectives (*mi, tu, su, nuestro, vuestro, su*) agree with the word that follows:

mi padre – **mis** padres
nuestra hija – **nuestras** hijas

See page 123.

Personality and physical appearance

El aspecto físico — *Physical appearance*

Tengo **los ojos marrones y grandes**. — *I have big, brown eyes.*

Llevo gafas. — *I wear glasses.*

Soy bastante delgado. — *I am quite slim.*

No soy débil; soy bastante fuerte e independiente. — *I am not weak; I am quite strong and independent.*

Teresa se parece mucho a su abuela. — *Teresa looks a lot like her grandmother.*

Las dos son morenas. — *They're both dark-skinned / dark-haired.*

Es **una chica hermosa**. — *She is a beautiful girl.*

Cuando era joven, tenía **el pelo corto y rubio**. — *When I was young, I used to have short blond hair.*

Mi hermana tiene un tatuaje pero es un poco feo. — *My sister has a tattoo, but it is a bit ugly.*

Tenemos **un perro bastante gordo**. — *We have quite a fat dog.*

La personalidad — *Personality*

Pienso que soy inteligente y práctico. — *I think I'm intelligent and practical.*

Mi hija es lista aunque a veces es perezosa. — *My daughter is clever, although sometimes she is lazy.*

Mi amiga es trabajadora y de carácter optimista. — *My friend is hard-working and of an optimistic character.*

¿Por qué pareces tan seria hoy? — *Why do you seem so serious today?*

Mi padre era muy serio. — *My father was very serious.*

Ella es famosa por su éxito deportivo. — *She is famous for her sporting success.*

Carlos no es muy simpático y, **además**, es tonto. — *Carlos is not very nice and he is silly as well.*

Nuestro jefe es gracioso; **sin embargo**, es responsable. — *Our boss is funny; however, he is responsible.*

Él se parece a su madre, pero tú te pareces a tu padre. — *He looks like his mother, but you look your father.*

¿Cómo son? *What are they like?*

Mi hermanito **es** bastante alto. **Tenía** el pelo largo, pero ahora **tiene** el pelo corto. Pienso que es muy artístico. En cambio, mi hermanita siempre es seria. Recuerdo que **era** muy tonta cuando era joven.

My little brother is quite tall. He used to have long hair, but now he has short hair. I think that he is very artistic. On the other hand, my little sister is always serious. I remember she used to be very silly when she was young.

GRAMMAR TIP

Be careful with Spanish word order. In the sentence 'I have big, brown eyes' in Spanish, 'big' and 'brown' are the adjectives and they go **after** the noun 'eyes'. See page 120.

SOUNDS TIP

The letter *o* in Spanish sounds like the English 'oh' and the letter *a* sounds like 'ah'. Many words in Spanish end in these letters, so it is important to get them right!

GRAMMAR TIP

Ser (to be) and *tener* (to have) are very common irregular verbs. Make sure you know them in different tenses and persons. See pages 154–155.

REMEMBER

The suffix *-ito* (on a masculine noun) or *-ita* (on a feminine noun) is used to mean that something is little or to imply affection. See page 161.

Knowledge  VOCABULARY

1.1 Identity and relationships with others

Couples and marriage

Las parejas	*Couples*
No tengo novio; estoy soltero.	I don't have a boyfriend; I'm single.
Busco una pareja graciosa y guapa.	I'm looking for a funny and good-looking partner.
Marta se divorcia de su mujer.	Marta is getting divorced from her wife.
Mi marido y yo **tenemos ganas** de vivir en el extranjero.	My husband and I want to live abroad.
Mañana él va a salir con Dani y está un poco nervioso.	Tomorrow, he's going to go out with Dani and he's a little nervous.
En España es tradición tener dos apellidos.	In Spain it is the tradition to have two surnames.
Ella está triste porque se separaron.	She is sad because they separated.

REMEMBER

The Spanish noun *ganas* means 'desire'. It is often used with the verb *tener* to mean 'to want' or 'to feel like'. See page 155.

El matrimonio	*Marriage*
Ana y Esteban se casaron el abril pasado.	Ana and Esteban got married last April.
La boda fue bonita.	The wedding was beautiful.
No es necesario tener una boda grande.	It is not necessary to have a big wedding.
No **estoy lista** para casarme o tener un bebé.	I'm not ready to get married or have a baby.
Hay más matrimonios del mismo sexo ahora.	There are more same-sex marriages these days.
Mi abuela se casó el año pasado. ¡Mejor tarde que nunca!	My grandmother got married last year. Better late than never!

REMEMBER

The adjective *listo* has two different meanings. Use it with *ser* to mean 'clever' or 'intelligent' and with *estar* to mean 'ready'.

Las relaciones *Relationships*

A veces visitamos a nuestros abuelos. Se casaron en 1978 y tuvieron su primer bebé al año siguiente. Yo estoy soltero, pero mi hermano tiene una novia. El nombre de su novia es Lucía. **Es lista** y muy alegre. Mi hermano dice que **está listo** para casarse. Quiere una boda tradicional y una fiesta grande.

Sometimes we visit our grandparents. They got married in 1978 and had their first baby the following year. I am single, but my brother has a girlfriend. Her name is Lucía. She's clever and very cheerful. My brother says he's ready to get married. He wants a traditional wedding and a big party.

Vocabulary learning

Learn this vocabulary and then use the 'look, cover, write, check' technique to make sure you really know it. Cover the English first and then the Spanish.

Useful adjectives and adverbs

Spanish	✓	English	✓
alemán(a)		German	
alto/a		tall	
argentino/a		Argentinian	
artístico/a		artistic	
bien		well	
bonito/a		pretty, nice, beautiful	
casado/a		married	
chileno/a		Chilean	
común		common	
corto/a		short, brief	
débil		weak	
delgado		slim, thin	
deportivo/a		sporty, sports	
duro/a		hard	
famoso/a		famous, well-known	
físico/a		physical	
fiel		faithful, loyal	
francés(a)		French	
fuerte		strong	
gordo/a		fat	
gracioso/a		funny	
grande		big, large	
guapo/a		good-looking	
hermoso/a		beautiful, handsome	
independiente		independent	
joven		young	
justo/a		fair, just	
largo/a		long	

Spanish	✓	English	✓
listo/a		ready; clever, intelligent	
marrón		brown	
mayor		older	
mejor		better, best	
menor		younger, youngest	
mismo/a		same	
moreno/a		brown (hair), dark skin	
muerto/a		dead	
musulmán(a)		Muslim	
necesario/a		necessary, required	
nervioso/a		nervous, uptight	
optimista		optimistic	
pequeño/a		small, little, young	
perezoso/a		lazy	
práctico/a		practical	
religioso/a		religious	
responsable		responsible	
rubio/a		blond, fair	
serio/a		serious	
simpático/a		nice, friendly	
solo		only, just	
soltero/a		single, unmarried	
tonto/a		silly	
trabajador(a)		hardworking	
tradicional		traditional	
transgénero		transgender	
triste		sad, unhappy, upset	

Knowledge

Knowledge — VOCABULARY

1.1 Identity and relationships with others

Vocabulary learning

Useful nouns for this topic

Spanish	✓	English	✓
el / la amigo/a		friend	
el / la abuelo/a		grandfather / grandmother	
el apellido		surname	
el aspecto		aspect	
la boda		wedding	
el / la bebé		baby	
el / la chico/a		boy / girl	
el extranjero		abroad, foreigner	
la familia		family	
las gafas		glasses	
el gato		cat	
el / la hermano/a		brother / sister	
el / la hijo/a		child; son / daughter	
el hombre		man	
el / la jefe		boss, manager	
el marido		husband	
la madrastra		stepmother	
la madre		mother	
el matrimonio		marriage	
la mujer		woman, wife	
el nacimiento		birth, origin	
el nombre		name	
el / la novio/a		boyfriend, groom; girlfriend, bride	
el ojo		eye	
el padrastro		stepfather	
el padre, los padres		father, parents	
la pareja		couple, partner	

Spanish	✓	English	✓
el pelo		hair	
la personalidad		personality, celebrity	
el primo		cousin	
la relación		relationship	
el sexo		sex	
el tatuaje		tattoo	
el / la tío/a		uncle / aunt	
la tradición		tradition	

Useful verbs and other expressions

Spanish	✓	English	✓
además		also, as well, besides	
buscar		to look for	
casarse		to get married	
conocer		to know (person / place)	
en cambio		on the other hand, whereas	
divorciarse		to get divorced	
llamar, llamarse		to call, be called	
llevar		to wear	
nacer		to be born	
parecerse a		to look like	
presentar		to introduce, present	
recordar		to remember, recall	
separarse		to separate (a couple)	
sin embargo		however	
también		also, too, as well	
tener ganas de		to feel like doing	

Retrieval

VOCABULARY 1.1

Answer the questions below. Cover the answers column with a piece of paper and write down as many answers as you can. Check and repeat.

Questions | Answers

#	Question	Answer
1	What is the difference in meaning between *parecer* and *parecerse*?	*Parecer* – to seem, *parecerse* – to look like
2	How do you say in Spanish: ugly?	*Feo/a*
3	Write a sentence to describe your appearance in Spanish.	*Tengo los ojos … y el pelo… / Soy…*
4	What is the difference in meaning between *estoy listo* and *soy listo*?	*Estoy listo* is 'I am ready' and *soy listo* is 'I am clever / intelligent'
5	Write *francés* in the feminine form.	*Francesa*
6	How do you say in Spanish: lazy?	*Perezoso /a*
7	How do you say in Spanish: our grandmother?	*Nuestra abuela*
8	What are the two meanings of *novia*?	'Girlfriend' and 'bride'
9	How do you say in Spanish: birthday?	*El cumpleaños*
10	Translate this sentence into Spanish: I want to go abroad.	*Quiero ir al extranjero*
11	Name two adjectives to describe something 'beautiful' or 'pretty'.	Possible answers include: *bonito, hermoso, guapo*
12	Answer this question in Spanish: *¿Cómo es un buen amigo?*	*Un buen amigo es…*

Previous questions

Use the questions below to check your knowledge from previous chapters.

Questions | Answers

#	Question	Answer
1	What is the next number in the sequence: *cincuenta y cuatro, cincuenta y seis, cincuenta y ocho…*?	*Sesenta*
2	Translate this sentence into English: *Pienso que mi trabajo actual es interesante.*	I think that my current job is interesting
3	Name three Spanish time phrases which refer to the past.	Possible answers include: *anoche, ayer, el mes pasado, la semana pasada*

Knowledge VOCABULARY

1.1 Identity and relationships with others

Family relationships

Vivir con mi familia — *Living with my family*

Siempre respeto a mi abuelo.	I always respect my grandad.
Tenemos confianza en nuestro padre.	We trust our father.
No me permiten salir tarde.	I am not allowed to go out late.
Mi madrastra es buena conmigo.	My stepmother is nice to me.
Mis abuelos nunca me critican.	My grandparents never criticise me.
No **me entiendo** bien con mi hermana.	I don't get on well with my sister.
Mi familia me da el espacio que necesito.	My family gives me the space I need.
Abuelo, ¿qué consejos tienes?	Grandad, what advice do you have?
Tengo que cuidar a mi primo.	I have to take care of my cousin.
Quiero ser más independiente.	I want to be more independent.
Mi hermano menor siempre **se pelea** con sus amigos.	My younger brother always fights with his friends.
Tienen un buen comportamiento en casa.	They behave well at home.

Los sentimientos — *Feelings*

Estoy feliz / alegre / contento.	I am happy.
Me siento enojada.	I feel angry.
Me preocupo por él.	I worry about him.
Se queja mucho.	He / she complains a lot.
Me molesta mucho.	It bothers me a lot.
No aguanto los secretos.	I can't stand / put up with secrets.
No me gusta cuando mi madre me grita.	I don't like it when my mother shouts at me.

¿Cómo es la relación con tu familia?
What is your relationship like with your family?

Me entiendo bien con mi familia. Mi hermano menor siempre **está** alegre, pero se siente enojado cuando pierde a un videojuego. En el futuro, escucharé los consejos de mi madre porque es fuerte e inteligente. De momento **estoy** triste y mi hermana no **está** contenta porque ayer discutimos mucho. ¡No es justo!

I get on well with my family. My younger brother is always cheerful, but he gets angry when he loses at a computer game. In the future, I will trust my mother's advice because she is strong and intelligent. At the moment, I am sad and my sister isn't happy because yesterday we argued a lot. It's not fair!

REVISION TIP

To improve the quality of your spoken answers, stress specific words and use intonation to express your feelings. Say it like you mean it!

GRAMMAR TIP

In all tenses, reflexive verbs work just like regular verbs, but they need the correct reflexive pronoun (*me, te, se, nos, os, se*), that is placed before the verb. See page 138.

SOUNDS TIP

The *j* in Spanish (*enojado, queja*) is always pronounced in the same way: from the throat, like the 'ch' in the Scottish word 'loch'.

GRAMMAR TIP

Use the verb *estar* to convey a temporary feeling or mood. See page 154.

REMEMBER

If followed by a word beginning with *i* or *hi*, *y* (and) becomes *e*:
Pedro e Isabel

1.1

Friends

Un amigo ideal / *An ideal friend*

Un amigo ideal	An ideal friend
Mi mejor amiga siempre me cuida.	My best friend always looks after me.
Mis amigos me entienden bien.	My friends understand me well.
Compartimos muchas cosas.	We share many things.
Tu mejor amigo debe escuchar tus problemas.	Your best friend must listen to your problems.
Estar soltero no me molesta.	Being single doesn't bother me.
Me gusta estar con mi grupo de amigos.	I like to be with my group of friends.
Hablamos de nuestras noticias.	We talk about our news.
Tenemos un sentido del **humor** muy **similar**.	We have a very similar sense of humour.
El amor y la amistad son **importantes**.	Love and friendship are important.
Debes mantener el contacto con los amigos.	You must keep in contact with friends.

El conflicto / *Conflict*

El conflicto	Conflict
Intentaré evitar discutir con mis amigos.	I will try to avoid arguing with my friends.
No me gustan las discusiones.	I don't like arguments.
Pienso que tienen una relación bonita.	I think that they have a beautiful relationship.
Tengo un amigo que se pone nervioso fácilmente.	I have a friend who gets nervous easily.
Él me muestra falta de respeto.	He shows me lack of respect.

> **REMEMBER**
>
> There are many English–Spanish cognates and they can help expand your vocabulary very quickly, but make sure you pronounce them correctly in Spanish.
>
> Although the spelling is the same or similar, the pronunciation is different. For example: *ideal, humor, similar, importante*.

¿Cómo es un amigo o una amiga ideal? *What is an ideal friend like?*

Un amigo ideal tiene que apoyar**me** y escuchar**me** cuando tengo problemas o estoy triste. Además, un amigo ideal **me** debe entender. Sin embargo, es importante tener siempre un sentido del humor porque quiero disfrutar de nuestra amistad.

An ideal friend has to support me and listen to me when I have problems or I am sad. Also, an ideal friend must understand me. However, it is important to always have a sense of humour because I want to enjoy our friendship.

> **GRAMMAR TIP**
>
> In structures with two verbs, put the reflexive pronoun before the first verb or attached to the infinitive: *Me tienes que apoyar. / Tienes que apoyarme.* See page 138.

> **REVISION TIP**
>
> Adapt the text above to give your own opinion of what an ideal friend is like. Then practise saying your Spanish text out loud.

Knowledge VOCABULARY

1.1 Identity and relationships with others

Vocabulary learning

Learn this vocabulary and then use the 'look, cover, write, check' technique to make sure you really know it. Cover the English first and then the Spanish.

Useful verbs for this topic

Spanish	✓	English	✓
aguantar		to put up with, stand	
apoyar		to support	
criticar		to criticise	
cuidar		to take care of	
deber		to have to, must	
discutir		to argue, discuss	
disfrutar		to enjoy	
entender		to understand	
entenderse (bien)		to get on (well)	
evitar		to avoid, prevent	
gritar		to shout	
guardar		to keep, save	
intentar		to try, attempt (to)	
molestar		to bother, annoy, upset	
mostrar		to show	
pelearse		to fight	
permitir		to allow, permit	
ponerse		to become	
proteger		to protect	
respetar		to respect	
sentirse		to feel (+ adj.)	

> **REVISION TIP**
>
> How many cognates can you spot on this page? Try learning Spanish words that look similar to English words (and which have the same meaning) first.

Features of a relationship

Spanish	✓	English	✓
alegre		happy, cheerful, lively	
la amistad		friendship	
el amor		love	
la confianza		trust	
el comportamiento		behaviour	
el consejo		(piece of) advice	
el contacto		contact	
contento/a		happy, pleased	
la decisión		decision	
la discusión		argument	
enojado/a		angry	
el espacio		space, room	
la falta		lack, shortage	
feliz		happy, glad	
la gente		people	
el grupo		group	
el humor		humour, mood	
importante		important	
independiente		independent	
(de) momento		(at the) moment	
la noticia		news	
el problema		problem	
el respeto		respect	
el sentido		sense, meaning	
el sentimiento		feeling, sentiment	
la vida		life	
el videojuego		computer game	

1.1 Identity and relationships with others

Retrieval

VOCABULARY

1.1

Answer the questions below. Cover the answers column with a piece of paper and write down as many answers as you can. Check and repeat.

Questions | Answers

#	Questions	Answers
1	Translate this question into English: *¿Discutes a veces con tus amigos?*	Do you fight with your friends sometimes?
2	How do you say in Spanish: trust?	*La confianza*
3	Choose the correct option: *Me molesta cuando mi amigo no está de buen problema / humor / espacio.*	*Me molesta cuando mi amigo no está de buen <u>humor</u>*
4	Translate this sentence into Spanish: I can't put up with my sister.	*No aguanto a mi hermana*
5	What does *el sentimiento* mean in English?	Feeling
6	What is the verb 'to get on with' in Spanish?	*Entenderse*
7	How do you say in Spanish: they need to listen to me?	*Me tienen que escuchar / Tienen que escucharme*
8	Say three synonyms for 'happy' in Spanish.	*Alegre, contento, feliz*
9	Translate this sentence into Spanish: I don't get on well with my stepfather.	*No me entiendo bien con mi padrastro*
10	What is the difference in meaning between *estoy feliz* and *soy feliz*?	*Estoy feliz* means 'I am happy right now'; *soy feliz* means 'I am a happy person'
11	How do you say in Spanish: My father never shouts?	*Mi padre nunca grita / Mi padre no grita nunca*
12	Which of the following is an example of a reflexive verb? *soy / me siento / apoyo*	*Me siento*

Previous questions

Use the questions below to check your knowledge from previous chapters.

Questions | Answers

#	Questions	Answers
1	Name three frequency phrases.	Possible answers include: *a veces, nunca, siempre, todos los días, cada…*
2	Write *francés* in the feminine form.	*Francesa*
3	How do you say in Spanish: lazy?	*Perezoso/a*

# Knowledge VOCABULARY

1.2 Healthy living and lifestyle

A balanced diet

Comidas	Meals
Siempre preparo la ensalada sin sal.	I always prepare the salad without salt.
Cuando tengo mucha hambre, ceno pollo con verdura.	When I am really hungry, I have chicken with vegetables for dinner.
El desayuno es muy importante.	Breakfast is very important.
Intento beber un vaso de agua cada dos horas.	I try to drink a glass of water every two hours.
Siempre tomo café con leche.	I always have coffee with milk.
Probé la comida chilena.	I tried Chilean food.
Casi nunca ceno jamón con huevos.	I hardly ever have ham and eggs for dinner.
El pescado con patatas fritas es un plato típico en Inglaterra.	Fish and chips is a typical dish in England.
La paella es un plato muy rico.	Paella is a very tasty dish.
Una dieta equilibrada	**A balanced diet**
¿Cómo es una dieta sana?	What is a healthy diet like?
Creo que el pescado es **más sano que** la carne.	I believe that fish is healthier than meat.
Quiero comer menos comida dulce.	I want to eat less sweet food.
¿Es verdad que la grasa no es **tan peligrosa como** el azúcar?	Is it true that fat is not as dangerous as sugar?
Evito la grasa animal porque soy vegetariana.	I avoid animal fat because I am a vegetarian.
Si tienes sed, el agua fría es la **mejor** bebida.	If you are thirsty, cold water is the best drink.

REMEMBER
Use the preposition *de* to separate two nouns. In Spanish, the nouns appear in the opposite order. For example: *ensalada de frutas* – fruit salad, *bocadillo de jamón* – ham sandwich.

REMEMBER
The verb *tomar* means 'to take', but with food and drink it can mean 'to have' or 'to drink'.

GRAMMAR TIP
To make comparisons, use *más … que* (more … than), *menos … que* (less … than) and *tan … como* (as … as). Also make sure you know *mejor* (better) and *peor* (worse). See page 121.

REMEMBER
Agua (water) is a feminine word, but in its singular form it takes the masculine article *el* instead of *la*: *el agua fría* – the cold water.

¿Tienes una dieta equilibrada? Have you got a balanced diet?

Es difícil comer sano, pero lo intento. De lunes a viernes, como una naranja, una manzana o unas uvas para el desayuno. Los fines de semana, siempre **tengo mucha hambre** y me gusta comer una hamburguesa. Me encanta probar diferentes tipos de comida. Mi mejor amigo es vegano. Entiendo y respeto sus razones.

It's difficult to eat healthily, but I try. From Monday to Friday, I have an orange, an apple or grapes for breakfast. At the weekends, I'm always very hungry, and I like to eat a burger. I love trying different types of food. My best friend is vegan. I understand and respect his reasons.

GRAMMAR TIP
The verb *tener* (to have) can be used to talk about a range of physical states that are expressed with the verb 'to be' in English:
tener hambre – to be hungry
tener sed – to be thirsty
tener frío – to be cold

Keeping fit

Mantenerse en forma — *Keeping in shape*

Vamos a jugar al baloncesto en el centro deportivo.	We are going to play basketball in the sports centre.
Para estar en forma, me gusta nadar.	To be fit, I like to swim.
Estoy cansado, pero voy a entrenar.	I am tired, but I am going to train.
¿**Juegas** en algún equipo?	Do you play in a team?
A veces mi tía y yo damos un paseo.	My aunt and I sometimes go for a walk.
¿Vais a montar a caballo?	Are you going to go horse riding?
Me gusta practicar deportes de equipo.	I like practising team sports.
Voy a ir al partido.	I am going to go to the match.
No estoy en mi peso ideal.	I am not at my ideal weight.
Si no **quieres** correr, **puedes** andar.	If you don't want to run, you can walk.
Vamos a hacer la carrera de diez kilómetros.	We are going to do the 10km race.

El cuerpo y las enfermedades — *The body and illness*

Me **duele** la cabeza.	I have a headache.
Me duele el diente.	I have toothache.
Me **duelen** los pies.	My feet hurt.
Cuido de mi cuerpo porque es importantísimo.	I take care of my body because it is very important.
Mi abuelo tiene un corazón fuerte.	My grandfather has a strong heart.
Está muy débil debido a su enfermedad.	She is very weak because of her illness.
Voy al hospital porque me siento peor.	I'm going to the hospital because I'm feeling worse.
Si estás enfermo, debes descansar y dormir.	If you are ill, you must rest and sleep.

Un accidente *An accident*

Normalmente juego al baloncesto con mis amigos en el equipo del instituto. **Tristemente**, me caí durante el partido esta tarde y ahora me duele el pie derecho. También me duelen las dos manos. Voy a ir al hospital **rápidamente** con mi padre y voy a descansar mucho este fin de semana antes del próximo partido.

Normally, I play basketball with my friends in the school team. Sadly, I fell during the match this afternoon and now my right foot hurts. Both my hands hurt as well. I am going to go to the hospital quickly with my father and I am going to rest a lot this weekend before the next game.

GRAMMAR TIP

The immediate future tense describes what is **going** to happen. Use the present tense of *ir + a +* infinitive. For example: *Voy a descansar.* I am going to rest. See page 150.

GRAMMAR TIP

Radical-changing verbs change their spelling in the 'I', 'you', 'he / she / it' and 'they' of the present tense. For example:
j*u*gar → j*ue*go
p*e*nsar → p*ie*nsas
qu*e*rer → qu*ie*re
p*o*der → p*ue*den.
See page 134.

SOUNDS TIP

The letter *v* in Spanish sounds just like the letter *b*. If the *v* is at the beginning of a word (*voy, vamos*), the *b* sound is hard, but in other positions, it is a little softer, as if your lips barely touch (*grave*).

GRAMMAR TIP

To form adverbs, you can often add the suffix *-mente* to the feminine form of the adjective. For example: *rápida* (quick) + *mente* = *rápidamente* (quickly). See page 126.

 Knowledge — VOCABULARY

1.2 Healthy living and lifestyle

Health issues

La salud pública	Public health
La salud física es un **gran** problema en nuestra sociedad.	Physical health is a big problem in our society.
Es importante respirar aire limpio.	It's important to breathe clean air.
Deben enseñar cocina en todas las escuelas.	They must teach cooking/ food technology in all schools.
Mucha gente dice que no tiene tiempo para ir al gimnasio.	Many people say they do not have time to go to the gym.
Hay que reducir el estrés en los niños.	We must reduce stress in children.
¿El ejercicio puede mejorar tu sueño?	Can exercise improve your sleep?
Los médicos recomiendan una vida activa.	Doctors recommend being active.
El amor ayuda a tener una vida más larga y sana.	Love helps you have a longer and healthier life.
Debes tener cuidado.	You must be careful.
La juventud no dura toda la vida.	Youth doesn't last a lifetime.
Tenemos que dormir más.	We must sleep more.

Un peligro para la salud	A danger to health
Hay una variedad de problemas sociales debido a las drogas.	There's a variety of social problems due to drugs.
Fumar es un riesgo. Causa problemas graves.	Smoking is a risk. It causes serious problems.
Sin embargo, mucha gente aun fuma.	However, many people still smoke.
Si tomas una copa de vino, no **debes** conducir.	If you have a glass of wine, you must not drive.

Llevar una vida sana   *To lead a healthy life*

¿Cuidas de tu salud? Hay que evitar comer demasiadas grasas y fumar. Debes beber suficiente agua. También **se necesita** dormir bien cada noche. Además, el ejercicio es muy importante, por eso intenta entrenar en el gimnasio una vez a la semana. En nuestra sociedad hay muchas presiones, pero **se puede** llevar una vida sana.

Do you take care of your health? You must avoid eating too much fat and smoking. You must drink enough water. You also need to sleep well every night. Exercise is very important as well, so try training in the gym once a week. In our society, there are lots of pressures but one can lead a healthy life.

REMEMBER

Grande means 'big' when placed after the noun. However, when placed before the noun, *gran* means 'great' (or 'big' in the sense of 'significant'). See page 120.

GRAMMAR TIP

The verbs *deber, tener que* and *hay que* are all used to express obligation and are followed by the infinitive form of the verb. See page 140.

GRAMMAR TIP

The impersonal *se* is followed by the third person singular form of a verb to make general statements that do not refer to a specific person:
se debe – you / one must
se puede – you / one can
se necesita – you need / one needs.

1.2

Vocabulary learning

Learn this vocabulary and then use the 'look, cover, write, check' technique to make sure you really know it. Cover the English first and then the Spanish.

Food and drink

Spanish	✓	English	✓
el agua (f.)		water	
el azúcar		sugar	
la bebida		drink	
el bocadillo		sandwich	
el café		coffee	
el caramelo		sweet	
la carne		meat	
la cocina		cooking/ food technology	
la comida		food, meal, lunch	
el desayuno		breakfast	
la ensalada		salad	
la fruta		fruit	
la grasa		fat, grease	
el hambre (f.)		hunger	
la hamburguesa		burger	
el huevo		egg	
el jamón		ham	
la leche		milk	
la paella		paella (rice dish)	
el pan		bread	
las patatas fritas		chips, fries	
el pescado		fish	
el plato		dish, plate	
el pollo		chicken	
la sal		salt	
la sed		thirst	
el tipo		type, kind	
la uva		grape	
el vaso		(drinking) glass	
la verdura		vegetable	
el vino		wine	

A balanced diet

Spanish	✓	English	✓
beber		to drink	
casi		almost, nearly	
cenar		to have dinner	
comer		to eat	
demasiado/a		too much / many	
la dieta		diet	
diferente		different	
dulce		sweet	
equilibrado/a		balanced	
fresco/a		fresh, cool	
frío/a		cold	
intentar		to try	
más		more	
probar		to taste, try	
rico/a		tasty	
sano/a		healthy, wholesome	
se necesita		you need (to), one needs (to)	
sin		without	
típico/a		typical	
tomar		to have, drink; take	
vegano/a		vegan	
vegetariano/a		vegetarian	

> **GRAMMAR TIP**
>
> Memorise the article with each noun you learn so that you know its gender. Make sure you know how to form plural nouns too. See page 116.

Knowledge   35

Knowledge
VOCABULARY

1.2 Healthy living and lifestyle

Vocabulary learning

Keeping fit

Spanish	✓	English	✓
andar		to walk	
antes		before, beforehand	
cansado/a		tired, tiring	
correr		to run	
cuidar		to take care of	
dar un paseo		to go for a walk, stroll	
descansar		to relax, rest	
difícil		difficult, hard	
durante		during	
entrenar; entrenarse		to train; to train, go training	
estar en forma		to be fit	
mantener		to keep, maintain	
mejorar		to improve, make better	
mental		mental	
montar		to ride	
nadar		to swim	
practicar		to practise	
recomendar		to recommend	
reducir		to reduce	
suficiente		sufficient, enough	

Useful nouns for this topic

Spanish	✓	English	✓
el baloncesto		basketball	
el caballo		horse	
la carrera		race	
el centro		centre, middle	
el centro deportivo		sports centre	
el cuidado		care, carefulness	
el deporte		sport	
el ejercicio		exercise	
el equipo		team, equipment	
el estrés		stress	
el gimnasio		gym	
el instituto		secondary school	
el juego		game	
el partido		(sports) match	
el peso		weight	
la razón		reason	
la sociedad		society	
la variedad		variety	

Vocabulary learning

The body and health

Spanish	✓	English	✓
bajar		to lower, go down	
caer; caerse		to fall; fall over	
continuar		to continue	
crear		to create	
debido (a)		owing (to), due (to)	
derecho/a		right	
doler		to hurt, be painful	
dormir		to sleep	
durar		to last	
enfermo/a		ill, sick	
es verdad (que)		it is true (that)	
fumar		to smoke	
grave		serious, grave	
hay que		you / one must	
llevar		to lead	
normalmente		normally	
peligroso/a		dangerous	
por eso		so, therefore	
público/a		public	
rápidamente		quickly	
respirar		to breathe	
seco/a		dry	
social		social	
tener que		to have to, must	

Useful nouns for this topic

Spanish	✓	English	✓
el accidente		accident	
el aire		air	
la cabeza		head	
el corazón		heart	
el cuerpo		body	
el diente		tooth	
la droga		drug	
la enfermedad		illness, disease	
el hospital		hospital	
la juventud		youth	
la mano		hand	
el / la médico/a		doctor	
el peligro		danger	
el pie		foot	
la piel		skin	
la presión		pressure	
el riesgo		risk	
la salud		health	
el sueño		sleep	

REVISION TIP

When revising topic words, you will remember them more easily if you group them into categories, such as types of food, parts of the body, etc. Focus on words that are on the AQA vocabulary list.

Retrieval — VOCABULARY

Answer the questions below. Cover the answers column with a piece of paper and write down as many answers as you can. Check and repeat.

Questions / Answers

#	Question	Answer
1	When talking about sport, what does *una carrera* mean?	A race
2	Name three body parts in Spanish.	Possible answers include: *la cabeza, el diente, la mano, el pie*
3	How do you say in Spanish: a chicken sandwich?	*Un bocadillo de pollo*
4	If the word *completo* means 'complete', what is the Spanish for 'completely'?	*Completamente*
5	How do you say in Spanish: we are going to train?	*Vamos a entrenar*
6	Name three ways to say 'you must' in Spanish.	*Debes / Se debe, tienes que, hay que*
7	Translate this sentence into Spanish: 'We must avoid sugar.'	*Tenemos que / Debemos evitar el azúcar*
8	How do you say in Spanish: to go for a walk?	*Dar un paseo*
9	Correct the error in this sentence: *Me duele las manos.*	*Me duele**n** las manos*
10	How do you say in Spanish: I am very hungry?	*Tengo mucha hambre*
11	Answer this question in Spanish and give a reason: *¿Cómo es tu dieta?*	Possible answers include: *Mi dieta (no) es muy sana / equilibrada porque como mucha verdura / comida dulce / Soy vegetariano/a, por eso no como carne*
12	Which two words in Spanish describe a person who does not eat meat?	*Vegano/a* and *vegetariano/a*

Previous questions

Use the questions below to check your knowledge from previous chapters.

#	Question	Answer
1	What is the difference in meaning between *estoy listo* and *soy listo*?	*Estar listo* is 'to be ready' and *ser listo* is 'to be clever / intelligent'
2	Translate this sentence into Spanish: I can't put up with my sister.	*No aguanto a mi hermana*
3	Say three synonyms for 'happy' in Spanish.	*Alegre, contento, feliz*

Knowledge — VOCABULARY — 1.3

1.3 Education and work

School subjects and facilities

Las asignaturas y el horario / *Subjects and the timetable*

Muchos alumnos llegan al instituto a las ocho y cuarto. / *Many pupils arrive at school at quarter past eight.*

Las clases empiezan a las ocho y media. / *Classes start at half past eight.*

¿Cuándo termina el recreo? / *When does break finish?*

Tengo que enviar mis deberes antes de las tres. / *I have to send in my homework before three o'clock.*

Voy a estudiar Bachillerato en septiembre. / *I am going to study for my A levels in September.*

El inglés es una asignatura dura. / *English is a hard school subject.*

Me encanta aprender idiomas. / *I love learning languages.*

Hago mis deberes de matemáticas **usando** el ordenador. / *I do my maths homework using the computer.*

¿Cuál es tu opinión sobre la geografía / el dibujo? / *What is your opinion about Geography / Art?*

Leer es mi actividad favorita. / *Reading is my favourite activity.*

Es más fácil resolver los problemas **trabajando** en grupo. / *It is easier to solve problems working in groups.*

El edificio y las instalaciones / *The building and facilities*

En mi instituto hay muchas instalaciones. / *In my school there are lots of facilities.*

¿Cuántas clases hay? / *How many classrooms are there?*

Estoy **escribiendo** en la biblioteca. / *I'm writing in the library.*

Mi silla está cerca de la ventana. / *My chair is near the window.*

Los baños están limpios. / *The bathrooms are clean.*

Construyen una nueva universidad. / *They are building a new university.*

Hay una escalera larga que lleva al patio. / *There is a long staircase that leads to the playground.*

> **REVISION TIP**
>
> It is often more effective to revise words from the word family. For example, if you learn that *estudiar* is 'to study', you can also learn the nouns *estudiante* (student) and *estudio* (study).

> **GRAMMAR TIP**
>
> In English, we form the present participle / gerund with '-ing' (studying). In Spanish, to form the present participle / gerund for *-ar* verbs, replace *-ar* with *-ando*. For *-er* and *-ir* verbs, use *-iendo*. See page 137.

De lunes a viernes *From Monday to Friday*

Yo prefiero los martes porque tengo ciencias. El año que viene, tengo la intención de escoger ciencias porque quiero estudiar medicina. Me gustan los viernes porque tengo economía, inglés e historia. Creo que **estudiar** es importante, pero ¡se necesita mucho esfuerzo! Las clases comienzan temprano. Durante el recreo, me gusta hablar con mis amigos.

I prefer Tuesdays because I have science. Next year, I intend to choose science because I want to study medicine. I like Fridays because I have Economics, English, and History. I believe that studying is important, but it requires a lot of effort! Classes start early. During break, I like talking with my friends.

> **REMEMBER**
>
> In Spanish, use the infinitive as the subject of the verb, not the gerund / -ing form (which is correct in English).

Knowledge 39

Knowledge  VOCABULARY

1.3 Education and work

Exams and rules

Pruebas y exámenes / *Tests and exams*

Asistir a clase es tan importante como repasar.
Attending lessons is as important as revising.

No estoy listo para aprobar mis exámenes.
I am not ready to pass my exams.

Estoy feliz con mis notas.
I'm happy with my grades.

Juan puede sacar buenas notas.
Juan can get good grades.

El profesor me ayuda si no apruebo mis exámenes.
The teacher helps me if I don't pass my exams.

Mi amiga es muy trabajadora en clase.
My friend is very hard-working in class.

Nadie sabe el resultado del examen.
No one knows the result of the exam.

De momento, **no** tengo presión, **o** estrés.
At the moment, I do not have pressure or stress.

Para tener éxito, hay que pedir ayuda a veces.
In order to be successful, you must ask for help sometimes.

Mi padre **no** tiene estudios de Bachillerato.
My father doesn't have A levels.

No sé cómo responder esta pregunta.
I don't know how to answer this question.

> **GRAMMAR TIP**
>
> Negative words can be used in two different ways in Spanish: either place *no* before the verb and the negative word after it, or just place the negative word before the verb. For example: **No** voy **nunca** a la biblioteca. / **Nunca** voy a la biblioteca. I never go to the library. See page 157.

Las reglas del instituto / *School rules*

En clase hay que callarse y escuchar.
In class, you must be quiet and listen.

Nunca se debe gritar en clase.
You must never shout in class.

No se puede grabar vídeos en el patio del colegio.
You cannot record videos on the school playground.

Los profesores mandan muchos deberes.
The teachers give a lot of homework.

Conseguir buenos resultados / *Getting good results*

Para mí, escuchar y poner mucho esfuerzo es necesario para sacar buenas notas en el colegio. Sin embargo, nada es tan sencillo como parece. **No** hay **ninguna** asignatura fácil. Nunca tengo suficiente tiempo para descansar. Ahora hay que trabajar duro porque en poco tiempo empiezan las vacaciones...

For me, listening and putting in a lot of effort is necessary to get good grades at school. However, nothing is as simple as it seems. There is no easy subject. I never have enough time to rest. I have to work hard now because in a short while the holidays begin...

> **GRAMMAR TIP**
>
> The negative word *ninguno* changes to agree with the gender of the noun it describes. For example: *No hablé con ningún alumno*. I didn't speak to any pupils / a single pupil. See page 124.

School life

La vida en el instituto — *Life at school*

Mi uniforme es una camisa blanca y falda o pantalón negros. — *My uniform is a white shirt and black skirt or trousers.*

Me gustaría llevar mi ropa al colegio. — *I would like to wear my clothes to school.*

Soy miembro del club de idiomas. — *I'm a member of the languages club.*

Llevo bolígrafos en mi mochila. — *I carry pens in my school bag.*

Su comportamiento es estupendo. — *Their behaviour is wonderful.*

Recibí el premio a la estudiante del año. — *I received the 'Student of the Year' award.*

Me preocupa el acoso. — *I am worried about bullying.*

Un compañero de clase a veces no sigue las reglas. — *A classmate doesn't follow the rules sometimes.*

> **SOUNDS TIP**
>
> The Spanish *g* sounds like the hard English *g* when it comes directly before an *a*, *o* or *u* (*gustar*, *grupo*), but when it precedes *i* or *e*, it sounds like the Spanish letter *j* (*colegio*).

Háblame de las fotos — *Tell me about the photos*

Photo 1

Photo 2

En la primera foto, **se puede ver** a un profesor y tres alumnos en una clase de música. El profesor parece muy contento. Está tocando una guitarra y lleva un pantalón, una camisa y unas gafas. Los alumnos no llevan uniforme; sin embargo, todos tienen un instrumento y están escuchando al profesor.

In the first photo, you can see a teacher and three pupils in a music class. The teacher seems very happy. He is playing a guitar and he is wearing trousers, a shirt and glasses. The pupils aren't wearing uniform; however, they all have an instrument and they are listening to the teacher.

En la segunda foto, **se puede ver** a tres alumnos que tienen doce o trece años. Llevan mochilas. A la izquierda, hay un alumno triste. Los otros alumnos no son muy simpáticos. Creo que el estudiante triste tiene una vida bastante dura porque hay acoso en el instituto.

In the second photo, you can see three pupils who are twelve or thirteen years old. They are carrying rucksacks. On the left, there is a sad pupil. The other pupils are not very nice. I think the sad student has quite a hard life because there is bullying in the school.

> **REVISION TIP**
>
> A useful phrase for the photo description task is *se puede ver* (you / one can see).

Knowledge

VOCABULARY

1.3 Education and work

Vocabulary learning

Learn this vocabulary and then use the 'look, cover, write, check' technique to make sure you really know it. Cover the English first and then the Spanish.

Useful verbs for this topic

Spanish	✓	English	✓
aprender		to learn	
aprobar		to pass (test)	
ayudar		to help	
callarse		to be quiet	
comenzar		to start, begin	
construir		to build	
empezar		to start, begin	
enseñar		to teach	
enviar		to send	
escribir		to write	
estudiar		to study	
grabar		to record	
llegar		to arrive	
llevar		to carry, wear	
organizar		to organise	
pedir		to ask for	
preparar		to prepare	
recibir		to receive	
repasar		to revise, review	
responder		to respond	
sacar		to get, obtain	
terminar		to finish, end	
tocar		to play (instrument)	
usar		to use	

Other useful words and expressions

Spanish	✓	English	✓
blanco/a		white	
cerca		near, close	
duro/a		hard, resilient	
fácil		easy	
(a la) izquierda		(on the) left	
nada		nothing, anything	
nadie		no one, nobody, anyone, anybody	
negro/a		black	
ninguno/a		no, not any / a single	
nunca		never	
sencillo/a		simple, easy	
sobre		about	
temprano/a		early	

> **REVISION TIP**
>
> When revising infinitives, learn their meaning in English and then practise conjugating them in different persons and tenses. For example: *recibir* – to receive, *recibí* – I received, *voy a recibir* – I am going to receive, etc.

1.3

Vocabulary learning

Useful nouns for this topic

Spanish	✓	English	✓
el acoso		bullying	
la actividad		activity	
la asignatura		(school) subject	
el Bachillerato		Baccalaureate / A levels	
la biblioteca		library	
el bolígrafo		pen	
la camisa		shirt	
las ciencias		Science(s)	
el club		club	
el colegio		(secondary) school	
el / la compañero/a		classmate, colleague	
el comportamiento		behaviour	
el dibujo		art, drawing	
la economía		economics, economy	
el edificio		building	
la educación		education	
el esfuerzo		effort	
el / la estudiante		student	
el examen		exam	
el éxito		success	
la falda		skirt	
la geografía		Geography	
la guitarra		guitar	
el horario		timetable, schedule	
el idioma		language	
el inglés		English	
la instalación		facility	

Spanish	✓	English	✓
el instituto		secondary school	
la intención		intention	
las matemáticas		Maths	
la medicina		medicine	
el miembro		member	
la mochila		rucksack, school bag	
la nota		grade, mark	
el pantalón		trousers	
el premio		award, prize	
el / la profesor(a)		teacher	
la prueba		test	
el recreo		break (at school)	
la regla		rule, ruler	
el resultado		result	
la revista		magazine	
la ropa		clothes, clothing	
la silla		chair, seat	
el teatro		drama, theatre	
el uniforme		uniform	
la universidad		university	
las vacaciones		holidays	
la ventana		window	
el vídeo		video	

REVISION TIP

Choose some of the vocabulary on these pages to describe the rules and routines at your school.

Knowledge 43

Retrieval — VOCABULARY

Answer the questions below. Cover the answers column with a piece of paper and write down as many answers as you can. Check and repeat.

Questions / Answers

#	Questions	Answers
1	How do you say in Spanish: learning is important?	*Aprender es importante*
2	Name at least three feminine school subjects in Spanish.	Possible answers include: *las ciencias, las matemáticas, la economía, la historia, la geografía, la música*
3	Translate this sentence into Spanish: I am going to finish my homework.	*Voy a terminar mis deberes*
4	Which Spanish verb means 'to pass an exam'?	*Aprobar (un examen)*
5	How do you say in Spanish: no one?	*Nadie*
6	Which word is the odd one out? *prueba / examen / regla*	*Regla* (rule) - the other two words mean 'test' / 'exam'
7	Name two words for 'secondary school' in Spanish.	*Colegio, instituto*
8	What is *la mochila* in English?	Rucksack / school bag
9	Translate this sentence into Spanish: I have to get very good grades.	*Tengo que sacar muy buenas notas*
10	Say three negative words in Spanish.	Possible answers include: *nadie, ninguno, no, nunca*
11	What is the name of the Spanish qualification similar to A level?	*Bachillerato*
12	Name two items of school uniform in Spanish.	Possible answers include: *la camisa, la falda, el pantalón*

Previous questions

Use the questions below to check your knowledge from previous chapters.

#	Questions	Answers
1	Say the verb *comer* in the 'I' form in the preterite, present and immediate future tenses.	*Comí* – I ate, *como* – I eat, *voy a comer* – I am going to eat
2	Name three ways to say 'you must' in Spanish.	*Debes / Se debe, tienes que, hay que*
3	If the word *completo* means 'complete', what is the Spanish for 'completely'?	*Completamente*

Knowledge — VOCABULARY — 1.3

1.3 Education and work

Jobs and future plans

Mis planes futuros	***My future plans***
Tengo la intención de trabajar en equipo.	I intend to work in a team.
Quiero **ser escritor** en una revista de moda.	I want to be a writer for a fashion magazine.
No estoy segura si quiero **ser policía / científica**.	I am not sure if I want to be a police officer / scientist.
Me interesa **ser periodista**.	I am interested in being a journalist.
Mi sueño es **ser cantante** famosa.	My dream is to be a famous singer.
El año que viene / El próximo año, voy a tener mi propio negocio.	Next year, I am going to have my own business.

El mercado laboral	***The job market***
Mi hermano es un peluquero muy conocido.	My brother is a very well-known hairdresser.
Pienso que ser camarera debe ser duro.	I think that being a waitress must be hard.
Para ser médico o enfermero, hay que estudiar medicina.	In order to be a doctor or a nurse, you have to study medicine.
No me gusta trabajar bajo presión.	I don't like to work under pressure.
No se puede trabajar de abogado sin estudiar mucho.	You cannot work as a lawyer without studying a lot.
¿Cuál es el papel de un jefe hoy?	What is the role of a boss nowadays?
Ella llegará a ser ingeniera.	She will become an engineer.
Sirvo a los clientes todo el día.	I serve customers all day.
Es posible ganar un buen salario sin ir a la universidad.	It is possible to earn a good salary without going to university.

¡No sé qué hacer! *I don't know what to do!*

En el futuro, quiero tener dinero suficiente **para vivir** bien. Puede ser difícil encontrar una carrera con un buen salario **sin viajar** al extranjero. **Para empezar** un negocio, no tengo que ir a la universidad. ¡Ya quiero ser parte del mundo laboral!

In the future, I want to have enough money to live well. It can be difficult to find a career with a good salary without travelling abroad. In order to start a business, I don't have to go to university. I want to be part of the world of work already!

GRAMMAR TIP

You do not use the article *un / una* after the verb *ser* when talking about professions. See page 117.

GRAMMAR TIP

The expressions *que viene* and *próximo* mean 'next' when used as part of a time phrase. *Próximo* is most often placed before the time period and must agree with it.

la **próxima** semana – next week
el **próximo** mes – next month
el año **que viene** – next year

REMEMBER

Nearly all professions have a masculine and feminine form (*el peluquero* – (male) hairdresser, *la peluquera* – (female) hairdresser). Some do not change spelling but do require a change of article (*el periodista* – (male) journalist, *la periodista* – (female) journalist). See page 116.

GRAMMAR TIP

Para + infinitive means 'in order to do something'. For example: *Trabajo para ganar dinero*. I work (in order) to earn money. *Sin* + infinitive means 'without + -ing': *sin practicar* – without practising.

Knowledge — VOCABULARY

1.3 Education and work

Getting a job

¡Quiero un trabajo!	I want a job!
Laura **buscará** un trabajo este verano.	Laura will look for a job this summer.
No quiero estar en el paro nunca.	I never want to be unemployed.
Pronto **tendré** una entrevista importante.	Soon I will have an important interview.
Pediré hablar con el dueño de la empresa.	I will ask to speak to the owner of the company.
Quiero ser la empleada del mes.	I want to be employee of the month.
La compañía **dará** trabajos de cuidador.	The company will give carer jobs.
Prepararé algunas preguntas para el director.	I will prepare a few questions for the manager.

El mundo del trabajo	The world of work
El paro **subirá** en marzo.	Unemployment will go up in March.
Los trabajadores quieren pedir mayores salarios.	The workers want to ask for larger salaries.
La jefa paga a los empleados cada mes.	The boss pays the employees every month.
Esta semana hay puente.	This week there is a long weekend.
Los abogados van a defender a los trabajadores.	The lawyers are going to defend the workers.

GRAMMAR TIP

To say what you 'will' do in Spanish, use the infinitive form of the verb and add the ending you need: é, ás, á.
See page 150.

Experiencia laboral *Work experience*

El lunes **empezaré** mi experiencia laboral en un teatro. Quiero ser actor en el futuro. **Tendré** que llegar temprano para hablar con el dueño del teatro. Él me **dirá** lo que **haré**. **Podré** aprender muchas cosas y será muy interesante.

On Monday, I will start my work experience in a theatre. I want to be an actor in the future. I will have to arrive early to talk to the theatre owner. He will tell me what I will do. I will be able to learn many things and it will be very interesting.

REVISION TIP

Cover up the English paragraph above and try translating the Spanish text into English yourself. Then compare your translation with the one above.

GRAMMAR TIP

Some common verbs in the future tense have an irregular stem, such as hacer → haré. Some add a d (poner → pon**d**ré, tener → ten**d**ré). The same verbs are irregular in the conditional. See page 151.

Vocabulary learning

Learn this vocabulary and then use the 'look, cover, write, check' technique to make sure you really know it. Cover the English first and then the Spanish.

The world of work

Spanish	✓	English	✓
el actor, la actriz		actor, actress	
el / la abogado/a		lawyer	
el / la artista		artist, performer	
el / la autor/a		author, writer	
bajo		under	
el / la cantante		singer	
la carrera		career, degree course	
el / la científico/a		scientist	
el / la cliente		customer, client	
la compañía		company	
conocido/a		known, well-known	
el / la cuidador(a)		carer	
el dinero		money	
el / la director(a)		manager, director	
el / la dueño/a		owner	
el ejército		army	
el / la empleado/a		employee	
el empleo		work, job	
la empresa		company, business	
encontrar		to find	
el / la enfermero/a		nurse	
la entrevista		interview	
el / la escritor(a)		writer	
la experiencia		experience	
ganar		to earn	

Spanish	✓	English	✓
el / la ingeniero/a		engineer	
el jefe / la jefa		boss	
laboral		(relating to) work	
llegar a + infinitive		to succeed in / to manage to	
la moda		fashion	
el mundo		world	
el negocio		business	
pagar		to pay (for)	
el papel		role, part, paper	
el paro		unemployment	
el / la peluquero/a		hairdresser	
el / la periodista		journalist	
el / la policía		police (officer)	
posible		possible	
el puente		long weekend	
la red (Red)		network (internet)	
la revista		magazine	
el salario		salary	
seguro/a		sure, safe, secure	
servir		to serve	
subir		to go up	
el sueño		dream	
el teatro		drama, theatre	
el trabajo		work, job, effort	
ya		already	

Knowledge

Retrieval

VOCABULARY

Answer the questions below. Cover the answers column with a piece of paper and write down as many answers as you can. Check and repeat.

Questions / Answers

#	Questions	Answers
1	How do you say in Spanish: I want to be a lawyer?	*Quiero ser abogado*
2	Name a job you can have in a hospital.	Possible answers include: *enfermero, médico*
3	Conjugate the verb *encontrar* (to find) in 1st, 2nd and 3rd singular in the future tense.	*Encontraré, encontrarás, encontrará*
4	Answer this question in a full sentence and give a reason: *¿Te gustaría ser profesor?*	Possible answers include: *Sí, me gustaría ser profesor porque es un trabajo interesante / No me gustaría ser profesor porque parece difícil*
5	What is the Spanish for 'to work' (verb), 'work' (noun) and 'hard-working' (adjective)?	*Trabajar, el trabajo, trabajador(a)*
6	Translate this sentence into Spanish: I want a job in order to earn a salary.	*Quiero un trabajo para ganar un salario*
7	How do you say in Spanish: owner?	*Dueño*
8	Mention two different meanings of *papel* in Spanish.	'Paper' or 'role'
9	Name a job that is the same in the masculine and feminine form.	Possible answers include: *el / la artista, el / la cantante, el / la periodista, el / la policía*
10	How do you say in Spanish: without having an interview?	*Sin tener una entrevista*
11	What is *un negocio* in English?	A business
12	When talking about work, what is a *puente*?	A long weekend

Previous questions

Use the questions below to check your knowledge from previous chapters.

Questions / Answers

#	Questions	Answers
1	Write the number 956 in Spanish.	*Novecientos cincuenta y seis*
2	How do you say in Spanish: our grandmother?	*Nuestra abuela*
3	How do you say in Spanish: no one?	*Nadie*

Practice EXAM

Theme 1 Listening practice

Section A: Listening comprehension

School

Two young people are talking about their school. Which aspect of school does each speaker like? Which aspect do they dislike? Write the correct letter in each box.

A	Teachers
B	School uniform
C	School location
D	Sports facilities
E	Drama
F	Library

       Likes   **Dislikes**

1. ☐ ☐ [2 marks]

2. ☐ ☐ [2 marks]

Family life

A Spanish-speaking friend, Marcela, is talking to you about her family. What does she say about each person? Write the correct letter in each box.

Write **A** if only statement **A** is correct

       B if only statement **B** is correct

       A + B if both statements **A** and **B** are correct.

3.1 Her aunt… [1 mark]

A	has a good sense of humour.
B	gives good advice.
C	has several problems.

3.2 Her younger sister… [1 mark]

A	can be argumentative.
B	is a good listener.
C	is not very clever.

3.3 Her cousin… [1 mark]

A	is a nice person.
B	currently lives abroad.
C	gets a lot of homework.

3.4 Her mother… [1 mark]

A	is normally quite serious.
B	works as a chef.
C	is very sociable.

Practice EXAM

Theme 1 Listening practice

Healthy lifestyles

Listen to two people talking about healthy lifestyles. Complete the sentences in **English**. Write **one** word in each space.

4. The speaker is worried about his .... because

   she .... too much.

   He says she will not be able to do .... if she

   cannot .... well. **[4 marks]**

5. Many young people must eat more .... and

   avoid .... food.

   The speaker is worried about the .... we eat

   because it affects our .... **[4 marks]**

Section B: Dictation

You will now hear 4 short sentences.

Listen carefully and using your knowledge of Spanish sounds, write down in **Spanish** exactly what you hear for each sentence. **[8 marks]**

Sentence 1

....

....

Sentence 2

....

....

Sentence 3

....

....

Sentence 4

....

....

> **EXAM TIP**
>
> You will hear each sentence **three** times: the first time as a full sentence, the second time in short sections and the third time again as a full sentence.

Practice EXAM

Theme 1 Speaking practice

Part 1: Role-play

Prepare the following role-play task. Then listen to the teacher's prompts and respond.

You are talking to your Spanish friend.

Your teacher will play the part of your friend and will speak first.

You should address your friend as *tú*.

When you see this – **?** – you will have to ask a question.

> **In order to score full marks, you must include a verb in your response to each task.**
>
> 1. Describe your personality. (Give **one** detail.)
> 2. Say what one of your friends looks like. (Give **one** detail.)
> 3. Say when you see your friend. (Give **one** detail.)
> 4. Say **one** activity you do with your family at the weekend.
> **? 5.** Ask your friend a question about their family.

> **EXAM TIP**
>
> Keep your answers short and simple but make sure you include a suitable verb.

> **EXAM TIP**
>
> For the question ('?') element of the role-play, try using one of these question starters.
>
> *¿Tienes…?* Do you have…?
> *¿Hay…?* Is there…?
> *¿Te gusta…?* Do you like…?

Part 2: Reading aloud task

Read aloud the following text in **Spanish**.

> Quiero llevar una vida sana.
> Es muy importante cuidar de la salud.
> Hago natación una vez a la semana.
> Cuando nado bien, gano premios.
> Mi amiga tiene una dieta equilibrada.
> Quiere probar la comida chilena.

Then listen and respond to the four questions on the topic of **Healthy living and lifestyle**.

In order to score the highest marks, you must try to **answer all four questions as fully as you can**.

> **EXAM TIP**
>
> When you are asked a question in the speaking exam, your answers don't need to be true. For example, if you are asked about food you eat and don't know the right vocabulary, just use the food words you have learnt in Spanish.

Practice EXAM

Theme 1 Speaking practice

Part 3: Photo card task

- Prepare a description of these two photos. You may make as many notes as you wish and use these notes during the test.
- Then record yourself talking about the content of these photos for approximately one minute. **You must say at least one thing about each photo.**
- After you have spoken about the content of the photos, you will be asked questions related to **any** of the topics within the theme of **People and lifestyle**. Listen to and respond to the example questions.

EXAM TIP
You could use your first sentence to say where each photo is set before giving more details. That ensures you have said at least one thing about each photo without worrying about running out of time.

Photo 1

Photo 2

52 Theme 1

Theme 1 Reading practice

Section A: Reading comprehension

Healthy living

You see this post in an online blog about healthy eating in Chile.

> En el pasado, muchos latinoamericanos tenían una dieta sana, pero ahora, comen mucha más sal y menos fruta y verduras. En mi país, Chile, los problemas de salud están aumentando entre los grupos de todas las edades, sobre todo entre los niños.
>
> Ya es momento de mejorar la dieta de los chilenos. Como padre, pienso que los institutos no deben vender comida dulce. Además, sería buena idea tener clases de cocina para los alumnos porque tienen que entender la importancia de comer comida sana.

EXAM TIP

It is important to practise multiple choice questions as much as possible. Often, the vocabulary in all three possible options, A, B and C, appears in the text, so finding the correct answer requires careful reading!

Complete these sentences. Write the letter for the correct option in each box.

1. Nowadays, many Latin Americans… **[1 mark]**

A	have a healthy diet.
B	consume a lot of salt.
C	are vegetarian.

2. In Chile, health problems… **[1 mark]**

A	are under control.
B	are on the rise.
C	affect only children.

3. The author of the blog… **[1 mark]**

A	works for the Chilean government.
B	attends a Chilean school.
C	is a parent.

4. He thinks that… **[1 mark]**

A	school meals should be less expensive.
B	it would be a good idea for children to cook at home.
C	cooking lessons in school would be beneficial.

News headlines

You see these headlines on a news website.

A	A los españoles no les interesa casarse.
B	Las familias mexicanas tienen menos hijos.
C	Nuevo estudio sobre el corazón.
D	Muchos jóvenes sufren acoso en el instituto.
E	El paro sube otra vez.

Which headline matches each description? Write the correct letter in each box.

5. Physical health research **[1 mark]**

6. Marriage in decline **[1 mark]**

7. Employment issues **[1 mark]**

Practice 53

Practice — EXAM

Theme 1 Reading practice

The world of work. You read these comments on an online forum about work.

A — AIDA
Estoy en una oficina de nueve a cinco, de lunes a viernes. Este tipo de trabajo es aburrido, pero el salario es bueno. Me preocuparía estar sin trabajo.

C — SALVADORA
La semana que viene tengo puente. Mi jefe me permite salir media hora antes el viernes. Voy a descansar en casa.

B — FRANCISCO
Trabajo en una tienda de ropa. Tenemos muchísimos clientes todos los días. La mayoría son agradables, pero ayudar a tanta gente puede ser duro.

Match the correct person with each of the following questions. Write the correct letter in each box.

8. Who finds helping so many customers difficult? ☐ [1 mark]
9. Who is finishing early on Friday? ☐ [1 mark]
10. Who is worried about being unemployed? ☐ [1 mark]
11. Who earns a good salary? ☐ [1 mark]
12. Who is looking forward to some time off? ☐ [1 mark]
13. Who deals with friendly people most of the time? ☐ [1 mark]

Section B: Translation into English.

14. Translate these sentences into **English**.

Me encanta el pescado porque es sano.   [2 marks]
....

Mi instituto tiene una biblioteca moderna.   [2 marks]
....

Mi amigo nunca me critica.   [2 marks]
....

El próximo año, trabajaré en otro país.   [2 marks]
....

Ayer la profesora me ayudó cuando tuve un problema. [2 marks]
....

Practice — EXAM

Theme 1 Writing practice

Section A

1. You post this photo on social media.

What is in this photo?

Write **five** sentences in **Spanish**.

1.1 .... [2 marks]

1.2 .... [2 marks]

1.3 .... [2 marks]

1.4 .... [2 marks]

1.5 .... [2 marks]

LINK
There is also a 50-word task in Section A of the writing paper. You can practise this on pages 79 and 194.

2. Using your knowledge of grammar, complete the following sentences in **Spanish**.

Choose the correct Spanish word from the three options in the grid.

Write the correct **word** in the space, as shown in the example below.

Example

Mi asignatura ......*favorita*...... es la historia.

| favorito | favoritas | favorita |

2.1 Mi hermana nunca .... pan.

| come | como | comemos | [1 mark]

2.2 Me .... mis profesores de dibujo.

| encanta | gusta | encantan | [1 mark]

2.3 Mañana, mis abuelos van a .... a Italia.

| viajan | viajar | viajamos | [1 mark]

2.4 María tiene un .... comportamiento en clase.

| buena | bueno | buen | [1 mark]

2.5 Para tener una dieta equilibrada, ... que comer más fruta.

| voy | hay | debes | [1 mark]

Practice EXAM

Theme 1 Writing practice

3. Translate the following sentences into **Spanish**. [10 marks]

I have three sisters.

....

....

She drinks fresh milk every day.

....

....

Normally, I don't eat a lot of red meat.

....

....

English is much more difficult than music.

....

....

Yesterday, I studied history and French in the library.

....

....

Section B

Answer **either** Question 4.1 **or** Question 4.2.

You must only answer **one** of these questions.

Either

Question 4.1

You are writing an article about being healthy.

Write approximately **90** words in **Spanish**.

You must write something about each bullet point.

Describe:

- what exercise you do to stay fit
- what you ate last weekend
- how you are going to stay healthy in the future. [15 marks]

Or

Question 4.2

You are writing to your Spanish friend about your school.

Write approximately **90** words in **Spanish**.

You must write something about each bullet point.

Describe:

- why you like your favourite subjects
- what you did in school yesterday
- your future career plans. [15 marks]

EXAM TIP

Remember to respond to all the bullet points, as this will give you a better chance of gaining high marks. If you only respond to two of the points, your overall mark will be lower.

56 Theme 1

Knowledge VOCABULARY 2.1

2.1 Free-time activities

Playing sports

Las actividades	Activities
participar en deportes en el agua	to participate in water sports
salir a bailar	to go out dancing
correr una carrera	to run a race
entrenar en el estadio	to train at the stadium
hacer ejercicio al aire libre	to exercise outdoors
nadar en la piscina	to swim in the pool
jugar al baloncesto / fútbol	to play basketball / football
montar a caballo / en bicicleta	to ride a horse / a bicycle
nadar en el mar	to swim in the sea
participar en actividades físicas	to take part in physical activities
subir una montaña	to go up a mountain

¡Soy muy activo!	I am very active!
Este año **estoy aprendiendo** a nadar.	This year I am learning to swim.
Preferimos los deportes de invierno.	We prefer winter sports.
Nadar en aguas calientes puede ser emocionante.	Swimming in warm waters can be exciting.
¿Cuál fue el resultado del partido?	What was the result of the match?
¡Perdimos, pero jugamos bien!	We lost, but we played well!
El precio de las entradas **está subiendo**.	The price of tickets is going up.
Ahora **estamos viendo** al Real Madrid.	Now we are watching Real Madrid.
El equipo de chicas español **está jugando** bien.	The Spanish female team is playing well.

GRAMMAR TIP

The present continuous tense describes an action in progress. Use the verb *estar* (to be) + the present participle of the verb: *estoy jugando* – I am playing; *están viendo* – they are watching. See page 137.

Una vida deportiva A sporting life

Normalmente nado dos veces a la semana, pero mi deporte favorito es el fútbol porque es divertido jugar en equipo. Este año, mi hermana mayor **está jugando** al baloncesto en el instituto y **está entrenando** mucho para ganar los partidos. Mis padres no son tan activos. Sin embargo, a veces compran entradas para ver a sus jugadores de fútbol favoritos, como Alexia Putellas.

I usually swim twice a week, but my favourite sport is football because it is fun to play in a team. This year, my older sister is playing basketball at school and she is training a lot to win the matches. My parents are not so active. However, sometimes they buy tickets to see their favourite football players, like Alexia Putellas.

REMEMBER

The verb *jugar* (to play) is used for sports played with a ball. Remember to follow it with *al*.

Juego al fútbol.
I play football.

Knowledge — VOCABULARY

2.1 Free-time activities

Different types of hobbies

Mis intereses	My interests
aprender a pintar	to learn to paint
comenzar / empezar a estudiar italiano	to start studying Italian
dejar de cantar	to stop singing
llegar a aprender una lengua	to manage to learn a language
ver una obra de teatro	to watch a theatre play
volver a hacer camping	to go camping again

El tiempo libre	Free time
Toco la guitarra todos los días.	I play the guitar every day.
Me gustaría ir al espectáculo de baile.	I would like to go to the dance show.
El arte me hace feliz.	Art makes me happy.
Nuestra amiga tiene entradas gratis para el parque temático.	Our friend has free tickets to the theme park.
Intento hacer fotos a los pájaros con mi cámara nueva.	I try to take photos of the birds with my new camera.
Las voy a subir a las redes sociales.	I am going to upload them on social media.
No puedo bailar si no sé las letras de las canciones.	I can't dance if I don't know the lyrics of the songs.
Me interesa leer, sobre todo las novelas de Isabel Allende.	I'm interested in reading, especially the novels of Isabel Allende.
No me gusta la música moderna.	I don't like modern music.
Los sábados, hacemos dibujos y escribimos cartas.	On Saturdays, we do drawings and write letters.

> **REMEMBER**
>
> Certain verbs change meaning when followed by the preposition *a* or *de*. For example:
>
> *volver* – to return; *volver* + *a* + infinitive – to do something again. See page 158.

¡No hay suficiente tiempo! *There is not enough time!*

¡Quiero hacer tantas cosas este fin de semana! Primero, voy a ir al gimnasio. Luego, iré a la piscina. Por la tarde, tengo que comprar una mochila. Ya tengo una, pero **la** rompí la semana pasada. El domingo, mis padres van a ir a una corrida de toros. Tienen una entrada para mí, pero no **la** quiero. Estoy en contra de las corridas porque **me** parecen peligrosas.

I want to do so many things this weekend! First, I am going to go to the gym. Then, I will go to the swimming pool. In the afternoon, I have to buy a rucksack. I already have one, but I broke it last week. On Sunday, my parents are going to go to a bullfight. They have a ticket for me, but I don't want it. I'm against bullfights because they seem dangerous to me.

> **GRAMMAR TIP**
>
> In Spanish, the direct object pronouns *me* (me), *te* (you), *lo / la* (him, her, it), *los / las* (them) are most often placed before the verb and agree in gender and number with the noun they replace. For example: *lo tengo* – I have it; *los compramos* – we buy them. See page 129.

Vocabulary learning

2.1

Learn this vocabulary and then use the 'look, cover, write, check' technique to make sure you really know it. Cover the English first and then the Spanish.

Free-time activities

Spanish	✓	English	✓
la actividad		activity	
al aire libre		in the open air, outdoors	
el arte		art	
bailar		to dance	
la bicicleta, bici		bicycle, bike	
caliente		warm, hot	
la cámara		camera	
el camping		campsite, camping	
la canción		song	
cantar		to sing	
la carta		letter	
como		like, as	
la copa		cup	
correr		to run	
la corrida		bullfight	
la cosa		thing	
dejar de (+ inf.)		to stop (+ -ing)	
en contra		against, in opposition	
la entrada		(admission) ticket	
el equipo		team	
el éxito		success	
la foto		photo, picture	
gratis		free (of charge)	
la guitarra		guitar	
italiano		Italian	

Spanish	✓	English	✓
el / la jugador(a)		player	
la lengua		language	
la letra		lyrics	
libre		free	
llegar a		to manage to, succeed in	
el mar		sea	
la montaña		mountain	
montar		to ride	
la novela		novel	
la obra		book, play, work (of art)	
el pájaro		bird	
el parque temático		theme park	
participar		to participate	
pintar		to paint	
la piscina		swimming pool	
el precio		price, cost, value	
el resultado		result	
romper		to break	
sobre		on top of, over	
tanto/a(s)		so much / many	
el toro		bull	
tratar de		to try to	
volver a		to do again	

> **REVISION TIP**
>
> Make a note of any 'false friends' when learning Spanish vocabulary. These are Spanish words that look or sound like English words but have a different meaning. For example: *el éxito* – success, *largo* – long.

Knowledge 59

Retrieval VOCABULARY

Answer the questions below. Cover the answers column with a piece of paper and write down as many answers as you can. Check and repeat.

Questions | Answers

1. Translate this question into Spanish: Do you want to play tennis? — *¿Quieres jugar al tenis?*
2. What does *una entrada* mean in English? — An (admission) ticket
3. What is *un equipo de baloncesto*? — A basketball team
4. Using the verb *volver*, how do you say in Spanish: I want to sing again? — *Quiero volver a cantar*
5. Write the present participle of the verbs *bailar*, *correr* and *escribir*. — *Bailando, corriendo, escribiendo*
6. Translate this sentence into Spanish: They are swimming in the sea. — *Están nadando en el mar*
7. Rewrite this sentence with a direct object pronoun: *El viernes, leo una novela.* — *El viernes la leo*
8. When followed by *de* and a verb in the infinitive form, what does *dejar* mean? — To stop (+ -ing)
9. How do you say in Spanish: I am going to read them? — *Voy a leerlas*
10. Translate this sentence into English: *Mi tío está bailando.* — My uncle is dancing
11. What is the difference in meaning between *gratis* and *libre*? — *Gratis* means 'free of charge', *libre* means 'free' in the sense of freedom or not being occupied
12. What does *al aire libre* mean in English? — Outside, in the open air

Previous questions

Use the questions below to check your knowledge from previous chapters.

Questions | Answers

1. Which hundreds are *not* formed by adding *-cientos* to the numbers 2–9? — *Quinientos* (500), *setecientos* (700), *novecientos* (900)
2. How do you say in Spanish: I am very hungry? — *Tengo mucha hambre*
3. How do you say in Spanish: I want to be a lawyer? — *Quiero ser abogado*

Knowledge VOCABULARY 2.1

2.1 Free-time activities

Viewing habits

¿Qué ponen esta noche?	What's on tonight?
Quiero ver la nueva temporada de mi serie favorita.	I want to watch the new season of my favourite series.
¡Vamos a ver un programa de telerrealidad **divertidísimo**!	We're going to watch a really fun reality show.
¿Cuál es tu programa favorito?	Which is your favourite programme?
A mí me gustan los musicales.	I like musicals.
Me encanta ver los concursos y responder a las preguntas de cultura.	I love watching quiz shows and answering the questions about culture.
Este nuevo grupo de rock es **emocionantísimo**.	This new rock group is really exciting.
No se puede grabar el concierto.	You can't record the concert.
A veces ver un programa infantil puede ser muy educativo.	Sometimes watching a children's programme can be very educational.

Las películas	Films
¿Prefieres el cine o la televisión?	Do you prefer the cinema or television?
En casa evitamos ver películas con violencia.	At home, we avoid watching violent films.
Los personajes en esta película son **aburridísimos**.	The characters in this film are really boring.
Las películas de acción son mi tipo favorito.	Action films are my favourite type.
Tiene escenas que no son buenas para los niños.	It has scenes that are not good for children.

GRAMMAR TIP

For greater originality in your speaking and writing, instead of using *muy* (very) with adjectives, try removing the last vowel and add *-ísimo / a*:

bueno / a (good) → *buenísimo / a* (very / really good)

SOUNDS TIP

The single *r* in the middle of a word is pronounced in a similar way to the soft *d* in English as in 'ladder'. However, *r* at the start of a word and *rr* sound more like the purr of a cat, such as in tele**rr**ealidad and **r**esponder.

¿Cómo ves la tele? How do you watch TV?

¿Cómo prefieres ver la televisión? En este momento, prefiero verla en mi móvil porque lo llevo a **todos** los sitios. Aunque la pantalla es un poco pequeña, funciona muy bien. **Poca** gente ve la tele en su ordenador, creo. **Muchos** de mis amigos la ven con sus familias.

How do you prefer to watch TV? At the moment, I prefer to watch it on my mobile because I carry it around everywhere. Although the screen is a bit small, it works very well. Few people watch TV on their computers, I think. Many of my friends watch it with their families.

GRAMMAR TIP

Indefinite adjectives such as *todos, poca* and *muchos* agree with the noun that follows. See page 124.

 Knowledge VOCABULARY

2.1 Free-time activities

Going out

Planes de fin de semana — *Weekend plans*

Me gusta dar un paseo solo los domingos. — *I like going for a walk alone on Sundays.*

El sábado pasado, **invité** a algunos amigos a mi casa. — *Last Saturday, I invited some friends to my house.*

No voy a salir porque tengo que ahorrar dinero. — *I'm not going to go out because I have to save money.*

Anoche lo **pasé** muy bien en la fiesta de cumpleaños. — *Last night, I had a very good time at the birthday party!*

Llevé mi pantalón nuevo. — *I wore my new trousers.*

Tendrás que esperar para comprar las entradas del teatro. — *You will have to wait to buy the theatre tickets.*

¿Hay una oferta en el supermercado? — *Is there an offer in the supermarket?*

¿Se permiten perros en el museo de ciencias? — *Are dogs allowed in the science museum?*

Comer fuera — *Eating out*

Reservé una mesa para dos. — *I reserved a table for two.*

Los camareros son simpatiquísimos. — *The waiters are really friendly.*

Ayer **gasté** mucho dinero en la cena. — *Yesterday I spent a lot of money on dinner.*

Cuando **llegó** la cuenta, ¡mi amiga se calló! — *When the bill arrived, my friend went quiet!*

No puedo recomendar ese restaurante. ¡Es malísimo! — *I can't recommend that restaurant. It's really bad!*

Aquí sirven tapas y bebidas frías. — *Here they serve tapas and cold drinks.*

Ese restaurante francés está de moda. — *That French restaurant is fashionable.*

Una fiesta horrible — *A horrible party*

La semana pasada **fui** a una fiesta de Navidad y **fue** un desastre total. Primero, **perdí** mi móvil, luego los camareros no **fueron** muy agradables y la comida **fue** horrible. Además, no **bailé** porque **no me gustó** nada la música y me puse unos zapatos que me hicieron daño en los pies. ¡Creo que el año que viene me quedaré en casa!

Last week I went to a Christmas party and it was a total disaster. First, I lost my mobile, then the waiters were not very pleasant, and the food was horrible. Furthermore, I didn't dance because I didn't like the music at all, and I wore shoes that hurt my feet. I think I'll stay at home next year!

GRAMMAR TIP

The preterite tense describes completed actions. For example: *cené* – I had dinner; *permitieron* – they allowed.
See pages 143–144.

SOUNDS TIP

The letters *cu* when followed by a vowel make a *kw* sound like the English *qu*: **cu**enta, **cu**ando. When followed by a consonant, *cu* sounds more like *koo*: **cu**mpleaños.

GRAMMAR TIP

Many important verbs are irregular in the preterite tense. The verbs *ir* (to go) and *ser* (to be) are identical:

fui – I went or I was;
fue – he / she / it went or he / she / it was.
See page 144.

REMEMBER

In the preterite tense, be careful with *gustar* and verbs like *gustar*: *me gustó* – I liked (it); *me encantó* – I loved (it).

Vocabulary learning

2.1

Learn this vocabulary and then use the 'look, cover, write, check' technique to make sure you really know it. Cover the English first and then the Spanish.

Viewing habits

Spanish	✓	English	✓
la (pelicula de) acción		action (film)	
aburrido/a		boring	
el concierto		concert	
el concurso		quiz, competition	
la cultura		culture	
el daño		harm, damage	
divertido/a		fun	
educativo/a		educational	
emocionante		exciting	
la escena		scene, stage	
funcionar		to function, work	
el grupo		group	
la moda, de moda		fashion, fashionable	
el móvil		mobile phone	
el musical		musical	
el ordenador		computer	
la pantalla		screen, monitor	
el personaje		character (in book / film)	
poner		to put on	
el programa		programme	
la serie		series	
la tele, televisión		TV, television	
la telerrealidad		reality TV	
la temporada		season (of sport, music)	
el tipo		type	
la violencia		violence	

Going out

Spanish	✓	English	✓
agradable		pleasant, nice	
ahorrar		to save (time, money)	
callarse		to quieten, to be quiet	
el / la camarero/a		waiter / waitress	
la cena		dinner, evening meal	
la cuenta		bill	
gastar		to spend (money)	
invitar		to invite	
mal		bad, badly	
la mesa		table	
la Navidad		Christmas	
la oferta		offer	
pasarlo bien / mal		to have a good / bad time	
el precio		price, cost, value	
quedar(se)		to stay	
recomendar		to recommend	
reservar		to reserve, book	
responder		to respond, answer	
el restaurante		restaurant	
el supermercado		supermarket	
las tapas		tapas (small dishes of food)	

Knowledge

Retrieval

VOCABULARY

Answer the questions below. Cover the answers column with a piece of paper and write down as many answers as you can. Check and repeat.

Questions / Answers

#	Question	Answer
1	How do you say in Spanish: screen?	*La pantalla*
2	Name three indefinite adjectives and say what they mean in English.	Possible answers include: *Tanto* (so much / so many), *cierto* (certain), *mucho* (much / many / a lot of)
3	Say these words aloud and translate them into English: *recomendar, ahorrar*	*Recomendar* – to recommend, *ahorrar* – to save (Note that the *r* should be rolled on both words)
4	How does the suffix *-ísimo/a* change the meaning of an adjective? Give an example.	It intensifies the meaning. For example: *buenísimo/a* – very / really good; *malísimo/a* – very / really bad
5	Which two verbs are identical in the preterite tense?	*Ser* (to be) and *ir* (to go)
6	Translate this sentence into English: *Me lo pasé bien el fin de semana pasado*.	I had a good time last weekend
7	Translate this sentence into Spanish: I liked the programme a lot.	*Me gustó mucho el programa*
8	Conjugate the verb *gastar* (to spend) in the preterite tense in the 1st singular person.	*Gasté*
9	Answer this question in Spanish: ¿Qué viste en la tele la semana pasada?	*La semana pasada vi...*
10	Translate this sentence into English: *La serie fue interesantísima*.	The series was very interesting
11	Complete the gap with the correct form of *encender* in the preterite tense. *Ellos _____ la tele*.	*Ellos encendieron la tele*
12	How do you say in Spanish: Waiter, the bill!	*¡Camarero, la cuenta!*

Previous questions

Use the questions below to check your knowledge from previous chapters.

Questions / Answers

#	Question	Answer
1	How do you say in Spanish: our grandmother?	*Nuestra abuela*
2	What is the name of the Spanish qualification similar to A Levels?	*Bachillerato*
3	What is the difference in meaning between *el lunes* and *los lunes*?	*El lunes* means 'on Monday' and *los lunes* 'on Mondays'

Knowledge **VOCABULARY** 2.2

2.2 Customs, festivals and celebrations

Celebrations with family

¡Celebramos!	We're celebrating
¡Enhorabuena por vuestra boda!	Congratulations on your wedding!
Vamos a comprar un regalo para celebrar **el cumpleaños de mi primo**.	We're going to buy a gift to celebrate my cousin's birthday.
Mis amigos me dieron caramelos **el día de mi cumpleaños**.	My friends gave me sweets on my birthday.
Este regalo es muy especial, gracias.	This is a very special gift, thank you.
¿Vienes a la fiesta conmigo o con tu novio?	Are you coming to the festival with me or your boyfriend?
¡Va a ser una celebración muy animada!	It's going to be a very lively celebration!
¿Llevaste tu disfraz a la fiesta?	Did you wear your costume / fancy dress to the party?
La novia llevó un vestido blanco bonito.	The bride wore a beautiful white dress.
También me gustó el traje negro de su pareja.	I also liked her partner's black suit.

Las celebraciones religiosas	Religious celebrations
Mis primos musulmanes estuvieron en la mezquita ayer.	My Muslim cousins were at the mosque yesterday.
Al final de una boda en la iglesia, la pareja puede besarse.	At the end of a church wedding, the couple can kiss.
Hay varias fiestas católicas durante el año.	There are several Catholic festivals during the year.
Sonia y Beltrán leerán en voz alta en la sinagoga.	Sonia and Beltrán will read aloud in the synagogue.
Estamos cantando en el templo.	We're singing in the temple.
Mis amigos judíos comen juntos los viernes.	My Jewish friends eat together on Fridays.

> **GRAMMAR TIP**
>
> In Spanish, *de* is used to indicate possession or ownership. Note that apostrophes don't exist in Spanish!
>
> *la fiesta **de** Ana* – Ana's party, *los libros **de** David* – David's books

A mi familia le gusta celebrar *My family likes celebrating*

Para los cincuenta años de casados de mis abuelos, el mes pasado **dimos** una fiesta sorpresa en un restaurante. Mis tíos **vinieron** desde Chile. Yo **me puse** mi vestido favorito y les **di** un regalo. La comida que compartimos fue deliciosa. **Estuvimos** allí cantando y bailando hasta las dos de la mañana. Lo mejor de la celebración fue la alegría de mis abuelos.

For my grandparents' fifty-year wedding anniversary, last month we gave a surprise party in a restaurant. My aunt and uncle came over from Chile. I put on my favourite dress and I gave them a gift. The food that we shared was delicious. We were there singing and dancing until two o'clock in the morning. The best thing about the celebration was my grandparents' happiness.

> **GRAMMAR TIP**
>
> Some of the most common irregular verbs in the preterite tense are *dar, estar, poner* and *venir*. See page 144.

Knowledge — VOCABULARY

2.2 Customs, festivals and celebrations

Festivals in the Hispanic world

Las fiestas	Festivals
En el Día de Muertos hay un desfile con muchas flores.	On the Day of the Dead, there is a parade with a lot of flowers.
¿Prefieres las celebraciones de Nochebuena o Nochevieja?	Do you prefer Christmas Eve or New Year's Eve celebrations?
En la Tomatina la gente se tira tomates en la calle.	At the Tomatina, people throw tomatoes at each other in the street.
Esta Navidad, comeremos todos juntos.	This Christmas, we will all eat together.
Los pasos de Semana Santa son tan bonitos.	The religious images in the Easter Week processions are so beautiful.
Los Reyes Magos traen regalos para el Día de Reyes el 6 de enero.	The Three Wise Men bring presents for Epiphany on 6 January.
Los Sanfermines son populares, pero no me gusta ir a la plaza de toros.	The Sanfermines festival is popular, but I don't like going to the bullring.
Los habitantes de Valencia celebran las Fallas en las calles.	Locals in Valencia celebrate the Fallas in the streets.
¿Cuándo es el día de tu santo?	When is your saint's day?

Las costumbres	Customs
Me interesan las costumbres españolas.	I am interested in Spanish customs.
Me encanta comer las doce uvas en Nochevieja.	I love eating the twelve grapes on New Year's Eve.
Vi un espectáculo de flamenco en Sevilla.	I saw a flamenco show in Seville.
¿Viste los fuegos artificiales y los fuegos?	Did you see the fireworks and the fires?
Hay puestos que venden platos dulces.	There are stalls that sell sweet dishes.

REVISION TIP

Words that end in -tion in English often end in -ción in Spanish. For example: *tradición, acción, celebración.*

SOUNDS TIP

The *ll* in Spanish sounds a bit like the *y* in 'yes' (particularly in Latin America) or the *j* in 'jump' (in many parts of central Spain).

¡Ya llega la Navidad! *Christmas is coming!*

Me encanta participar en las celebraciones de Navidad. En Nochebuena, **me gusta** ver la televisión y ayudar a mis padres a cocinar. Cenamos todos juntos y, por la mañana, abrimos los regalos. **No me molesta** ser la última en abrir un regalo. Navidad **me parece** una fiesta emocionante para niños y gente mayor.

I love to participate in the Christmas celebrations. On Christmas Eve, I like to watch television and help my parents to cook. We have dinner together and, in the morning, we open presents. I don't mind being the last one to open a present. Christmas seems to me like an exciting holiday for children and older people.

GRAMMAR TIP

Notice how verbs like *me encanta, me gusta, (no) me molesta* and *me parece* translate into English. Take care when translating these verbs from English to Spanish! See page 133.

2.2

Vocabulary learning

Learn this vocabulary and then use the 'look, cover, write, check' technique to make sure you really know it. Cover the English first and then the Spanish.

Celebrations

Spanish	✓	English	✓
abrir		to open, unwrap	
la alegría		joy, happiness	
alto/a		loud	
animado/a		lively	
besar		to kiss	
católico/a		catholic	
celebrar		to celebrate	
la celebración		celebration	
compartir		to share	
conmigo		with me	
el disfraz		costume, fancy dress	
¡Enhorabuena!		Congratulations!	
especial		special	
el final		end, ending	
la iglesia		church	
judío/a		Jewish	
la mezquita		mosque	
musulmán/a		Muslim	
el regalo		present, gift	
la sinagoga		synagogue	
la sorpresa		surprise	
el templo		temple	
traer		to bring	
el traje		suit, costume	
último/a		last	
el vestido		dress	
la voz		voice	

Festivals in the Hispanic world

Spanish	✓	English	✓
la calle		street	
la costumbre		custom, habit, tradition	
el desfile		parade, procession	
el Día de Muertos		Day of the Dead	
el Día de Reyes		Epiphany (6 Jan)	
dulce		sweet	
el flamenco		flamenco (dance / music)	
la flor		flower	
los fuegos artificiales		fireworks	
el / la habitante		local (person), inhabitant	
las Fallas		Valencian celebration	
la Nochebuena		Christmas Eve	
la Nochevieja		New Year's Eve	
el paso		religious image carried in Holy Week processions	
la plaza de toros		bullring	
el puesto		stall (market)	
los Reyes Magos		the Three Wise Men / Kings	
los Sanfermines		festival in Pamplona with bull runs	
el santo		saint, saint's day	
la Semana Santa		Holy Week, Easter Week	
tirar		to throw, pull	
el tomate		tomato	
la Tomatina		Spanish tomato festival	
la uva		grape	
vender		to sell	

Knowledge

Retrieval

VOCABULARY

Answer the questions below. Cover the answers column with a piece of paper and write down as many answers as you can. Check and repeat.

Questions | Answers

#	Question	Answer
1	What are the two meanings of *fiesta*?	Party, festival
2	Name three religious buildings in Spanish.	Possible answers include: *una mezquita* (mosque), *una iglesia* (church), *una sinagoga* (synagogue), *un templo* (temple)
3	How do you say in Spanish: Congratulations!	¡Enhorabuena!
4	Answer this question in Spanish and give a reason: *¿Cuál es tu fiesta favorita?*	Sample answer: *Me gusta celebrar la Navidad con mi familia porque comemos todos juntos*
5	What date is *Nochebuena* celebrated in Spain?	Christmas Eve (24 December)
6	Choose the correct option. Then translate the sentence. *Me parece / parecen un regalo bonito.*	*Me parece un regalo bonito* — It seems like a nice present to me
7	Name three festivals that take place in Spain.	Possible answers include: *las Fallas, la Tomatina, los Sanfermines, la Semana Santa, la Navidad, el Día de Reyes*
8	What are *fuegos artificiales*?	Fireworks
9	Translate this sentence into Spanish: We gave you a costume.	*Te dimos un disfraz*
10	What's the noun of the verb *celebrar*?	*Celebración*
11	When talking about the *Semana Santa* festival, what is a *paso*?	It is a religious image carried in Holy Week processions
12	How do you say in Spanish: parade?	*El desfile*

Put paper here

Previous questions

Use the questions below to check your knowledge from previous chapters.

Questions | Answers

#	Question	Answer
1	Name three body parts in Spanish.	Possible answers include: *la cabeza, el diente, la mano, el pie*
2	Translate this sentence into Spanish: I have to get very good grades.	*Tengo que sacar muy buenas notas*
3	How do you say in Spanish: screen?	*La pantalla*

Put paper here

Knowledge

VOCABULARY — 2.3

2.3 Celebrity culture

Hispanic icons

Famosos del pasado y presente / **Celebrities past and present**

Esta actriz tiene muchos premios.	This actress has many awards.
Mi tío **era** seguidor del actor Javier Bardem.	My uncle was a fan of the actor Javier Bardem.
Le **encantaba** el cine.	He used to love the cinema.
Este director hace películas muy buenas.	This film director makes very good films.
El año pasado, **veía** muchas series.	Last year, I watched a lot of series.
El cantante colombiano Maluma tiene un nuevo proyecto.	The Colombian singer Maluma has a new project.
Ella tuvo un papel importante en esta serie.	She had an important role in this series.
El jugador de fútbol Lamine Yamal tiene mucho éxito.	The football player Lamine Yamal is very successful.
¡Antes, él **iba** a mi instituto!	Before, he used to go to my school!
Rosalía es una estrella de la música actual.	Rosalía is a star of current music.
Algunos influencers ponen anuncios en sus cuentas de TikTok.	Some influencers put adverts on their TikTok accounts.
Karol G **vivía** en Colombia.	Karol G lived in Colombia.
No **era** tan famosa entonces.	She wasn't as famous then.

GRAMMAR TIP

The imperfect tense describes what you 'used to do' or 'were doing'.

REMEMBER

The imperfect tense has just three irregular verbs: *ser* (era, eras, era…), *ir* (iba, ibas, iba…), *ver* (veía, veías, veía…). See page 146.

¿Te gustaría ser famoso? / Would you like to be famous?

Mi sueño es tener una gran voz y grabar música como Shakira.	My dream is to have a great voice and record music like Shakira.
No me importa ser famoso, pero me gustaría ser rico.	Being famous doesn't matter to me, but I would like to be rich.
Ser famoso puede traer muchos problemas.	Being famous can cause many problems.

REVISION TIP

Learn the endings of each tense by heart. Make sure you pronounce the endings clearly, as a mistake can lead to misunderstanding.

Una modelo a seguir / A role model

Mi cantante favorita es Ana Mena. Cuando Ana **era** pequeña, **cantaba** todo el rato. Cuando **tenía** 12 años, **actuaba** en una serie de televisión. Le **veía** cada semana y siempre **escuchaba** su música en mi casa. Mi sueño es cantar como ella, pero no tengo una voz muy bonita.

My favourite singer is Ana Mena. When Ana was little, she used to sing all the time. When she was 12 years old, she was acting in a television series. I would watch her every week and I would always listen to her music at home. My dream is to sing like her, but I haven't got a nice voice.

GRAMMAR TIP

To form the imperfect tense with **-ar** verbs, use the ending *-aba*.
For **-er** / **-ir** verbs, use the ending *-ía*. See page 146.

Knowledge VOCABULARY

2.3 Celebrity culture

The pros and cons of fame

En el ojo público	In the public eye
Anoche vi una entrevista con el artista Sebastián Yatra.	Last night, I watched an interview with the performer Sebastián Yatra.
Hay muchas desventajas de ser modelo.	There are lots of disadvantages to being a model.
Es verdad que esos mensajes no eran justos.	It's true that those messages were unfair.
Muchos famosos dicen mentiras en la tele.	Many celebrities lie on TV.
Hay revistas que no dicen la verdad sobre los famosos.	There are magazines that don't tell the truth about celebrities.
Si soy famosa en el futuro, protegeré mi identidad en Internet.	If I am famous in the future, I will protect my identity on the internet.
No leo los periódicos que hablan de la vida de los famosos.	I don't read newspapers that talk about celebrities' lives.
Hay que mostrar respeto a los famosos online.	We must show respect for celebrities online.
Un actor chileno dijo que recibió acoso.	A Chilean actor said that he was bullied.
Muchas jugadoras no comparten información online.	Many players do not share information online.
A veces parece que está de moda criticar a los famosos.	Sometimes it seems that it is fashionable to criticise celebrities.

La imagen lo es todo	Image is everything
Llevan ropa de marca cara.	They wear expensive brands.
La organización **que** creó Shakira ayuda a los colegios.	The organization that Shakira set up helps schools.
Pienso que los famosos deben tener un buen comportamiento.	I think that celebrities have to have good behaviour.
Hay programas en la tele **que** muestran las casas de los famosos.	There are TV programmes that show celebrities' houses.

REMEMBER
Some nouns change only the article to indicate the masculine or feminine form. For example: **el / la** modelo, **el / la** artista.

REVISION TIP
It's a good idea to learn some set phrases in Spanish which you can then use and adapt in your own writing and speaking on different topics.

GRAMMAR TIP
Use relative clauses with *que* to make more complex sentences. See page 131.

Una mala experiencia A bad experience

Un actor famoso que **estaba** de vacaciones **tuvo** una mala experiencia. Alguien le **pidió** una foto y luego **empezó** a grabarle. Ese actor **explicó** que un día sus amigos le **dijeron** que no **disfrutaban de** ir a lugares públicos con él.

A famous actor who was on holiday had a bad experience. Someone asked him for a photo and then started to film him. This actor explained that one day his friends said to him that they didn't enjoy going to public places with him.

GRAMMAR TIP
Use the preterite and imperfect tenses together to narrate a story. See page 147.

Vocabulary learning

Learn this vocabulary and then use the 'look, cover, write, check' technique to make sure you really know it. Cover the English first and then the Spanish.

Celebrities

Spanish	✓	English	✓
actual		current	
colombiano/a		Colombian	
conocido/a		well-known, known	
el / la director(a)		director, manager	
la estrella		star	
explicar		to explain	
el / la famoso/a		celebrity, famous person	
me / te / le gustaría		I / you / he / she / it would like	
el / la influencer		influencer	
influir		to influence	
joven		young	
el / la modelo		model	
nuevo/a		new	
online		online	
el papel		role	
el premio		award	
el proyecto		project, plan	
el rato		time, moment, while	
seguir		to follow	

Fame

Spanish	✓	English	✓
alguien		someone	
caro/a		expensive	
el comentario		comment, remark	
crear		to create	
de moda		in fashion, fashionable	
la identidad		identity	
la imagen		image	
la información		information	
el / la Internet		internet	
justo/a		fair	
el lugar		place, position	
la marca		brand	
la mentira		lie	
mostrar		to show	
online		online	
la organización		organisation	
el periódico		newspaper	
el público		public	
el respeto		respect, regard	
el / la seguidor(a)		follower, fan, supporter	
sobre		about	
la (des)ventaja		(dis)advantage	
la verdad		truth	

Knowledge

Retrieval — VOCABULARY

Answer the questions below. Cover the answers column with a piece of paper and write down as many answers as you can. Check and repeat.

Questions / Answers

#	Question	Answer
1	Translate this sentence into English: *Su papel era muy bueno.*	Her / His role was very good
2	Complete the sentence with the correct form of the verb *ver* in the imperfect tense: *Mi padre _____ a los famosos en el cine, no en Internet.*	*Mi padre veía a los famosos en el cine, no en Internet*
3	Translate into Spanish: When I was little, my dream was to present a television programme.	*Cuando era pequeño/a, mi sueño era presentar un programa de televisión*
4	Which of the following words is a cognate? star / influencer / film	*El / la influencer* is a cognate Star – *la estrella* Film – *la película*
5	Translate *modelo a seguir* into English.	Role model (literally: a model to follow)
6	What is the noun 'follower' in Spanish?	*El / la seguidor(a)*
7	Identify the tenses and translate this sentence. *La actriz que hablaba se casó con el director.*	*Hablaba* – imperfect; *se casó* – preterite The actress who was talking got married with the director
8	What does the Spanish word *actual* mean in English?	Current
9	What are the three irregular verbs in the imperfect tense?	*Ir (iba), ser (era), ver (veía)*
10	What is the feminine form of 'model' in Spanish?	*La modelo*
11	How do you say in Spanish: respect?	*El respeto*
12	Which word is exactly the same in Spanish? identity / online / private	Online

Previous questions

Use the questions below to check your knowledge from previous chapters.

#	Question	Answer
1	If the word *completo* means 'complete', what is the Spanish for 'completely'?	*Completamente*
2	How do you say in Spanish: unemployment?	*El paro*
3	Name three religious buildings in Spanish.	Possible answers include: *una mezquita* (mosque), *una iglesia* (church), *una sinagoga* (synagogue), *un templo* (temple)

Practice EXAM

Theme 2 Listening practice

Section A: Listening comprehension

A famous sportsperson

You hear a famous sportsperson talking about her life on Spanish radio. What is her opinion on the following aspects?

Write **P** for a **positive** opinion

N for a **negative** opinion

P+N for a **positive** and **negative** opinion.

Write the correct letter in each box.

1. Riding her bike [1 mark]
2. Going to football matches [1 mark]
3. Christmas holidays [1 mark]
4. Easter holidays [1 mark]

A family celebration

You listen to an audio message from Aurelio to his best friend about his birthday party.

Complete the sentences.

Choose the correct answer and write the letter in each box.

5.1 Aurelio's birthday party… [1 mark]

A	is on 3 March.
B	has been organised by his boyfriend.
C	is going to be held in a restaurant.

5.2 Aurelio's mother… [1 mark]

A	has bought him a new phone.
B	is on holiday.
C	cannot attend the party in person.

6.1 Aurelio asks his friend… [1 mark]

A	to come to the party in fancy dress.
B	to tell jokes at the party.
C	to arrive at 10pm.

6.2 Aurelio says… [1 mark]

A	he would like lots of presents.
B	he is saving up.
C	he is going to Mexico next month.

Practice

Theme 2 Listening practice

The pros and cons of fame

You are listening to a Spanish podcast. The speaker is talking about the pros and cons of fame.

Answer the questions in **English**.

7. What do many celebrities say is their biggest problem?

   .... **[1 mark]**

8. As well as a lot of money, what can successful celebrities earn?

   .... **[1 mark]**

9. What have several famous singers been criticised about in the media?

   .... **[1 mark]**

10. Where do many celebrities choose to live?

    .... **[1 mark]**

EXAM TIP
Underline key words in the questions as you read them, such as 'who', 'what', 'where', 'when' question words.

Section B: Dictation

You will now hear 4 short sentences. Listen carefully and using your knowledge of Spanish sounds, write down in **Spanish** exactly what you hear for each sentence. **[8 marks]**

Sentence 1

....

....

Sentence 2

....

....

Sentence 3

....

....

Sentence 4

....

....

EXAM TIP
You will hear each sentence **three** times: the first time as a full sentence, the second time in short sections and the third time again as a full sentence.

 **Practice** EXAM

Theme 2 Speaking practice

Part 1: Role-play

Prepare the following role-play task. Then listen to the teacher's prompts and respond.

You are talking to your Spanish friend.

Your teacher will play the part of your friend and will speak first.

You should address your friend as *tú*.

When you see this – **?** – you will have to ask a question.

> **In order to score full marks, you must include a verb in your response to each task.**
>
> 1. Say what your favourite festival is. (Give **one** detail.)
> 2. Say why you like this festival. (Give **one** reason.)
> 3. Say how you celebrated your last birthday. (Give **one** detail.)
> ? 4. Ask your friend a question about their birthday.
> 5. Say one thing about your favourite celebrity.

EXAM TIP

You could mention a festival you celebrate or a Hispanic festival you have learned about.

Part 2: Reading aloud task

Read aloud the following text in **Spanish**.

> No me gusta ver corridas de toros en la tele.
>
> Es una actividad muy peligrosa.
>
> Mucha gente en España va a la plaza.
>
> Disfruta del espectáculo al sol.
>
> Yo prefiero otros deportes al aire libre.

Then listen and respond to the four questions on the topic of **Free-time activities**.

In order to score the highest marks, you must try to **answer all four questions as fully as you can**.

 **EXAM TIP**

To get the best marks you should try and extend each response to give three bits of information, including suitable verbs.

Theme 2 Speaking practice

Part 3: Photo card task

- Prepare a description of these two photos. You may make as many notes as you wish and use these notes during the test.
- Then record yourself talking about the content of these photos for approximately one minute. **You must say at least one thing about each photo.**
- After you have spoken about the content of the photos, you will be asked questions related to **any** of the topics within the theme of **Popular culture**. Listen to and respond to the example questions.

Photo 1

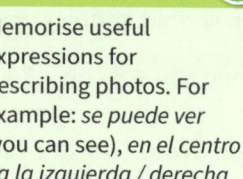

> **EXAM TIP**
> Memorise useful expressions for describing photos. For example: *se puede ver* (you can see), *en el centro / a la izquierda / derecha hay* (in the centre / on the left / right there is / are).

> **EXAM TIP**
> You can use the present continuous to describe what people are doing. For example: *está hablando / sonriendo / mirando...* (he / she is talking / smiling / looking at).

Photo 2

Practice EXAM

Theme 2 Reading practice

Section A: Reading comprehension

A famous singer

You read about the singer, Álvaro de Luna, on a Spanish website.

> El cantante Álvaro de Luna dijo en su última entrevista que los medios de comunicación le están causando mucho estrés. Explicó que todos los días hay periodistas que le hacen preguntas en la puerta de su casa sobre su familia.
>
> Álvaro explicó que el año pasado decidió dejar de usar su cuenta en Instagram. Continúa sin usarla y dice que se siente mejor.

Answer the following questions in **English**.

1. What is causing Álvaro de Luna stress at the moment?
   .... [1 mark]

2. Where do journalists ask Álvaro questions?
   .... [1 mark]

3. What did Álvaro decide to do last year?
   .... [1 mark]

4. How do we know his decision worked?
   .... [1 mark]

EXAM TIP

Don't worry if you don't understand all of the vocabulary in the text. Focus on finding the key words that relate to each question.

Childhood activities

You read an article about how children spend their free time.

> De momento, en las ciudades casi no se puede ver a niños jugando en grupo al aire libre como siempre hacían en el pasado. Ahora, sus padres prefieren organizar paseos en familia. En los años ochenta, millones de familias pasaban horas delante de la pantalla viendo películas en la televisión.
>
> Era una actividad social. Hoy, muchos niños ven sus películas favoritas solos en sus tabletas. Muchos jóvenes hacen deporte en su tiempo libre, pero en poco tiempo veremos que el número de niños que participan en deportes de equipo caerá.

What does the article say about these aspects of children's free time?

Write **P** for something that happened in the **past**
N for something that is happening **now**
F for something that is going to happen in the **future**.

5. Playing outside together all the time ☐ [1 mark]
6. Going on organised family walks ☐ [1 mark]
7. Watching films alone ☐ [1 mark]
8. Spending less time on team sports ☐ [1 mark]

Practice — EXAM

Theme 2 Reading practice

Weekend plans

Some friends are chatting on their mobile phones about their weekend plans.

Complete these sentences. Write the letter for the correct option in each box.

9. Jesús asks if they are going to the cinema this…

A	morning.
B	afternoon.
C	evening.

[1 mark]

10. Alejandra does not want to go to the cinema because she wants to be…

A	outside.
B	at home.
C	alone.

[1 mark]

11. Paula recommends going to the concert in the park because…

A	her mum likes live music.
B	she can drive them there.
C	it is free.

[1 mark]

Jesús
¿Vamos al cine? Es más barato por la mañana.

Alejandra
Me gustaría salir, sí, pero prefiero hacer una actividad al aire libre.

Paula
¿Por qué no vamos al concierto de música en el parque? ¡Es gratis! Mi madre nos llevará en coche.

Jesús
¡Buena idea!

Section B: Translation into English

12. Translate these sentences into **English**.

A veces mi hermano nada en el mar. [2 marks]

....

....

Me gustan los deportes de invierno porque son divertidos. [2 marks]

....

....

Mañana vamos a ir a una fiesta de cumpleaños. [2 marks]

....

....

Los fuegos artificiales son muy emocionantes. [2 marks]

....

....

Ayer vi a mi jugador favorito en un restaurante. [2 marks]

....

....

Practice **EXAM**

Theme 2 Writing practice

Section A

1. Write an email to your Mexican friend about free-time activities.

   Write approximately **50** words in **Spanish**.

   You must write something about each bullet point.

Mention:
- art
- computer games
- sport
- music
- cinema [10 marks]

> **LINK**
> There is also a photo description task in Section A of the writing paper. You can practise this on pages 55, 114 and 194.

2. Using your knowledge of grammar, complete the following sentences in **Spanish**.

Choose the correct Spanish word from the three options in the grid.

Write the correct **word** in the space, as shown in the example below.

Example

Yo ......voy...... al partido de fútbol.

| vas | vamos | voy |

2.1 Hay .... ruido en la fiesta.

| mucha | mucho | muy | [1 mark]

2.2 El .... día, vamos al mercado.

| primero | primer | primera | [1 mark]

2.3 ¿..................... empieza la película?

| Cuánto | Cuándo | Cuál | [1 mark]

2.4 Ayer, ... ejercicio en el jardín.

| hago | voy a hacer | hice | [1 mark]

2.5 Escucho música tres .... al día.

| tiempos | horas | vez | [1 mark]

Practice   EXAM

Theme 2 Writing practice

3. Translate the following sentences into **Spanish**. **[10 marks]**

I'm going to the concert on Sunday.

....

....

I prefer to celebrate my birthday at home.

....

....

It is difficult to organise a party.

....

....

I played basketball in the park.

....

....

My sister sings every day.

....

....

> **EXAM TIP**
>
> When translating sentences into Spanish, if you don't know a particular word try to think of a very similar one. Reasonable alternatives are accepted.

Section B

Answer **either** Question 4.1 **or** Question 4.2.

Either

Question 4.1

You are writing an article about free time.

Write approximately **90** words in **Spanish**.

You must write something about each bullet point.

Describe:

- an activity you like doing with family or friends
- an activity you enjoyed recently
- an activity you would like to try in the future.   **[15 marks]**

Or

Question 4.2

You are writing to your Spanish friend about celebrations and festivals.

Write approximately **90** words in **Spanish**.

You must write something about each bullet point.

Describe:

- your opinion on music concerts
- something you celebrated last month
- how you are going to celebrate your next birthday.   **[15 marks]**

> **EXAM TIP**
>
> Before you start writing, make notes for each bullet point of your chosen question. Write down useful words and phrases you can include to cover each prompt.

Knowledge — VOCABULARY — 3.1

3.1 Travel and tourism, including places of interest

Going on holiday

¡Vamos de vacaciones!	We're going on holiday!
Vamos de excursión al bosque en coche.	We're going on a trip to the forest by car.
¿Organizamos un viaje cultural a China?	Shall we organise a cultural trip to China?
Me gusta ver la naturaleza.	I like seeing nature.
¡Hay tantas comunidades que hablan español en Florida!	There are so many Spanish-speaking communities in Florida!
Me gustaría hablar con los habitantes.	I would like to talk to the locals.
En Egipto, **visitaríamos** templos bonitos.	In Egypt, we'd visit beautiful temples.
Los paisajes están tan hermosos.	The landscape is so beautiful.

De camino — On the way

El **aeropuerto** está lleno de turistas hoy.	The airport is full of tourists today.
Cogimos un **vuelo** directo a la isla.	We took a direct flight to the island.
El tren iba a 300 kilómetros por hora.	The train was going at 300 kilometres per hour.
El alojamiento está cerca de las montañas.	The accommodation is near the mountains.
¡Aquí está el plano de **nuestro** hotel!	Here's our hotel map!
¿Pusiste tu ropa en la maleta?	Did you put your clothes in the suitcase?

Un viaje al extranjero — A trip abroad

Para conocer bien la cultura latina, **tendrías** que viajar al extranjero. **Podrías** ir a México, por ejemplo. Está lejos de España, pero creo que sería un viaje bonito. Necesitarías bastante dinero porque el vuelo es largo y caro. Yo **pondría** poca ropa en una mochila para poder moverme fácilmente. **Haría** viajes cortos dentro del país en tren o autobús.

To truly get to know the Latin culture, you would need to travel abroad. You could go to Mexico, for example. It's far from Spain, but I think it would be a beautiful trip. You would need quite a lot of money because the flight is long and expensive. I would pack a few clothes in a backpack to be able to move around easily. I would make short trips in the country by train or by bus.

GRAMMAR TIP

Use the conditional to talk about probabilities, wishes and recommendations.

¡Aprenderíamos a montar a caballo!

We'd learn to go horseriding!

See page 151.

SOUNDS TIP

The *ue* sound in Spanish blends and is similar to the English sound in 'way'. For example: *bue*no, *pue*do. However, if the *ue* follows the letters *g* or *q*, the *u* is silent. For example: hambur**gue**sa, **que**so.

GRAMMAR TIP

There are five key verbs that are irregular in the conditional: tener – tendría, hacer – haría, poder – podría, poner – pondría, haber – habría. See page 151.

REMEMBER

The future tense and the conditional are formed in a similar way and they share the same irregular verbs. For example: *haré* (I will do) and *haría* (I would do).

Knowledge VOCABULARY

3.1 Travel and tourism, including places of interest

A staycation

Vacaciones en casa — *Holidays at home*

Este verano me quedo en casa.	This summer I'm staying at home.
Vamos a disfrutar de la cocina de tu región.	We are going to enjoy the cuisine of your region.
Voy a hacer una visita cultural en mi ciudad.	I'm going on a cultural visit in my city.
Iremos al museo a ver el arte local.	We will go to the museum to see the local art.
Voy a aprender sobre la comida mexicana.	I'm going to learn about Mexican food.
Tengo entradas para el concierto de música cubana.	I have tickets to the Cuban music concert.
Voy a participar en un espectáculo tocando la guitarra.	I'm going to take part in a show playing the guitar.

¿Qué tiempo hace hoy? — *What's the weather like today?*

Hace buen / mal tiempo.	The weather is good / bad.
Hace sol y calor.	It's sunny and hot.
Esta mañana, hacía fresco.	This morning, it was cool / mild.
Ayer por la noche, hizo mucho frío.	Last night, it was very cold.
Hará un poco de viento.	It's going to be a bit windy.
Llueve ahora.	It's raining now.
El cielo está gris hoy.	The sky is grey today.

SOUNDS TIP

When *g* is followed by *ui* or *uí* in Spanish, the *g* is a hard sound and the *u* is not pronounced. For example:
se**gui**r – to follow

REMEMBER

Use *mucho* or *un poco de* before nouns that describe the weather. For example:
Hace mucho calor.
Va a hacer un poco de frío.

Un verano en mi pueblo *A summer in my town*

El verano pasado, pasé unas vacaciones buenísimas, sin salir de mi pueblo. Mis amigos y yo quedábamos casi todos los días. ¡Fuimos a un festival de comida y lo pasamos genial! **Hizo** mucho calor. Este verano viene de visita mi primo mexicano. ¡Va a ser una experiencia bonita! Lo llevaré de camping y a un concierto porque **hará** muy buen tiempo.

Last summer, I had an amazing holiday without leaving my town. My friends and I met almost every day. We went to a food festival and had a great time! It was very hot. This summer, my Mexican cousin is visiting. It's going to be a lovely experience. I'm going to take him camping and to a concert because the weather will be great.

GRAMMAR TIP

In certain weather expressions, *hace* means 'it is':
Hace sol. It's sunny.

If you are describing past or future weather conditions, *hace* should also change to a past or future form:
Hizo calor. It was hot.
Hará frío. It will be cold.

REVISION TIP

Try reading the Spanish paragraph above out loud to practise your pronunciation.

Vocabulary learning

Learn this vocabulary and then use the 'look, cover, write, check' technique to make sure you really know it. Cover the English first and then the Spanish.

Going on holiday

Spanish	✓	English	✓
el aeropuerto		airport	
el alojamiento		accommodation	
el avión		plane, aeroplane	
el barco		boat, ship	
el billete		ticket (for transport)	
el bosque		forest, wood	
el camping		campsite, camping	
el campo		countryside	
la comunidad		community	
la entrada		ticket (for an event)	
el espectáculo		show	
la excursión		trip, excursion	
el extranjero		abroad	
la guitarra		guitar	
el habitante		local (person), inhabitant	
hermoso/a		beautiful	
lleno/a de		full of	
la maleta		suitcase	
la naturaleza		nature	
organizar		organize	
el paisaje		scenery, landscape	
el plano		map	
quedar		to meet	
quedarse		to stay	
el templo		temple	
el tren		train	
el / la turista		tourist	
las vacaciones; de vacaciones		holidays; on holiday	
el viaje		trip, journey	
el vuelo		flight	

Weather

Spanish	✓	English	✓
Hace / Hizo / Hará…		It is / was / will be…	
calor		hot	
frío		cold	
fresco		cool	
sol		sunny	
viento		windy	
el cielo		sky	
llover		to rain	

> **REVISION TIP**
>
> Use the weather vocabulary above to say what the weather **was** like yesterday, **is** like today and **will be** like tomorrow.

Retrieval

VOCABULARY

Answer the questions below. Cover the answers column with a piece of paper and write down as many answers as you can. Check and repeat.

Questions | Answers

#	Question	Answer
1	Name at least three modes of transport in Spanish.	Possible answers include: *tren, avión, barco, metro, coche*
2	Which of the following words is related to travelling? *el paisaje / la montaña / el vuelo*	*El vuelo* (flight)
3	Which of the following verbs is in the conditional? *quedaba / viajará / visitaría*	*Visitaría* (would visit)
4	What is the meaning of *fresco* when describing the weather?	Cool / mild
5	Translate this sentence into Spanish: The sky is blue today.	*El cielo está azul hoy*
6	Which of the following phrases means 'It will be hot.'? *Hace calor. / Hizo calor. / Hará calor.*	*Hará calor*
7	How do you say in Spanish: accommodation?	*El alojamiento*
8	Which is a shorter trip: *excursión* or *viaje*?	*Excursión*
9	Choose the correct word to complete the sentence: *En mi plano / maleta / turista hay mucha ropa.*	*En mi maleta hay mucha ropa*
10	Translate this sentence into Spanish: It was too windy yesterday.	*Hizo demasiado viento ayer*
11	Name three verbs with an irregular conditional form.	Possible answers include: *tener (tendría), hacer (haría), poder (podría), poner (pondría), haber (habría)*
12	If the noun 'rain' is *la lluvia*, what is the verb 'to rain' in Spanish?	*Llover*

Previous questions

Use the questions below to check your knowledge from previous chapters.

Questions | Answers

#	Question	Answer
1	How does the suffix *-ísimo/a* change the meaning of an adjective? Give an example.	It intensifies the meaning. For example: *buenísimo/a* – very / really good; *malísimo/a* – very / really bad
2	How do you say in Spanish: Congratulations!	*¡Enhorabuena!*
3	Translate *modelo a seguir* into English.	Role model (literally: a model to follow)

Knowledge VOCABULARY 3.1

3.1 Travel and tourism, including places of interest

Past holidays

¡Me lo pasé genial!	I had a great time!
Encontramos un hotel en la isla.	We found a hotel on the island.
Me gustaron mucho las actividades en la capital.	I really liked the activities in the capital city.
Compramos recuerdos para toda la familia.	We bought souvenirs for the whole family.
Hice fotos de la plaza mayor.	I took photos of the main square.
Descubrimos una playa hermosa.	We discovered a beautiful beach.
Me gustó el espectáculo de baile.	I liked the dance show.
Pasé la tarde descansando.	I spent the afternoon relaxing.

REMEMBER
The reflexive verb *gustar* agrees with the object (not the subject) in present and past tenses, e.g. *Me gustó el hotel. Me gustaron las playas.*

¡Me lo pasé mal!	I didn't have a good time!
Las luces en el hotel no funcionaban.	The lights in the hotel weren't working.
Se perdió mi maleta.	My suitcase got lost.
Tomé mucho el sol y me dolió la cabeza.	I sunbathed too much and my head hurt.
El camping estaba demasiado sucio.	The campsite was too dirty.
La mujer de la recepción no era nada agradable.	The woman at the reception wasn't nice.
Dejé mi móvil en el metro y alguien me lo robó.	I left my mobile phone in the undeground and someone stole it.
No disfrutamos de las vistas.	We didn't enjoy the view.
El viaje de vuelta fue horrible.	The return trip was horrible.

REVISION TIP
Practise using a range of verbs in different past tenses. Make sure you know how each one translates into English.

Problemas en un viaje *Problems on a trip*

¡Es mi último día en España! He viajado **por dos semanas**. Es un viaje guay, pero no sin problemas. Para empezar, el vuelo salió tarde. Luego, la primera noche, me perdí en Madrid. Estuve buscando un restaurante chino **durante una hora**. Otro día, se me olvidó mi mochila en el museo. ¡Y hoy, no deja de llover!

It's my last day in Spain! I've been travelling for two weeks. It's a cool trip, but not without problems. To begin with, the flight was late. Then, on the first evening, I got lost in Madrid. I was looking for a Chinese restaurant for an hour. On another day, I forgot my backpack in the museum. And today it won't stop raining!

GRAMMAR TIP
Use *por* or *durante* + time expression to say how long you have been doing something.

Knowledge

Knowledge

3.1 Travel and tourism, including places of interest

Vocabulary learning

Learn this vocabulary and then use the 'look, cover, write, check' technique to make sure you really know it. Cover the English first and then the Spanish.

Past holidays

Spanish	✓	English	✓
agradable		pleasant, nice	
el camping		campsite, camping	
la capital		capital (city)	
dejar		to leave	
dejar de + infinitive		to stop -ing	
demasiado		too	
descubrir		to discover	
doler		to hurt	
durante		for (time), during	
el espectáculo		show	
la estación		station	
funcionar		to function, work	
guay		cool	
la isla		island	
el metro		underground, metro, tube	

Spanish	✓	English	✓
olvidar		to forget	
perderse		to get lost	
por		for + time period	
la recepción		reception	
el recuerdo		souvenir	
robar		to steal	
sin		without	
tomar el sol		(to) sunbathe / sunbathing	
la vista		view	
la vuelta		return	

REVISION TIP

Practise using some of the Spanish vocabulary on this page to talk about a holiday that you have had or would like to have.

Retrieval — VOCABULARY — 3.1

Answer the questions below. Cover the answers column with a piece of paper and write down as many answers as you can. Check and repeat.

Questions | Answers

1. Choose the correct option:
   Me gustó / gustaron los espectáculos.
   → *Me <u>gustaron</u> los espectáculos*

2. Translate this sentence into English:
   Dejé mi móvil en el metro.
   → I left my mobile phone in the underground

3. If *funcionar* and *trabajar* can both be translated as 'to work', what is the difference in their meaning?
   → *Funcionar* is 'to work' in the sense of 'to function'; *trabajar* refers to someone doing a job or task

4. Translate this sentence into Spanish:
   I sunbathed.
   → *Tomé el sol*

5. In the context of holidays, what is the meaning of *el recuerdo*?
   → Souvenir

6. What does the word *la vista* mean in English?
   → View

7. If *volver* is the verb 'to return', what is the noun 'return'?
   → *La vuelta*

8. How do you say in Spanish: underground train?
   → *El metro*

9. Translate this sentence into English: *Se me olvidó mi billete.*
   → I forgot my ticket

10. Choose the correct option to complete the sentence:
    Estuve en Sevilla en / durante / de tres días.
    → *Estuve en Sevilla <u>durante</u> tres días*

11. Which of the following adjectives is negative in meaning?
    guay / sucio / agradable
    → *Sucio*

12. What is the difference in meaning between *perder* and *perderse*?
    → *Perder* means 'to lose something'
    Perderse means 'to get lost'

Previous questions

Use the questions below to check your knowledge from previous chapters.

Questions | Answers

1. Which of the following words is a cognate (the same word in Spanish and English)?
   star / influencer / film
   → *El/la influencer* is a cognate

2. How do you say in Spanish: respect?
   → *El respeto*

3. Which of the following verbs is in the conditional?
   veía / viajará / visitaría
   → *Visitaría* (would visit)

Knowledge  VOCABULARY

3.2 Media and technology

Media and technology

Las actividades online	**Online activities**
¿Quieres escribir un artículo para mi página web?	Do you want to write an article for my webpage?
Debo mandar un mensaje.	I have to send a message.
Sé cómo enviar emails / correos electrónicos.	I know how to send emails.
Normalmente grabo videos en mi móvil.	I normally record videos on my mobile phone.
Quiero jugar a los videojuegos.	I want to play computer games.
Puedo hablar con amigos que viven lejos.	I can talk to friends who live far away.
Tengo que leer más libros online.	I have to read more books online.
¿Sabes cómo compartir vídeos en TikTok?	Do you know how to share videos on TikTok?
Quisiera trabajar desde casa.	I would like to work from home.
Podría comprar productos en la app.	I could buy products on the app.
Debemos ver menos vídeos cortos.	We must watch fewer short videos.
¿Qué tipos de tecnología digital usas?	**What types of digital technology do you use?**
el móvil / el reloj / la televisión inteligente	smartphone / smartwatch / smart TV
el ordenador	computer
la tableta	tablet
las redes sociales	social media
la app (las apps)	app(s)
la cámara digital	digital camera
Internet	internet

GRAMMAR TIP

Use modal verbs + infinitive to talk about need, obligation, permission or probability: *poder* (to be able to / can), *deber / tener que* (to have to, must), *querer* (to want to) and *saber* (to know how to). See page 140.

REVISION TIP

There is a lot of topic vocabulary and grammar to cover for GCSE. Remember: 10–15 minutes of revision a day is better than cramming once every few weeks!

¿Para qué usas la tecnología? What do you use technology for?

La tecnología es muy importante en mi vida. En casa tenemos tres tabletas. Mi tableta tiene una pantalla muy grande así que es ideal para ver vídeos. **Quisiera** tener un reloj inteligente porque me gustaría mantenerme en forma y tiene algunas apps muy útiles.

Technology is very important in my life. At home, we have three tablets. My tablet has a very large screen, so it's ideal for watching videos. I would like to have a smartwatch because I would like to keep fit and it has some very useful apps.

REMEMBER

Use *quisiera* + infinitive (I would like to) to make wishes or polite requests.

3.2

Viviendo en un mundo digital — *Living in a digital world*

Muchas personas suben vídeos para compartir información.
Many people upload videos to share information.

Es útil poder leer en el ordenador.
It's useful to be able to read on the computer.

Tenemos muchas apps para ayudar a los jóvenes con sus estudios.
We have many apps to help young people with their studies.

El uso de las redes sociales podría causar daño a los jóvenes en el futuro.
The use of social media could cause harm to young people in the future.

Mi reloj inteligente me dice la hora y si estoy cansado.
My smartwatch tells me the time and whether I'm tired.

¿Qué has hecho online en la última semana? — *What have you done online in the past week?*

He bajado una app para hacer ejercicio.
I've downloaded an app for doing exercise.

He creado una página web.
I've created a web page.

He pasado seis horas online. ¡Demasiado!
I've spent six hours online. Too much!

He visitado varios sitios web para investigar un proyecto.
I've visited several websites to research a project.

Mi amigo y yo hemos diseñado una app.
My friend and I have designed an app.

He decidido comprar un reloj inteligente.
I've decided to buy a smart watch.

He escrito sobre mis vacaciones en Internet.
I've written about my holiday on the internet.

He seguido algunas cuentas nuevas en Instagram.
I've followed some new accounts on Instagram.

He comprado entradas para un festival.
I've bought tickets for a festival.

Ayudando a mi abuela — *Helping my grandmother*

Mi abuela nunca **ha usado** un móvil inteligente o un ordenador en su vida. **Ha decidido** que quiere aprender cómo hacerlo y yo **he respondido** que le voy a enseñar. Ella quiere leer el periódico online y recibir mensajes y fotos. **Hemos hablado** y mi madre piensa que podría ser una tarea difícil. Es mejor ir poco a poco.

My grandmother has never used a smartphone or a computer in her life. She has decided that she wants to learn how to do it and I have replied that I am going to teach her. She wants to read the newspaper online and receive messages and photos. We have spoken and my mother thinks that it could be a difficult task. It is better to do it bit by bit.

> **REMEMBER**
> To talk about possessions, use the verb *tener* (not *haber*).
> *Tengo un ordenador.* (not *he un ordenador.*)

> **SOUNDS TIP**
> In most of Spain, the *c* in *ce* and *ci* is pronounced like the 'th' in English. In Latin America and in some areas of southern Spain, it is pronounced more like the English 's'.

> **GRAMMAR TIP**
> Use the perfect tense (*haber* + past participle) to talk about things that have happened recently.
> To form the past participle of a verb: remove the *-ar* of the infinitive and add *-ado*, or remove the *-er/-ir* and add *-ido*. See page 148.

Knowledge 89

Knowledge

VOCABULARY

3.2 Media and technology

Vocabulary learning

Learn this vocabulary and then use the 'look, cover, write, check' technique to make sure you really know it. Cover the English first and then the Spanish.

Useful verbs

Spanish	✓	English	✓
compartir		to share	
crear		to create	
diseñar		to design	
enviar		to send	
grabar		to record	
quisiera		I would like	
recibir		to receive	
seguir		to follow	
subir		to upload	

Different types of technology

Spanish	✓	English	✓
la app		app	
el blog		blog	
la cámara		camera	
el correo electrónico		email	
la cuenta		account	
inteligente		smart (device)	
el móvil		mobile phone	
el ordenador		computer	
la página web		web page	
la pantalla		screen	
el reloj		watch	
la tableta		tablet	

Other useful words

Spanish	✓	English	✓
el artículo		article	
cansado/a		tired	
desde		from, since	
los estudios		studies	
los jóvenes		young people, the youth	
el mensaje		message	
el periódico		newspaper	
el producto		product	
el proyecto		project	
el sitio (web)		(web)site	
útil		useful	

> **REVISION TIP**
>
> When you revise verbs, say them aloud with nouns that you can use with them. For example: *recibir – un mensaje, un correo, una foto, un vídeo*. This will help you remember whole phrases.

Retrieval — VOCABULARY — 3.2

Answer the questions below. Cover the answers column with a piece of paper and write down as many answers as you can. Check and repeat.

Questions / Answers

#	Question	Answer
1	Translate this sentence into Spanish: She has used a computer.	(Ella) ha usado un ordenador
2	Choose the correct verb to complete the sentence. *Me gusta charlar / grabar / trabajar vídeos.*	Me gusta <u>grabar</u> vídeos
3	Say the Spanish words for four different devices.	Possible answers include: *móvil, tableta, ordenador, reloj inteligente, televisión*
4	How do you say in Spanish: web page?	La página web
5	Translate this sentence into English: *Quisiera escribir un mensaje.*	I would like to write a message
6	Which of these is <u>not</u> an electronic device? *la cuenta / el ordenador / la tableta*	La cuenta
7	Name two verbs that mean 'to send'.	Mandar, enviar
8	If *seguidor* means 'follower', how do you say 'to follow'?	Seguir
9	What does *quisiera* mean in English?	I would like
10	Choose the correct word to complete the sentence. *Tengo / He / Soy usado mi móvil esta mañana.*	<u>He</u> usado mi móvil esta mañana
11	Change the verb in this sentence to the perfect tense: *Pasé una hora online.*	He pasado una hora online
12	Translate this sentence into English: *Hemos diseñado una app.*	We have designed an app

Previous questions

Use the questions below to check your knowledge from previous chapters.

Questions / Answers

#	Question	Answer
1	What is the verb 'to get on with' in Spanish?	Entenderse
2	Translate this sentence into English: *He mandado una carta a mi tío.*	I have sent a letter to my uncle
3	In the context of holidays, what is the meaning of *el recuerdo*?	Souvenir

Knowledge  VOCABULARY

3.2 Media and technology

The advantages of technology

Soy un aficionado a la tecnología — *I'm a fan of technology*

No apago nunca mi móvil.	I never switch off my mobile phone.
Existen apps útiles de todo tipo.	There are all kinds of useful apps.
Tengo muchos seguidores en mis cuentas de redes sociales.	I have many followers on my social media accounts.
Mucha gente las utiliza para hacer negocios.	Many people use them to do business.
Es divertido buscar nuevos amigos online.	It's fun looking for new friends online.

¿Cómo te ayuda la tecnología? — *How does technology help you?*

Es posible hacer tareas rápidamente.	It is possible to do tasks quickly.
Los científicos pueden compartir información.	Scientists can share information.
Puedes mantenerte en contacto con la familia fácilmente.	You can easily keep in touch with family.
Da tanto apoyo para estudiantes como para trabajadores.	It gives so much support for students and workers alike.
Internet es ideal para personas que quieren aprender cosas nuevas.	The internet is ideal for people who want to learn new things.

GRAMMAR TIP

The verbs *esperar* (to wait for) and *buscar* (to look for) are **not** followed by *para* or any other preposition.

SOUNDS TIP

The Spanish *z* sounds like the English 'th'. In Latin America it sounds more like the letter 's'.

Note that there is no difference in sound between the letter *z* and the letter *c* when followed by an *e* or *i*.

La tecnología que cambia vidas *Technology that changes lives*

Para los jóvenes colombianos que viven lejos de ciudades, la tecnología puede cambiarles la vida. La familia de mi amigo Juan **le dió** una tableta y ahora, puede comunicarse con sus amigos, leer las noticias y disfrutar de sus libros favoritos. Sus profesores también **le han recomendado** aplicaciones útiles para mejorar su experiencia.

For young Colombians who live far from cities, technology can be life-changing. My friend Juan's family gave him a tablet, and now, he can communicate with his friends, read the news and enjoy his favourite books. His teachers have also recommended useful apps to him to improve his experience.

GRAMMAR TIP

Use indirect object pronouns (*me*, *te*, *le*) to indicate to whom or for whom an action is performed.

Le envié un mensaje.
I sent a message to him.
See page 129.

The disadvantages of technology

3.2

Las desventajas de la tecnología	The disadvantages of technology
Paso demasiado tiempo delante de la pantalla.	I spend too much time in front of the screen.
Me preocupa mucho el ciberacoso.	I am really worried about cyberbullying.
Hay demasiados anuncios aburridos.	There are too many boring adverts.
No puedo encender mi tableta.	I can't switch on my tablet.
He recibido mensajes negativos online.	I have received negative messages online.
Si te roban la cuenta tienes que llamar a la policía.	If your account is stolen, you have to call the police.
Tuve problemas para entrar a Internet.	I had problems getting on the internet.
Mucha gente comparte demasiada información.	Many people share too much information.
Tenemos que proteger nuestra identidad.	We must protect our identity.

¿Estás a favor o en contra?	Are you for or against?
Estoy de acuerdo. / No estoy de acuerdo.	I agree. / I don't agree.
Es mejor / peor …	It is better / worse …
Por un lado,… / Por otro lado,…	On one hand,… / On the other hand,…
Apoyo la idea de…	I support the idea of…
Me parece que…	It seems to me that…
Hay que aceptar que…	You have to accept that…

REMEMBER

Nouns that end in –*dad* usually end in –*ty* in English and are feminine:
la identidad – identity,
la sociedad – society

REVISION TIP

Learn some short phrases to use in your own writing and speaking. This will also help you understand vocabulary and grammar in context.

¿Estoy seguro online? Am I safe online?

Ayer **estaba pensando** en subir una foto en Instagram, pero tuve un problema. Intenté conectarme, pero me daba error. Por fin, me conecté. Luego, mi foto **se estaba subiendo** y la app se cerró. No pude conectarme otra vez. ¿Y si alguien ha robado mi cuenta? Me voy a poner en contacto con la policía. Estoy triste porque mi cuenta es muy importante.

Yesterday, I was thinking about uploading a photo on Instagram, but I had a problem. I tried to log in, but it gave me an error. At last, I logged in. Later, my photo was uploading and the app closed. I couldn't log in again. What if someone has stolen my account? I'm going to get in touch with the police. I am sad because my account is very important.

GRAMMAR TIP

Use the imperfect continuous tense (*estaba* + present participle) to describe an action that was in progress at a specific moment in the past. See page 146.

Knowledge 93

Knowledge — VOCABULARY

3.2 Media and technology

Vocabulary learning

Learn this vocabulary and then use the 'look, cover, write, check' technique to make sure you really know it. Cover the English first and then the Spanish.

The pros and cons of technology

Spanish	✓	English	✓
abrir		to open	
aceptar		to accept	
el anuncio		advert	
apagar		to turn off	
apoyar		to support	
el apoyo		support, backing	
cambiar		to change	
conectarse a		to connect to	
el ciberacoso		cyberbullying	
el / la científico/a		scientist	
dar		to give	
delante (de)		in front (of)	
digital		digital	
el error		error	
estar de acuerdo		to agree	
hacer negocio		to do business	
la identidad		identity	
mantenerse en contacto con alguien		to keep in touch with someone	

Spanish	✓	English	✓
negativo/a		negative	
el / la policía		police	
ponerse en contacto con alguien		to contact / get in touch with someone	
por fin		finally, at last	
proteger		to protect	
recomendar		to recommend	
robar		to steal, rob	
el / la seguidor(a)		follower	
seguro/a		safe, sure, secure	
la tarea		task	

REVISION TIP

Practise using some of the Spanish vocabulary on this page to talk about the advantages and disadvantages of technology.

Retrieval

VOCABULARY

3.2

Answer the questions below. Cover the answers column with a piece of paper and write down as many answers as you can. Check and repeat.

Questions | Answers

#	Question	Answer
1	How do you say in Spanish: do business online?	*Hacer negocio online*
2	Translate this sentence into English: *Yo estaba usando mi ordenador.*	I was using my computer
3	Complete the sentence with the correct preposition. *Voy a ponerme en contacto ____ mi amigo.*	*Voy a ponerme en contacto* <u>*con*</u> *mi amigo*
4	If *actividad* means 'activity', how do you say 'identity' in Spanish?	*La identidad*
5	Choose the correct option to complete the sentence. *Algo no va bien. Hay un error / apoyo / anuncio.*	*Algo no va bien. Hay un* <u>*error*</u>
6	Translate this sentence into English: *Tenemos que proteger a los niños.*	We have to protect (the) children
7	Which of the following is a possible danger of using social media? *el reloj / el ciberacoso / el apoyo*	*El ciberacoso* (cyberbullying)
8	If *por un lado* is 'on the one hand', how do you say 'on the other hand'?	*Por otro lado*
9	What does *un anuncio aburrido* mean in English?	A boring advert
10	How do you say in Spanish: I agree?	*Estoy de acuerdo*
11	Choose the correct pronoun to convey the meaning 'I gave him the book'. *Me / Te / Le di un libro*.	<u>*Le*</u> *di un libro*
12	What is the opposite of the verb *apagar*?	*Encender*

Previous questions

Use the questions below to check your knowledge from previous chapters.

Questions | Answers

#	Question	Answer
1	Name at least three feminine school subjects in Spanish.	Possible answers include: *las ciencias, las matemáticas, la economía, la historia, la geografía, la música*
2	When followed by *de* and a verb in the infinitive form, what does *dejar* mean?	To stop (+ -ing)
3	Translate this sentence into English: *Su papel era muy bueno.*	Her / His role was very good

Knowledge VOCABULARY

3.3 The environment and where people live

House and home

Describe tu casa	Describe your house
En la planta baja, hay …	On the ground floor, there is / are…
En el primer / segundo / tercer piso, hay …	On the first / second / third floor, there is / are…
Mi casa / piso tiene …	My house / flat has…
un salón / una cocina.	a living room / kitchen.
dos cuartos de baño pequeños.	two small bathrooms.
tres dormitorios modernos.	three modern bedrooms.
tres plantas y siete habitaciones.	three floors and seven rooms.
un jardín bonito.	a pretty garden.
La escalera es muy bonita.	The staircase is very pretty.
El dormitorio de mi hermano no está muy limpio.	My brother's bedroom is not very clean.

REMEMBER

Some words have more than one meaning. When translating, use context to work out which one to use.

el piso – floor (of house), flat

la planta – plant, floor (of house)

Mi dormitorio / My bedroom

Mi dormitorio	My bedroom
Comparto mi dormitorio con mi hermana.	I share my room with my sister.
Tengo un dormitorio con un baño.	I have a bedroom with a bathroom.
Mi gato duerme encima de mi cama.	My cat sleeps on top of my bed.
Una silla amarilla está delante de la mesa.	A yellow chair is in front of the table.
Hay un montón de libros al lado de la mesa.	There are lots of books next to the table.
Desde la ventana se puede ver una sinagoga y un árbol.	From the window you can see a synagogue and a tree.

SOUNDS TIP

In Spanish, the letter *i* sounds like the 'ee' in the English word 'see'. For example: *dormitorio, libros*. It never sounds like the English 'eye'!

Como en casa ningún sitio There's no place like home

La casa de mis padres **está delante del** parque y me da mucha alegría. Es de los años treinta y tiene mucho carácter. En la planta baja hay una cocina tradicional **al lado de** un salón cómodo. En la primera planta están las habitaciones. Todas las paredes están pintadas de color blanco. También, tenemos un jardín grande. ¡Me encantaría tener una piscina al aire libre!

My parents' house is in front of the park and it makes me really happy. It's from the 30s and it has a lot of character. On the ground floor, there's a traditional kitchen next to a comfortable living room. The bedrooms are on the first floor. All the walls are painted a white colour. We also have a big garden. I'd love to have an open-air pool!

GRAMMAR TIP

Use the verb *estar* (not *ser*) with prepositions of place to talk about location. For example: *delante de, al lado de, encima de*, etc. See page 154.

Where I live

¿Dónde vives?	Where do you live?
Vivo en una ciudad animada e histórica.	I live in a lively and historic city.
Mi pueblo está en el norte de Inglaterra.	My town is in the north of England.
Nuestra casa está a las afueras.	Our house is on the outskirts.
Cuando era pequeña, vivía en el sur de Francia.	When I was little, I used to live in the south of France.
Me gustaría vivir en el este de España.	I would like to live in the east of Spain.
Es mejor vivir en la costa que en el campo.	It is better to live on the coast than in the countryside.

REMEMBER

In Spanish, the word *y* (and) changes to *e* when it is followed by a word starting with *i* or *hi* to avoid repetition of the 'i' sound: *animada e histórica*.

Describe tu pueblo / Describe your town

Es precioso y tranquilo.	It is beautiful and tranquil.
Hay tantos sitios de interés.	There are so many places of interest.
No hay muchos delitos, entonces es un lugar seguro.	There isn't much crime, so it's a safe place.
No hay mucho que hacer allí.	There isn't much to do there.
Hay demasiado ruido en el centro.	There is too much noise in the centre.
Las carreteras están llenas de tráfico. Por eso, son bastante peligrosas.	The roads are full of traffic. Therefore, they're quite dangerous.
Está claro que hay una falta de espacio.	Clearly, there's a lack of space.
En el pasado, nuestro barrio era industrial.	In the past, our neighbourhood was industrial.
Habrá un nuevo puerto en mi ciudad.	There will be a new port in my city.

REVISION TIP

Extend your ideas when you are speaking and writing. Use phrases like *por eso* (therefore) and *entonces* (then, so) to talk about results.

¿Vivirías en otro país? Would you live in another country?

Vivo en el oeste de Inglaterra. En el futuro, me encantaría vivir en España. Es un país precioso con una historia única. Allí, podré disfrutar del clima y la cultura. Espero descubrir muchos sitios de interés y **conocer a gente** nueva. Me gustaría quedarme por un tiempo. Este verano, voy a **ver a mi amigo** en Portugal, luego voy a **visitar a mi abuela** en Barcelona.

I live in the west of England. In the future, I would love to live in Spain. It's a beautiful country with a unique history. There, I will be able to enjoy the climate and the culture. I hope to discover many places of interest and meet new people. I would like to stay for a while. This summer, I am going to see my friend in Portugal, then I am going to visit my grandmother in Barcelona.

GRAMMAR TIP

Use the personal *a* in Spanish when the object is a person or a group of people.

*Ayer vi **a** Marta.*
I saw Marta yesterday.

See page 159.

Knowledge VOCABULARY

3.3 The environment and where people live

Pros and cons of where I live

Los aspectos positivos de mi ciudad	The positive aspects of my city
El estadio de fútbol no está lejos de aquí.	The football stadium isn't far from here.
Me encanta la red de transporte de mi ciudad.	I love the transport network in my city.
Los martes, hay un mercado al aire libre.	On Tuesdays, there is an open-air market.
Me encantan los puestos de comida.	I love the food stalls.
Una ventaja de vivir cerca del mar es respirar aire fresco.	One advantage of living near the sea is breathing fresh air.
La iglesia en esta plaza es preciosa.	The church in this square is beautiful.

Los aspectos negativos de mi ciudad	The negative aspects of my city
La carretera que lleva a la costa está cerrada.	The road leading to the coast is closed.
Una desventaja es que hay zonas con paro.	A disadvantage is that there are areas with unemployment.
La arquitectura en el centro es demasiado moderna.	The architecture in the city centre is too modern.
El museo es caro y de un tamaño pequeño.	The museum is expensive and small.
Me molestan los turistas en verano.	The tourists annoy me in the summer.
En las afueras, ciertos barrios no están tan limpios como deberían.	On the outskirts, certain neighbourhoods are not as clean as they should be.
Los pisos en el centro son muy caros.	The flats in the city centre are very expensive.

¿Qué piensas de tu ciudad? What do you think of your city?

Vivo en una ciudad histórica con muchos espacios verdes. Sin embargo, la red de transporte es muy lenta y vieja. Esto **no** es bueno para **nadie**. Mucha gente está enojada porque el ayuntamiento **no** hace **nada** para mejorar las instalaciones públicas y la contaminación del aire que tenemos es peligrosa.

I live in a historic city with many green spaces. However, the transport network is very slow and old. This is no good for anyone. Many people are angry because the city council does nothing to improve public facilities, and the air pollution we have is dangerous.

REMEMBER

In Spanish, written accents are important! *Está* means 'he / she / it is', whereas *esta* is 'this' for feminine nouns. Note also: *sí* (yes), *si* (if); *mí* (me), *mi* (my).

REVISION TIP

Summarise the main postitive and negative aspects of a city near you by adapting some of these Spanish sentences.

GRAMMAR TIP

Double negative structures are grammatically correct in Spanish, even though they are considered wrong in English.

No quiero *nada*.
I don't want anything.
No vi a *nadie*.
I didn't see anyone.
See page 157.

3.3 A visit to my city

¡No te lo puedes perder! / You can't miss it!

¡Hay que visitar el puerto!	You have to visit the port!
Puedes subir una montaña muy alta.	You can go up a very tall mountain.
Es posible disfrutar de un espectáculo de flamenco.	It's possible to enjoy a flamenco show.
La arquitectura es hermosa.	The architecture is beautiful.
Se pueden encontrar muchos restaurantes.	You can find many restaurants.
Las tiendas abren hasta tarde.	The shops are open until late.
El centro comercial tiene de todo.	The shopping centre has everything.
Las instalaciones deportivas son muy buenas.	The sports facilities are very good.
Pronto, abrirá un hotel de cuatro estrellas aquí.	Soon, a four-star hotel will open here.
No te puedes ir sin visitar la mezquita.	You can't leave without visiting the mosque.

Direcciones / Directions

¿Hay algunas tiendas por aquí cerca?	Are there any shops near here?
¿Por dónde se va al museo?	How do I get to the museum?
Tienes que pasar por esa plaza.	You have to go through that square.
Sigue hasta el final de la calle y está allí.	Carry on to the end of the road and it is there.
Toma la primera / segunda / tercera calle.	Take the first / second / third road.
Está a mano derecha / izquierda.	It is on the right / left hand side.
El teatro está entre al ayuntamiento y la universidad.	The theatre is between the town hall and the university.
La playa no está lejos. Está a un kilómetro de aquí.	The beach isn't far. It's one kilometre from here.

¡Una visita a San Carlos del Valle! / A visit to San Carlos del Valle!

Bienvenidos a **este** pueblo hermoso. Aquí hay varios sitios de interés que no os podéis perder. **Este** lugar histórico tiene **esta** maravillosa Plaza Mayor. En **esta** esquina está el ayuntamiento y **esa** iglesia con un reloj grande es muy antigua.

Welcome to this beautiful town. Here, there are several places of interest that you can't miss. This historic place has this wonderful main square. In this corner is the town hall, and that church with a large clock is very old.

> **REVISION TIP**
> When revising expressions, group them together by meaning. For example giving recommendations: *hay que* (you have to), *es posible* (it is possible), *se puede* (you can).

> **GRAMMAR TIP**
> *Este* (this) and *ese* (that) are demonstrative adjectives. They indicate the distance of a noun from the speaker or listener. In Spanish, demonstrative adjectives agree in gender and number with the noun.
> See page 123.

 # Knowledge VOCABULARY

3.3 The environment and where people live

Vocabulary learning

Learn this vocabulary and then use the 'look, cover, write, check' technique to make sure you really know it. Cover the English first and then the Spanish.

My house

Spanish	✓	English	✓
al aire libre		open air	
el ambiente		atmosphere	
el árbol		tree	
el baño, el cuarto de baño		bathroom	
el carácter		character	
la cocina		kitchen	
cómodo/a		comfortable	
el cuarto / la habitación		room	
el dormitorio		bedroom	
la escalera		staircase	
el jardín		garden	
la mesa		table	
moderno/a		modern	
un montón de		lots of	
la pared		wall	
la piscina		swimming pool	
el piso		flat, floor	
la planta baja		ground floor	
la primera / segunda / tercera planta		first / second / third floor	
el salón		living room	
la silla		chair	
tradicional		traditional	
la ventana		window	

Prepositions

Spanish	✓	English	✓
cerca de		near	
debajo de		underneath	
delante de		in front of	
detrás de		behind	
desde		from	
encima de		on top of	
entre		between	
al lado de		next to	

REMEMBER

Not all prepositions are followed by *de*. Be careful with those that are, but are only translated by one word in English. For example: *cerca de* (near), *detrás de* (behind).

GRAMMAR TIP

If *de* is followed by *el*, the words are contracted and become *del*. For example: *al lado del baño* (next to the bathroom).

REMEMBER

Some words are easily confused because they look similar. For example: *cuarto* (room / quarter), *cuatro* (four); *casado* (married), *cansado* (tired). Be careful with the spelling!

Vocabulary learning

Places and facilities

Spanish	✓	English	✓
las afueras		outskirts, suburbs	
la arquitectura		architecture	
el ayuntamiento		town hall	
el barrio		neighbourhood	
el campo		countryside	
la calle		street	
la carretera		road	
el centro		city centre	
el centro comercial		shopping centre	
el cine		cinema	
la costa		coast	
el espacio verde		green space	
el espectáculo		show	
la esquina		(street) corner	
el estadio		stadium	
la estación		station	
la iglesia		church	
las instalaciones		facilities	
el lugar		place, position	
la mezquita		mosque	
el mercado		market	
el museo		museum	
el paisaje		landscape	
la plaza		square	
el puente		bridge	
el puerto		port, harbour	
el puesto		stall (market)	
el restaurante		restaurant	
la sinagoga		synagogue	
el sitio		place	
el supermercado		supermarket	
el teatro		theatre	

Spanish	✓	English	✓
la tienda		shop	
el transporte		transport	
la universidad		university	

Describe your town / city

Spanish	✓	English	✓
alto/a		high	
animado/a		lively	
barato/a		cheap	
de (cuatro) estrellas		a (four)-star	
deportivo/a		sports (adj.)	
hermoso/a		beautiful	
histórico/a		historic	
industrial		industrial	
interesante		interesting	
lento/a		slow	
limpio/a		clean	
lleno/a de		full of	
peligroso/a		dangerous	
pequeño/a		small	
precioso/a		beautiful	
seguro/a		safe	
el tamaño		size, dimension	
tranquilo/a		tranquil	

> **SOUNDS TIP**
>
> The Spanish *a* is pronounced like the English 'ah', though shorter. For example: *casa*. It never sounds like the English 'ay'.

Knowledge VOCABULARY

3.3 The environment and where people live

Vocabulary learning

Where is it?

Spanish	✓	English	✓
allí		there	
aquí		here	
cerca		near	
lejos		far	
el norte		north	
el sur		south	
el este		east	
el oeste		west	
¿Por dónde se va al / a la…?		How do I get to the …?	
a mano derecha / izquierda		on the right- / left-hand side	
a (un) kilómetro		(one) kilometre from	
metro		metre	
el final de la calle		the end of the road	
por aquí		around here	
primero/a		first	
segundo/a		second	
tercero/a		third	

> **GRAMMAR TIP**
>
> *Primero* (first) and *segundo* (second) lose the final –o when placed before any masculine noun e.g. *el primer piso* the first floor.

Advantages and disadvantages

Spanish	✓	English	✓
casi		almost	
la contaminación		pollution	
el delito		crime	
la desventaja		disadvantage	
enojado/a		angry	
el paro		unemployment	
el / la turista		tourist	
la ventaja		advantage, benefit	

Useful verbs

Spanish	✓	English	✓
abrir		to open	
compartir		to share	
construir		to build	
descubrir		to discover	
encontrar		to find	
molestar		to annoy	
perder, perderse		to lose, to get lost	
quedarse		to stay	
respirar		to breathe	
seguir		to continue, carry on	

Retrieval — VOCABULARY — 3.3

Answer the questions below. Cover the answers column with a piece of paper and write down as many answers as you can. Check and repeat.

Questions / Answers

#	Question	Answer
1	Complete the sentence with the correct demonstrative adjectives. *El edificio más antiguo en* (this) ___ *pueblo es* (that) ___ *iglesia*.	*El edificio más antiguo en* <u>este</u> *pueblo es* <u>esa</u> *iglesia*
2	What are the two words that are the opposite of *lejos* and *delante*?	*Cerca* and *detrás*
3	Write two ways of saying 'the second floor' in Spanish.	*La segunda planta, el segundo piso*
4	Say the Spanish words for four rooms inside a house.	*El salón, la cocina, el baño, el dormitorio*
5	Translate this sentence into Spanish: My house has many bedrooms.	*Mi casa tiene muchos dormitorios*
6	How do you say 'first, second, third' in Spanish?	*Primero, segundo, tercero*
7	Name the four compass points in Spanish.	*Norte, sur, este, oeste*
8	How do you say in Spanish: here and there?	*Aquí y allí*
9	Which word does <u>not</u> mean 'room'? *el árbol / la habitación / el cuarto*	*El árbol*
10	Choose the correct preposition to complete the sentence. *El supermercado está entre / detrás / en de la plaza*.	*El supermercado está* <u>detrás</u> *de la plaza*
11	Complete the sentence with the missing word. *Hay un mercado cerca _____ castillo*.	*Hay un mercado cerca* <u>del</u> *castillo*
12	Choose the correct verb to complete the sentence. *La sinagoga no es / tiene / está muy lejos de aquí*.	*La sinagoga no* <u>está</u> *muy lejos de aquí*

Previous questions

Use the questions below to check your knowledge from previous chapters.

#	Question	Answer
1	Rewrite this sentence with a direct object pronoun: *El viernes, leo una novela*.	*El viernes, la leo*
2	Choose the correct word to complete the sentence: *En mi plano / maleta / excursión hay mucha ropa*.	*En mi* <u>maleta</u> *hay mucha ropa*
3	Identify the tenses and translate this sentece. *La actriz que hablaba se casó con el director*.	*Hablaba* – imperfect; *Se casó* – preterite. The actress who was talking got married with the director

Knowledge VOCABULARY

3.3 The environment and where people live

Protecting the environment

Problemas de medio ambiente	*Environmental problems*
Hay demasiado tráfico.	There's too much traffic.
La contaminación me preocupa.	I'm worried about pollution.
La gente tira basura en la calle.	People throw litter in the street.
Los ríos están muy sucios.	The rivers are very dirty.
Hay una falta de espacios verdes.	There's a lack of green spaces.
Me preocupo por el cambio climático.	I worry about climate change.
Las temperaturas no dejan de aumentar.	Temperatures keep rising.
Debido a la falta de lluvia, la tierra está seca.	Due to the lack of rain, the land is dry.
Algunas especies pueden desaparecer.	Some species can disappear.
La Tierra está en peligro por el plástico.	The earth is in danger because of plastic.
La naturaleza no va a durar siempre.	Nature won't last forever.

Posibles soluciones	*Possible solutions*
Es mejor conducir un coche eléctrico.	It's better to drive an electric car.
Tenéis que recoger la basura.	You have to pick up rubbish.
Debemos apagar las luces.	We must turn off the lights.
Los jóvenes tienen que ser más responsables.	Young people must be more responsible.
Hay que cerrar esa fábrica porque produce humo y contamina el aire.	That factory must be closed because it produces smoke and pollutes the air.

SOUNDS TIP

Practice your pronunciation of words that end in **-ción**, such as *contaminación* and *información*.

REVISION TIP

To expand your vocabulary, create a list of synonyms on each topic. For example: *La Tierra* and *el planeta*.

¡Vamos a trabajar! Let's get to work!

En casa, todos hacemos algo para el planeta. Mi **hermanita** y yo reciclamos papel y cajas. Además, apoyamos el proyecto de Greenpeace para salvar los **animalitos** en peligro. Mis amigos están haciendo un gran esfuerzo también, y mis padres intentan usar un **poquito** menos de agua en casa.

At home, we all do something for the planet. My little sister and I recycle paper and boxes. Additionally, we support the Greenpeace project to save little animals in danger. My friends are also making a great effort, and my parents try to use a bit less water at home.

GRAMMAR TIP

In Spanish, *-ito* / *-ita* can be added to the end of a noun, or can replace the *o/a* at the end of a noun, to make it sound smaller or more affectionate. For example: *hermano* – brother, *hermanito* – little brother. See page 161.

REMEMBER

Un poco changes to *un poquito* to mean 'a little bit'.

3.3

Social issues

Problemas sociales / Social problems

Me parece que hay una falta de oportunidades.	It seems to me that there's a lack of opportunities.
El uso de drogas es un problema grave.	The use of drugs is a serious problem.
Tengo miedo de la violencia en las calles.	I'm scared of the violence on the streets.
El paro afecta a la mayoría de los jóvenes.	Unemployment affects the majority of young people.
Cada vez hay más personas sin casa.	There are more and more homeless people.

Soluciones políticas / Political solutions

¡Organiza un proyecto!	Organise a project!
¡Cuida tu zona!	Take care of your area!
¡Ayuda a tus vecinos!	Help your neighbours!
¡Comparte tu tiempo!	Share your time!
¡Crea más trabajo para la juventud!	Create more work for the youth!
¡Pon presión al ayuntamiento!	Put pressure on the local government!
¡Protege la naturaleza!	Protect nature!

SOUNDS TIP

In Spanish, the *e* sounds like a shorter version of the 'e' in the English words 'bed' and 'pet'. The *i* sounds like the *ee* in 'see'. Note the clear difference in sound between *me* and *mi*. For example: **me** *parece*, **mi** *miedo*.

¡Haz un cambio! Make a change!

Querido amigo, es hora de mejorar nuestra sociedad. Todos debemos vivir felices en una sociedad justa con trabajo, casa, hospitales y naturaleza. **Entra** en acción ahora y **pon** presión a los partidos. **Trabaja** duro para ayudarte a ti y a tu gente. ¡**Protege** tu futuro! **Sal** a la calle y **di** '¡Queremos un cambio ya!'

Dear friend, it's time to improve our society. We should all live happily in a fair society with jobs, houses, hospitals, and nature. Take action now and put pressure on parties. Work hard to help yourself and your people. Protect your future! Go out on the street and say 'We want a change now!'

GRAMMAR TIP

Use the imperative for commands or instructions. For the *tú* form, use the third person singular of the present tense. For example: ¡*Recicla!* (Recycle!), ¡*Come!* (Eat!) See page 153.

REMEMBER

Several *tú* imperative forms are irregular: *sé* (ser), *haz* (hacer), *di* (decir), *ten* (tener), *pon* (poner), *sal* (salir), *ve* (ir), *ven* (venir). See page 153.

Knowledge

VOCABULARY

3.3 The environment and where people live

Vocabulary learning

Learn this vocabulary and then use the 'look, cover, write, check' technique to make sure you really know it. Cover the English first and then the Spanish.

Environmental problems and solutions

Spanish	✓	English	✓
la basura		rubbish	
el cambio climático		climate change	
eléctrico/a		electric	
la especie		species	
la fábrica		factory	
el humo		smoke, fumes	
el peligro		danger	
el plástico		plastic	
responsable		responsible	
el río		river	
seco/a		dry	
la temperatura		temperature	
la tierra		land, earth	
el tráfico		traffic	

Social problems and solutions

Spanish	✓	English	✓
la acción		action	
la droga		drug	
grave		serious	
justo/a		fair	
la juventud		youth	
la mayoría		majority	
la oportunidad		opportunity	
el miedo		fear	
la persona sin casa		homeless person	
la presión		pressure	
responsable		responsible	
la sociedad		society	
la violencia		violence	

Useful verbs

Spanish	✓	English	✓
afectar		to affect	
aumentar		to increase	
cerrar		to close	
conducir		to drive	
contaminar		to pollute, contaminate	
crear		to create	
desaparecer		to disappear	
durar		to last	
luchar		to fight	
mejorar		to improve	
organizar		to organise	
producir		to produce	
reciclar		to recycle	
recoger		to collect, pick up	
salvar		to save	
tirar		to throw, pull	

> **REVISION TIP**
>
> Practise talking in Spanish for one minute about environmental problems and solutions. Use as many words as possible from the vocabulary on this page.

Retrieval — VOCABULARY — 3.3

Answer the questions below. Cover the answers column with a piece of paper and write down as many answers as you can. Check and repeat.

	Questions	Answers
1	Which of the following verbs is in the imperative form? *haz / tengo / ayudáis*	*Haz*
2	What's a synonym for *el planeta*?	*La Tierra*
3	How do you say in Spanish: a lack of?	*Una falta de*
4	Translate the sentence into Spanish: I will buy an electric car.	*Compraré / Voy a comprar un coche eléctrico*
5	What does *hermanita* mean in English?	Little sister
6	What are the two meanings of the verb *tirar*?	To throw, to pull
7	Which letter in *humo* is silent?	The letter '*h*'
8	How would you say 'Listen!' informally to a friend in Spanish?	*¡Escucha!*
9	How do you say in Spanish: due to?	*Debido / a*
10	Complete the sentence with the correct verb: *Mi ciudad está sucia. Mucha gente apaga / dura / tira basura.*	*Mi ciudad está sucia. Mucha gente <u>tira</u> basura*
11	What does *tener miedo* mean in English?	To be afraid / scared
12	Translate this sentence into English: *¡Cuida tu ciudad!*	Take care of / look after your city!

Previous questions

Use the questions below to check your knowledge from previous chapters.

	Questions	Answers
1	Which of these words means 'there was / were'? *Hay / Habrá / Había*	*Había*
2	Name two words for 'secondary school' in Spanish.	*Instituto, colegio*
3	If *Voy a leer las novelas* means 'I am going to read the novels', how do you say, 'I am going to read them'?	*Voy a leerlas*

Retrieval 107

Practice EXAM

Theme 3 Listening practice

Section A: Listening comprehension

The environment

You are listening to an environmental campaigner give tips on a Spanish radio station. Complete the sentences in **English**. Write **one** word in each space.

1. In our society, we consume too much ...., therefore we need more .... **[2 marks]**

2. It is clear that many young people want to care for .... However, the current situation is .... **[2 marks]**

> **EXAM TIP**
> Use the five minutes' preparation time at the start of the exam to read through the questions carefully and note down possible key vocabulary.

Technology

You hear Hugo, Lucía and Isabel talking to their teacher.
What problem does each person mention?
Choose the correct answer and write the letter in each box.

3. Hugo **[1 mark]**

A	His keyboard isn't working.
B	There is no sound.
C	The screen is dirty.

4. Lucía **[1 mark]**

A	The computer is broken.
B	She forgot to save her work.
C	She can't download the homework.

5. Isabel **[1 mark]**

A	The computer screen is blank.
B	She cannot find her test.
C	She did not have time to finish.

6. The teacher **[1 mark]**

A	He has lost his mobile phone.
B	He received a message from another teacher.
C	He cannot turn on his computer.

Exploring Bilbao, Spain

You hear Sofía talking about the city of Bilbao in Spain.
Answer the questions in **English**.

7.1 Which aspect of the city is popular with tourists in summer?
.... **[1 mark]**

7.2 What is special about the *La Ribera* market?
.... **[1 mark]**

7.3 What fact is given about the *Iberdrola* building?
.... **[1 mark]**

7.4 How does Sofía describe the people of Bilbao?
.... **[1 mark]**

> **EXAM TIP**
> You will hear the answers to the questions in order. If you miss an answer, stay focused for the next one. When you listen for the second time, you can focus on the answer you missed.

A phone conversation

You hear Soraya telling you about her experience at the airport.

Write the correct letter in each box.

Answer both parts of question 8.

8.1   What is Soraya's problem?

A	A missing passport.
B	A delayed flight.
C	A heavy suitcase.

[1 mark]

8.2   What is she going to do?

A	Seek help.
B	Call her mum.
C	Watch a film.

[1 mark]

Section B: Dictation

You will now hear 4 short sentences. Listen carefully and using your knowledge of Spanish sounds, write down in **Spanish** exactly what you hear for each sentence.

[8 marks]

Sentence 1

....

....

Sentence 2

....

....

Sentence 3

....

....

Sentence 4

....

....

EXAM TIP

The only double letters in Spanish are *c*, *r*, *l* and *n*. If you're not sure whether a Spanish word contains a double letter, use the acronym CaRoLiNa to help!

Practice

Practice  EXAM

Theme 3 Speaking practice

Part 1: Role-play

Prepare the following role-play task. Then listen to the teacher's prompts and respond.

You are talking to your Cuban friend.

Your teacher will play the part of your friend and will speak first.

You should address your friend as *tú*.

When you see this - **?** - you will have to ask a question.

> **In order to score full marks, you must include a verb in your response to each task.**
>
> 1. Say how you use technology in class. (Give **one** detail.)
> 2. Say what technology you use at home. (Give **one** detail.)
> 3. Say how much time you spend each day on the Internet. (Give **one** detail.)
> 4. Say what you think about the internet. (Give **one** opinion.)
> **? 5.** Ask a friend a question about mobile phones.

EXAM TIP

At Foundation, you are required to provide **one** detail for each bullet point. Make sure you communicate it clearly and accurately, using a verb.

Part 2: Reading aloud task

Read aloud the following text in **Spanish**.

> Vivo en un pueblo con casas antiguas.
>
> Me gusta dar paseos por mi pueblo.
>
> En casa, siempre reciclamos la basura.
>
> Mi hermana quiere comprar una bici nueva.
>
> El paro es un problema que me preocupa.

EXAM TIP

Practise reading sentences aloud in Spanish. This will not only be useful for the reading aloud task, but also for your answers to the role play and photo cards when you may be reading out notes you made during the preparation time.

Then listen and respond to the four questions on the topic of **The environment and where people live**.

In order to score the highest marks, you must try to **answer all four questions as fully as you can**.

Part 3: Photo card task

- Prepare a description of these two photos. You may make as many notes as you wish and use these notes during the test.
- Then record yourself talking about the content of these photos for approximately **one minute**. **You must say at least one thing about each photo**.
- After you have spoken about the content of the photos, you will be asked questions related to **any** of the topics within the theme of **Communication and the world around us**. Listen to and respond to the example questions.

> **EXAM TIP**
>
> If you don't understand a particular question, ask the examiner to repeat it: *Repite la pregunta, por favor.* Be polite and avoid using English in your exam!

Photo 1

Photo 2

Theme 3 Reading practice

Section A: Reading comprehension

A popular destination

You see an advert on social media about a popular tourist area of Spain.

Complete these sentences. Write the letter for the correct option in each box.

> ¡Bienvenidos a la Playa de la Barrosa!
> Puedes visitar esta zona en el suroeste de España todo el año, porque el tiempo casi siempre es agradable, con temperaturas buenas aun en invierno.
>
> Allí puedes…
>
> - visitar la ciudad de Cádiz, a menos de una hora en coche. Llena de arquitectura hermosa, esta ciudad tiene iglesias históricas en cada esquina
> - probar sus tapas riquísimas, conocidas en todas partes de España y a muy buen precio
> - conocer los pueblos blancos. Con sus calles antiguas, casas tradicionales y vistas increíbles, ¡es como viajar en el tiempo!

1. The weather in the *Playa de la Barrosa* area is usually… **[1 mark]**

A	pleasant all year round.
B	hot and humid.
C	warm, except in winter.

2. The city of Cádiz is… **[1 mark]**

A	just over an hour away by car.
B	full of beautiful architecture.
C	known for having a few historic churches.

3. The tapas in Cádiz… **[1 mark]**

A	are expensive.
B	have a great reputation.
C	are given for free.

4. It's worth visiting the *pueblos blancos* in Cádiz because… **[1 mark]**

A	the streets are broad.
B	the houses are modern.
C	the views are amazing.

Social media

You read this extract from an online article.
The extract gives advice to young people about how to use social media safely.

> ¿Eres uno de los muchos jóvenes españoles que usan las redes sociales para comunicarse y ver información actual? Puedes pasarlo bien hablando con tus amigos en las redes, pero nunca debes compartir tu dirección. Además, siempre debes evitar tener una cuenta abierta y aceptar la amistad de personas que no conoces. Otro consejo: piensa bien antes de mandar un mensaje.
> Para proteger tu salud mental, es recomendable reducir el tiempo que pasas delante de la pantalla. ¡Quítate los **auriculares** y habla con tu gente mirándola a los ojos!

112 Theme 3

Answer the following questions in **English**.

5. What must you never share online?

   .... [1 mark]

6. What two things should you always avoid doing?

   ....
   .... [2 marks]

7. What should you do before sending a message?

   .... [1 mark]

8. What should young people do when they talk to someone?

   .... [1 mark]

9. Read the last sentence again. What are **auriculares**?
   Write the correct letter in the box.

A	Something you wear
B	Something you play
C	Something you eat

   [1 mark]

> **EXAM TIP**
> The answers to the questions will always be in the same order as they appear in the text.

Section B: Translation into English

10. Translate these sentences into **English**.

Mis abuelos van de vacaciones hoy. [2 marks]

....
....

Hay edificios antiguos a las afueras de la ciudad. [2 marks]

....
....

Voy a comprar un ordenador con mi dinero. [2 marks]

....
....

Viajé al extranjero en avión y en coche. [2 marks]

....
....

Siempre debes tener cuidado online. [2 marks]

....
....

> **EXAM TIP**
> This task always contains a range of different tenses, so be as precise as possible when translating them into English. You have to be exactly right to get the mark!

Practice EXAM

Theme 3 Writing practice

Section A

1. You send this photo on WhatsApp to a friend in Spain.

What is in this photo?

Write **five** sentences in **Spanish**.

1.1 .... [2 marks]

1.2 .... [2 marks]

1.3 .... [2 marks]

1.4 .... [2 marks]

1.5 .... [2 marks]

LINK
There is also a 50-word task in Section A of the writing paper. You can practise this on pages 79 and 194.

2. Using your knowledge of grammar, complete the following sentences in **Spanish**.

Choose the correct Spanish word from the three options in the grid.

Write the correct **word** in the space, as shown in the example below.

Example

Hay ......*demasiado*...... ruido en la calle.

| mucha | demasiado | algo |

2.1 Mi hermana nunca .... su ropa vieja.

| tirar | tira | tirando |

[1 mark]

2.2 Hoy .... mucho frío.

| es | hace | está |

[1 mark]

2.3 ¡Apaga las ...., por favor!

| luces | televisión | ordenadores |

[1 mark]

2.4 No me gusta .... pueblo.

| esta | esos | este |

[1 mark]

2.5 Si tienes Internet, puedes .... vídeos.

| ver | veo | viendo |

[1 mark]

114 Theme 3

3. Translate the following sentences into **Spanish**. [10 marks]

I always go to a beach in the south.

....

....

I prefer a modern hotel with a pool.

....

....

I use my tablet more than my computer.

....

....

My stepfather bought a new bicycle.

....

....

I would like to breathe clean air.

....

....

Section B

Answer **either** Question 4.1 **or** Question 4.2.

You must only answer **one** of these questions.

Either

Question 4.1

You are writing about technology.

Write approximately **90** words in **Spanish**.

You must write something about each bullet point.

Describe:

- what you think about social media
- what you used your phone for last weekend
- something you would like to buy in the future. [15 marks]

Or

Question 4.2

You are writing an article about the summer holidays.

Write approximately **90** words in **Spanish**.

You must write something about each bullet point.

Describe:

- why holidays are important to you
- what you did last summer
- a place you would like to go on holiday. [15 marks]

EXAM TIP

There is no need to cover each bullet point equally, but you should provide reasonable detail for each, and make sure the content is relevant.

EXAM TIP

Make sure you leave enough time near the end of your exam to carefully check your work.

Knowledge — GRAMMAR

Nouns and articles

Nouns: gender and plurals

Gender of nouns

All nouns in Spanish are either masculine or feminine, singular or plural. Masculine nouns often end in -o and feminine nouns in -a, but there are many exceptions.

- Masculine singular nouns are introduced with the articles *el* (the) or *un* (a).
  - **el** *piso* = the flat
  - **un** *perro* = a dog
- Feminine singular nouns are introduced with the articles *la* (the) or *una* (a).
  - **la** *casa* = the house
  - **una** *familia* = a family
- Some nouns have masculine **and** feminine forms, for example nouns that refer to people:
  - **el** *niño* = the boy
  - **la** *niña* = the girl
  - **un** *francés* = a French man
  - **una** *francesa* = a French woman
- Nouns that refer to people and end in -ante, -ente or -ista have the same form for both genders, but the article changes.
  - **el / la** *estudiante* = the (male / female) student
  - **el / la** *cliente* – the (male / female) customer
  - **un / una** *artista* = a (male / female) artist
- Some nouns referring to people have irregular endings to indicate gender.
  - **el** *rey* = the king
  - **la** *reina* = the queen
  - **un** *actor* = an actor
  - **una** *actriz* = an actress

Plural nouns

- Singular nouns ending in a vowel add -s for plural:
  - *el coche* = the car
  - *los coche***s** = the cars
- Singular nouns ending in a consonant add -es for plural.
  - *la ciudad* = the city
  - *las ciudad***es** = the cities
  - *el español* = the Spanish man
  - *los español***es** = the Spanish people
- Singular nouns ending in -z change the z for a c and add -es for plural.
  - *un pez* = a fish
  - *tres pe***ces** = three fish
- Singular nouns ending in -ción lose the accent and add -es.
  - *la habitación* = the room
  - *las habitac***iones** = the rooms

> **REMEMBER**
> Many nouns ending in -ma and -pa are masculine, even though their endings suggest they ought to be feminine. For example: *el problema, el mapa*.

> **REVISION TIP**
> Practise saying different nationalities in Spanish. See page 25.

> **REMEMBER**
> The feminine form of *el jefe* (boss) can be either *el jefe* or *la jefa*.

Articles: definite and indefinite

Indefinite articles

- There are four indefinite articles in Spanish that match the gender and number of the noun. They are equivalent to 'a' or 'an' (singular) in English, and 'some' (plural).

Singular	Plural
un (masculine)	unos (masculine)
una (feminine)	unas (feminine)

- **un** *libro* = a book
- **una** *mujer* = a woman
- **unos** *libros* = some books
- **unas** *mujeres* = some women

REMEMBER

Don't use an indefinite article in Spanish when talking about someone's job:

Mi hermana es una secretaria. My sister is a secretary.

Definite articles

- There are four definite articles in Spanish that refer to nouns matching their gender and number. The equivalent article in English is 'the'.

Singular	Plural
el (masculine)	los (masculine)
la (feminine)	las (feminine)

- **el** *hermano* = the brother
- **la** *ventana* = the window
- **los** *hermanos* = the brothers
- **las** *ventanas* = the windows

- In Spanish, the definite article is used to make general statements or talk about concepts, whereas in English it is omitted.

La comida española es deliciosa. Spanish food is delicious.

REMEMBER

When the article *el* follows the prepositions *a* and *de*, the words blend together to form *al* and *del*:

Voy al parque. I go to the park.

Vivo cerca del estadio. I live near the stadium.

El papel de la familia — *The role of the family*

Para mí, pasar tiempo con la familia es importante. ¡Me encanta estar en mi **casita**! A veces hay discusiones, pero siempre tengo el amor de mis padres. Mi madre es médica y trabaja cerca del centro. También tengo una **hermanita**. ¡Es estudiante y ¡mi mejor amiga! Nos gusta dar paseos en el parque. Además, tengo unos primos geniales. Mi **primito** Juan es mi favorito.

For me, spending time with family is important. I love being at my little house. Sometimes there are arguments, but I always have the love of my parents. My mother is a doctor, and she works near the centre. Also, I have a little sister. She is a student and my best friend! We like going for walks in the park. I've also got some great cousins. My little cousin Juan is my favourite.

GRAMMAR TIP

Use the suffix *-ito* / *-ita* to convey the meaning of 'little' or as a term of affection. For example: el *gatito* (little cat). See page 161.

REVISION TIP

Try learning one new noun a day and use it in a sentence with the correct article (*el* / *la* / *un* / *una*). Practise saying it out loud.

Retrieval

GRAMMAR

Answer the questions below. Cover the answers column with a piece of paper and write down as many answers as you can. Check and repeat.

	Questions	Answers
1	What are the four indefinite articles in Spanish and what is their equivalent in English?	*Un, una* (a) *Unos, unas* (some)
2	Are these words masculine or feminine? *problema, mapa*	They are all masculine (despite ending in *-a*)
3	How do you say in Spanish: little boy?	*El niñito*
4	Write these four words in the plural form: *la casa, el hijo, el mes, la luz*	*Las casas, los hijos, los meses, las luces*
5	What is the feminine form of *el turista* (the tourist)?	*La turista*
6	What are the four definite articles in Spanish and what do they mean in English?	*El, la, los, las* (the)
7	What is the Spanish for 'king' and 'queen'? Include the definite article.	*El rey, la reina*
8	What is the missing word in this sentence? *Voy ___ museo.* (I go to the museum.)	*Voy al museo*
9	Translate this sentence into Spanish: My mum is a teacher.	*Mi madre es profesora*
10	Write the plural form of *la acción*.	*Las acciones*
11	Write 'near the centre' in Spanish.	*Cerca del centro*
12	What is the missing word in this sentence? *Dinero es importante.*	*El* (*El dinero es importante*)

Previous questions

Now go back and use these questions to check your knowledge of previous topics.

	Questions	Answers
1	How do you say in Spanish: 600 pages?	*Seiscientas páginas*
2	Which letter is almost always silent in Spanish?	The letter '*h*'
3	What is *la mochila* in English?	Rucksack / school bag

Knowledge  GRAMMAR

Adjectives

Adjective agreement

Regular agreement patterns

- In Spanish, an adjective changes to agree with the noun it describes. It matches the gender (masculine or feminine) and the number (singular or plural).
- The masculine singular form often ends in *-o*:
  - *El piso es bonito.* The flat is pretty.
- The feminine singular form often ends in *-a*:
  - *La casa es bonita.* The house is pretty.
- With plural nouns, an *-s* is usually added to the adjective:
  - *Los pisos son bonitos.* The flats are pretty.
  - *Las casas son bonitas.* The houses are pretty.
- If the adjective describes a group of masculine and feminine nouns, the masculine plural form is used:
  - *Mis padres son simpáticos.* My parents are nice.

Other agreement patterns

- Adjectives ending in *-ente* or *-ista* are the same in the masculine and feminine form:
  - *Mi hermano es inteligente y optimista.* My brother is intelligent and optimistic.
  - *Mi hermana es inteligente y optimista.* My sister is intelligent and optimistic.
- Adjectives that end in a consonant generally do not change in the feminine form, but add *-es* in the plural:
  - *el hombre joven* = the young man
  - *la mujer joven* = the young woman
  - *las mujeres jóvenes* = the young women
- However, adjectives ending in *-r* add an *-a* in the feminine form:
  - *Mi padre es trabajador y mi madre es trabajadora también.*
    My father is hard-working and my mother is hard-working, too.
- Adjectives of nationality are not written with a capital letter in Spanish. If they end in a consonant, add *-a* for the feminine singular form, *-es* for the masculine plural form, and *-as* for the feminine plural form:
  - *un chico inglés* = an English boy
  - *una chica inglesa* = an English girl
  - *unos chicos ingleses* = some English boys
  - *unas chicas inglesas* = some English girls

Note the removal of the accent over the *-e* in the feminine and plural forms.

> **REMEMBER**
> Although 'water' in Spanish is *el agua*, it is in fact a feminine noun so the adjective used to describe it must also be in the feminine form:
> *el agua fría* – cold water

> **REMEMBER**
> Adding *-ísimo* / *-ísima* to the end of an adjective intensifies its meaning.
> *(bueno) buenísimo* – very good
> *(caro) carísimo* – very expensive

Knowledge — GRAMMAR

Adjectives

Position of adjectives

Adjectives after the noun

- In Spanish, most adjectives are placed after the noun they describe:
  - *mi amigo mexicano* = my Mexican friend
- The following adjectives are placed before the noun, and lose their final *–o* when the noun that they describe is masculine singular:
  - *(alguno) algún día* = one day
  - *(bueno) un buen chico* = a good boy
  - *(malo) mal tiempo* = bad weather
  - *(ninguno) ningún libro* = no book
  - *(primero) mi primer trabajo* = my first job
  - *(tercero) el tercer mes* = the third month

Adjectives before or after the noun

- Some adjectives change meaning depending on their position (before or after the noun):
  - *una **gran** ciudad* = a great city
  - *una ciudad **grande*** = a big city
  - *la **única** persona* = the only person
  - *una persona **única*** = a unique person
  - *mi **nuevo** coche* = my new car (new to me)
  - *mi coche **nuevo*** = my (brand) new car

Adjectives before the noun

- The following adjectives are always placed before the noun:
  - *bastante(s)* = enough
  - *mucho(s) / mucha(s)* = many
  - *demasiado(s) / demasiada(s)* = too many
  - *otro(s) / otra(s)* = another, other
  - *poco(s) / poca(s)* = few
  - *tanto(s) / tanta(s)* = so much, so many
  - *varios / varias* = several, various
- Here are some examples:
  - ***bastante** información* = enough information
  - ***demasiadas** personas* = too many people
  - ***otras** ideas* = other ideas
  - ***tantas** tiendas* = so many shops
  - ***varias** opciones* = several options

REMEMBER

When placed before an adjective, *bastante* means 'quite' and *demasiado* means 'too':

***bastante** grande* – quite big

***demasiado** tranquilo* – too quiet

Comparatives

Using comparatives with adjectives

- In Spanish, the following structures are used with adjectives to compare people, things and places:

  - *más ... que* = more ... than

  *Mi tío es **más** alto **que** mi padre.* My uncle is taller than my father.
  *Madrid es **más** grande **que** Málaga.* Madrid is bigger than Malaga.

  - *menos ... que* = less ... than

  *Tengo **menos** dinero **que** tú.* I have less money than you.
  *La falda es **menos** cara **que** la camisa.* The skirt is less expensive than the shirt.

  - *tan ... como* = as ... as

  *Mi amigo es **tan** alto **como** su hermano mayor.*
  My friend is as tall as his older brother.

  *El cine es **tan** antiguo **como** el teatro.* The cinema is as old as the theatre.

Using comparatives with quantity and numbers

- *Más de* can also mean 'more than', but only when referring to quantity and numbers:

  *Tengo **más de** cien euros.* I have more than a hundred euros.
  *He viajado a **más de** diez países.* I've travelled to more than ten countries.

Using *mejor* and *peor*

- The comparative form of *bueno/a* (good) is *mejor* (better).

  *Es **mejor** hablar **que** discutir.* Talking is better than arguing.
  *El clima en España es **mejor que** en Inglaterra.*
  The climate in Spain is better than in England.
  *Mi hermana canta **mejor que** yo.* My sister sings better than me.

- The comparative form of *malo/a* (bad) is *peor* (worse).

  *El tráfico aquí es **peor que** en mi ciudad.* The traffic here is worse than in my city.
  *Este restaurante es **peor que** el otro.* This restaurant is worse than the other one.
  *El tiempo hoy es **peor que** ayer.* The weather today is worse than yesterday.

> **GRAMMAR TIP**
>
> Use the same structures and irregular forms for comparative adverbs. See pages 127–128.
>
> *Hablan **más rápidamente que** ustedes.* They speak faster than you.
>
> *Canto **peor que** María.* I sing worse than María.

Un viaje a Perú *A trip to Peru*

El año **pasado**, fui a Perú. El **primer** día, conocí a **otras** estudiantes **españolas**. ¡Visitamos **tantos** sitios **interesantes** y sacamos **muchas** fotos allí! Perú es más **grande** que Colombia y en mi opinión, como país es más **bonito**. En la capital, hay **algunas** tiendas **baratísimas** y **muchos** museos **históricos**.

Last year, I went to Peru. On the first day, I met other Spanish students. We visited so many interesting sites and we took lots of photos there! Peru is bigger than Colombia and, in my opinion, as a country it is more beautiful. In the capital, there are some very cheap shops and lots of historic museums.

> **REVISION TIP**
>
> Remember to check for adjective agreement, especially when you're using comparative structures.

Retrieval — GRAMMAR

Answer the questions below. Cover the answers column with a piece of paper and write down as many answers as you can. Check and repeat.

#	Questions	Answers
1	What does *tan … como* mean in English?	As … as
2	How do you say in Spanish: better, worse?	*Mejor, peor*
3	Name three adjectives that shorten when placed before a masculine noun.	Possible answers include: *alguno* (one / some), *bueno* (good), *malo* (bad), *ninguno* (no, not a single), *primero* (first), *tercero* (third), *grande* (big)
4	Translate this sentence into English: *Es una gran ciudad.*	It is a great city
5	What is the feminine form of the adjective *joven* (young)?	*Joven* (it does not change)
6	What is the plural form of *feliz* (happy)?	*Felices*
7	Write *francés* in the plural form.	*Franceses*
8	Translate this sentence into Spanish: There is a new house.	*Hay una casa nueva*
9	How do you say in Spanish: cold water?	*El agua fría*
10	Translate this sentence into Spanish: I have more than twenty books.	*Tengo más de veinte libros*
11	What does *carísimo* mean in English?	Very expensive
12	Translate this sentence into English: *Hay pocas casas en el centro de la ciudad.*	There are few houses in the city centre

Previous questions

Use the questions below to check your knowledge from previous chapters.

#	Questions	Answers
1	How do you say in Spanish: learning is important?	*Aprender es importante*
2	Write these four words in the plural form: *la casa, el hijo, el mes, la luz*	*Las casas, los hijos, los meses, las luces*
3	What are the four definite articles in Spanish and what do they mean in English?	*El, la, los, las* (the)

Knowledge  GRAMMAR

Adjectives

Demonstrative, possessive and indefinite adjectives

Demonstrative adjectives

- Demonstrative adjectives indicate the relative distance of a noun in relation to the speaker and listener. In Spanish, they must agree with the noun to which they refer.

Singular		Plural	
Masculine	Feminine	Masculine	Feminine
este this	*esta* this	*estos* these	*estas* these
ese that	*esa* that	*esos* those	*esas* those

- **este** *niño* = this boy
- **esta** *niña* = this girl
- **esos** *pájaros* = those birds
- **esas** *montañas* = those mountains

Possessive adjectives

- Possessive adjectives agree in number and sometimes in gender with the noun that follows, not the possessor.

Singular	Plural
mi my	*mis* my
tu your	*tus* your
su his / her	*sus* his / her
nuestro/a our	*nuestros/as* our
vuestro/a your	*vuestros/as* your
su their	*sus* their

- **mi** *vestido* = my dress
- **tu** *chaqueta* = your jacket
- **nuestros** *zapatos* = our shoes
- **vuestras** *bolsas* = your (plural) bags

REMEMBER

Tu (without an accent) is a possessive adjective, but *tú* (with an accent) is a personal pronoun that precedes a verb.
Tú sabes la respuesta.
You know the answer.

REVISION TIP

Try explaining key grammar points to a friend or family member to help them stick in your memory.

Knowledge 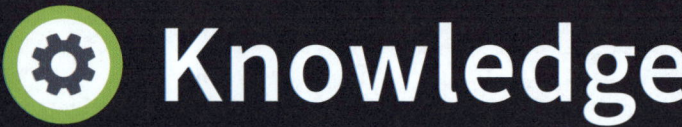 GRAMMAR

Adjectives

Indefinite adjectives

Using indefinite adjectives

- Indefinite adjectives are used to describe nouns in a general sense.
- The following adjectives agree in gender and number with the noun that follows them:
  - *algún, alguna, algunos, algunas* (some)
  - *demasiado, demasiada, demasiados, demasiadas* (too much, too many)
  - *mismo, misma, mismos, mismas* (same)
  - *mucho, mucha, muchos, muchas* (many, a lot of)
  - *otro, otra, otros, otras* (other, another)
  - *poco, poca, pocos, pocas* (few, little)
  - *tanto, tanta, tantos, tantas* (so much, so many)
  - *todo, toda, todos, todas* (all, every)

  algunas preguntas = some questions   **pocas** oportunidades = few opportunities
  demasiada comida = too much food   **tantas** personas = so many people
  las **mismas** cosas = the same things   **todos** los estudiantes = all the students
  mucho trabajo = a lot of work

- *bastante, bastantes* (quite a lot of, enough) only exists in one singular and plural form:
  - **bastante** *tiempo* = enough time
  - **bastantes** *razones* = quite a few reasons
- *ningún, ninguna* (no, not a single) is generally only used in the singular form:
  - **ningún** *cambio* = no change
  - **ninguna** *solución* = no solution
- *varios, varias* (several, various) only exists in the plural form:
  - **varios** *platos* = several dishes
  - **varias** *opciones* = several options
- *cada* (every) does not change with gender:
  - **cada** *semana* = every week
  - **cada** *mes* = every month

REMEMBER

Cada uno and *cada una* mean 'each one'.

Cada uno de los estudiantes tiene un libro.
Each of the students has a book.

Cada una de las flores es bonita.
Each of the flowers is pretty.

Mucho trabajo y poco tiempo   *A lot of work and little time*

Esta semana, tengo **mucho** trabajo en el instituto y **demasiados** deberes que hacer en casa. **Mis** padres dicen que es importante evitar el estrés, pero en este momento, yo tengo **poco** tiempo. **Todos** mis exámenes empiezan **este** mayo y no tengo **ninguna** oportunidad de descansar.

This week, I have a lot of work in school and too much homework to do at home. My parents say that it is important to avoid stress, but at the moment, I have little time. All of my exams start this May and I don't have any opportunity to rest.

REVISION TIP

Cover the English text on the left and try translating the Spanish text yourself. Take care with the words in bold!

Retrieval — GRAMMAR

Answer the questions below. Cover the answers column with a piece of paper and write down as many answers as you can. Check and repeat.

Questions / Answers

#	Question	Answer
1	Which is far from you: *este vaso* or *ese vaso*	*Ese vaso*
2	Choose the correct option to fill the gap: ¿Te gustan mi / mis / tu pantalones?	¿Te gustan <u>mis</u> pantalones?
3	Translate this sentence into Spanish: There are too many books in his bedroom.	*Hay demasiados libros en su dormitorio / habitación*
4	Complete the question with the correct option and translate into English: ¿Tienes otro / otra / otros ejemplos?	¿Tienes <u>otros</u> ejemplos? Do you have other examples?
5	In Spanish, 'every day' is *todos los días* or…	*Cada día*
6	Which are the only two possessive adjectives that have a feminine form?	*Nuestra(s)* and *vuestra(s)*
7	How do you say in Spanish: so many houses?	*Tantas casas*
8	Translate into Spanish: Where are our shoes?	¿Dónde están nuestros zapatos?
9	If 'vegetables' are *verduras*, how do you say 'these vegetables' in Spanish?	*Estas verduras*
10	Which of the following adjectives is only used in the plural form? *varios / bastantes / algunos*	*Varios*
11	What are the three meanings of the possessive adjective *su*?	His, her, their
12	How do you say in Spanish: those houses?	*Esas casas*

Previous questions

Use the questions below to check your knowledge from previous chapters.

#	Question	Answer
1	Are these words masculine or feminine? *problema, mapa*	They are all masculine (despite ending in -a)
2	What is the plural form of *feliz* (happy)?	*Felices*
3	What does *carísimo* mean in English?	Very expensive

Knowledge

GRAMMAR

Adverbs

Different type of adverbs

Adverbs of manner

- Adverbs of manner describe how something is done. There are several different types.
- Adverbs in Spanish are often formed by adding *-mente* (*-ly*) to the feminine form of the adjective:
  - *rápida* → *rápida***mente** = quick → quickly
  - *lenta* → *lenta***mente** = slow → slowly
- Adjectives that end in *-e, -l, -z* simply add *-mente* to form the adverb:
  - *final* → *final***mente** = end → finally
  - *probable* → *probable***mente** = probable → probably
- Other adjectives have an irregular adverb:
  - *bueno/a* → **bien** = good → well
  - *malo/a* → **mal** = bad → badly
- We usually place an adverb after the verb it describes. It can also be placed at the beginning of a sentence for emphasis.
  - *Cocináis muy **bien**.* You cook really well.
  - ***Lentamente** salió del coche.* Slowly she got out of the car.
- The comparative form of adverbs follows the same structures and patterns as the adjectives. (See pages 123–124.)
  - *Nadas **tan bien como** tu padre.* You swim as well as your dad.
  - *Hablo en inglés **mejor que** antes.* I speak in English better than before.

Adverbs of time

- Adverbs of time indicate when an action occurs and are often placed at the beginning or end of a sentence.
  - *hoy* = today
  - *mañana* = tomorrow
  - *ayer* = yesterday
  - *anoche* = last night
  - *ahora* = now
  - *ya* = already

  ***Anoche** salí con mis amigos.* Last night, I went out with my friends.

Adverbs of frequency

- Adverbs of frequency indicate how often an action occurs and are often placed at the beginning or end of a sentence.
  - *a veces* = sometimes
  - *siempre* = always
  - *nunca* = never

  ***Nunca** voy al supermercado.* I never go to the supermarket.

REMEMBER

Rápido can be used both as an adjective and an adverb.

*Ese coche va **rápido**.* That car is going fast.

Notice that if an adjective has an accent, so does the adverb.
práctico – practical
prácticamente – practically

REVISION TIP

Try to avoid using *bien* (well), *mal* (badly), *bueno/a* (good) and *malo/a* (bad) too often in your speaking or writing. Replace them with synonyms like *genial* (great), *estupendo* (wonderful) and *horrible* (horrible).

Adverbs of sequence

- Adverbs of sequence indicate the order in which an action occurs in relation to other actions.
  - *primero* = first
  - *antes* = before
  - *después* = after
  - *luego* = then, later
  - *mientras* = while
  - *finalmente* = finally

  - **Primero**, *hago mis deberes y* **luego** *ceno.*
    First, I do my homework and then I have dinner.

Adverbs of place

- Adverbs of place are often used with *estar* to denote position or location.
  - *aquí* = here
  - *allí* = there
  - *debajo* = underneath
  - *delante* = in front
  - *detrás* = behind
  - *al lado* = next to
  - *cerca* = near
  - *lejos* = far
  - *entre* = between
  - *sobre* = on top of, over, about

  - *Tu mochila* **está aquí**. Your rucksack is here.

- They are also often used with the preposition *de* to provide more precise descriptions:
  - *La mesa está al lado* **de** *la cama.* The table is next to the bed.

- Note that whenever *de* and *el* appear next to each other, they merge to make *del*:
  - *Los libros están dentro* **del** *coche.* The books are inside the car.

Quantifiers and intensifiers

- These words modify both verbs and adjectives:
  - *bastante* = quite
  - *demasiado* = too
  - *mucho* = a lot
  - *muy* = very
  - *un poco* = a bit

- *Muy* and *mucho* are often confused. *Muy* means 'very' when used with adjectives and adverbs:
  - *Son* **muy** *bonitos.* They are very pretty.
  - *Hablas español* **muy** *bien.* You speak Spanish very well.

- *Mucho* means 'a lot', 'many' or 'much' when used with nouns and verbs:
  - *Tienen* **mucho** *trabajo.* They have a lot of work.
  - *Estudio* **mucho**. I study a lot.

REMEMBER

Unlike many other adverbs of position, *entre* is never followed by *de*:

El parque está **entre** *el instituto y el ayuntamiento.* – The park is between the school and the town hall.

GRAMMAR TIP

Un poco before an adjective means 'a bit', but *poco* before an adjective means 'not very'. *Poco* before a noun means 'little' or 'few'.

Es **un poco** *difícil.*
It is a bit difficult.

Es **poco** *difícil.*
It is not very difficult.

Tengo **poco** *dinero.*
I have little money.

Retrieval — GRAMMAR

Answer the questions below. Cover the answers column with a piece of paper and write down as many answers as you can. Check and repeat.

Questions / Answers

#	Question	Answer
1	How do you say in Spanish: here, there?	*Aquí, allí*
2	If *tranquilo* means 'calm', how do you say 'calmly' in Spanish?	*Tranquilamente*
3	Translate this sentence into English: *Anoche salí con mis amigos.*	Last night I went out with my friends
4	Translate this sentence into Spanish: It is too easy.	*Es demasiado fácil*
5	What is the missing word in this sentence? *Tu teléfono está debajo ___ libro.* (Your phone is under the book.)	*Tu teléfono está debajo del libro*
6	If *malo/a* is the adjective, what is the adverb?	*Mal* (badly)
7	Translate this sentence into English: *Veo la televisión mientras ceno.*	I watch television while I have dinner
8	What is the opposite of *detrás*?	*Delante* (in front)
9	Which of these adverbs of place is never followed by the preposition *de*? *debajo / entre / al lado*	*Entre*
10	Which of the following adjectives indicates frequency? *después / lejos / a veces*	*A veces* (sometimes)
11	What are the two words for 'never' in Spanish?	*Nunca* and *jamás*
12	Complete the sentence with the correct word: *El examen fue muy / mucho / mejor fácil.*	*El examen fue muy fácil*

Previous questions

Use the questions below to check your knowledge from previous chapters.

#	Question	Answer
1	What is the missing word in this sentence? *Voy ___ museo.* (I go to the museum.)	*Voy al museo*
2	In Spanish, 'every day' is *todos los días* or…	*Cada día*
3	What are the three meanings of the possessive adjective *su*?	His, her, their

Knowledge GRAMMAR

Pronouns

Subject pronouns: direct and indirect object pronouns

Subject pronouns

- Subject pronouns take the place of one of more nouns, and carry out the action expressed by the verb.

yo	I	nosotros / nosotras	we
tú	you	vosotros / vosotras	you (plural)
él / ella	he / she / it	ellos / ellas	they
usted	you (formal)	ustedes	you (formal)

> **GRAMMAR TIP**
> Subject pronouns are often omitted in Spanish as the verb endings generally make clear who or what the subject is: *Vivo en Madrid.* (yo)

- Subject pronouns show a change in the focus of the sentence. They also show contrast or emphasis when there is more than one subject in the sentence.

  ¡**Yo** he terminado ya! I have finished already!

  Él estudia y **yo** escucho música. He studies and I listen to music.

Direct and indirect object pronouns

- Direct object pronouns replace the noun that directly receives the action of the verb. They are placed directly before the conjugated verb.

| me | me | lo / los | him, it / them |
| te | you | la / las | her, it / them |

  Compro el libro. **Lo** compro. I buy the book. I buy it.

  Ella ve a María. Ella **la** ve. She sees María. She sees her.

- When there are two verbs, the direct object can be placed before the first verb or attached to the end of an infinitive or present participle.

  Puedes comprar **el libro** aquí. You can buy the book here.

  Lo puedes comprar aquí. / Puedes comprar**lo** aquí. You can buy it here.

- Object pronouns are also attached to imperative constructions and gerunds. Note the addition of the accent:

  ¡Compra los zapatos! ¡Cómpra**los**! Buy the shoes! Buy them!

  Ese hombre **te** está mirando. That man is looking at you.

- Indirect object pronouns indicate 'to whom' or 'for whom' the action of the verb is done:

| me | to / for me | le | to / for him, her |
| te | to / for you | les | to / for them |

> **REMEMBER**
> Use the form *conmigo* to say 'with me'.
> *Mi hermano vive* **conmigo**. My brother lives with me.

  Les compramos una bici nueva. We bought them a new bike.

- When there are two verbs, the indirect object can be placed before the first verb, or attached to the end of an infinitive or present participle:

  Voy a dar el dinero a mis padres. Voy a dar**les** el dinero. / **Les** voy a dar el dinero.

  I'm going to give my parents the money. / I'm going to give them the money.

Knowledge — GRAMMAR

Pronouns

Interrogative and indefinite pronouns

Interrogative pronouns

- Interrogative pronouns normally appear at the beginning of a question and always have a graphic accent (*tilde*).

  *¿**Cuánto** cuesta este libro?* How much does this book cost?

- The pronoun *quién* is used to ask about people. It means 'who' or 'whom' and it has a plural form, *quiénes*.

  *¿**Quién** quiere jugar conmigo?* Who wants to play with me?

  *¿**Quiénes** te han dicho eso?* Who has told you that?

- The pronoun *qué* is used to ask about things or ideas. It means 'what'.

  *¿**Qué** es esta caja?* What's this box?

- The pronoun *cuál* is used to ask about two or more things. It means 'what' or 'which' and it has a plural form, *cuáles*.

  *¿**Cuál** camisa prefieres, la blanca o la gris?*

  Which shirt do you prefer, the white one or the grey one?

  *Hay muchos museos. ¿**Cuáles** has visitado?*

  There are many museums. Which ones have you visited?

- The pronoun *cuánto* is used to ask about quantity or number. It means 'how much' or 'how many' and it has singular and plural forms, *cuánto(s)* and *cuánta(s)*.

  *¿**Cuánto** tiempo tenemos?* How much time do we have?

  *¿**Cuántos** minutos hay en un día?* How many minutes are there in a day?

  *¿**Cuántas** hermanas tienes?* How many sisters do you have?

> **REMEMBER**
>
> When these pronouns are used with a preposition, it is the preposition that comes first in the sentence.
>
> *¿**Con** quién vives?*
> Who do you live with?
> *¿**Para** cuánto tiempo necesitas el coche?*
> How long do you need the car for?

Indefinite pronouns

- Indefinite pronouns substitute nouns and refer to people or things in a non-specific way.

Masculine singular	Feminine singular	Masculine plural	Feminine plural	English
algún	*alguna*	*algunos*	*algunas*	a / an / some / any
ningún	*ninguna*	*ningunos*	*ningunas*	no / not … any

- The indefinite pronouns *algún* and *ningún* agree in gender and in number with the noun they are replacing:

  *Tiene buenas canciones. ¿Has escuchado **alguna**?*

  He's got good songs. Have you listened to any?

  *Tengo tres hermanos, pero **ninguno** vive cerca.*

  I have three brothers, but none live nearby.

- Indefinite pronouns are similar to indefinite adjectives (see page 124). However, while an indefinite adjective will accompany and modify a noun, indefinite pronouns substitute nouns.

Relative and demonstrative pronouns

Relative pronouns

- Relative pronouns refer to a noun or another pronoun previously mentioned. Relative pronouns allow two sentences to be combined into a single new one.
- *que* (who, that, which)

    *La tía **que** vive en Madrid tiene dos perros.*
    The aunt who lives in Madrid has two dogs.

    *El libro **que** estoy leyendo es interesante.*
    The book (that) I am reading is interesting.

Demonstrative pronouns

- Demonstrative pronouns agree with the nouns they replace.

Singular		Plural	
Masculine	**Feminine**	**Masculine**	**Feminine**
este (this)	*esta* (this)	*estos* (these)	*estas* (these)
ese (that)	*esa* (that)	*esos* (those)	*esas* (those)

LINK

Demonstrative pronouns are not used in the same way as demonstrative adjectives, which describe the nouns that follow them. See page 123.

***Esta** es la dirección correcta.* This is the correct address.

*Busco unos zapatos. Quiero probar **esos**.*
I'm looking for shoes. I'd like to try those (ones).

- *Esto* (this) and *eso* (that) are neutral demonstrative pronouns in Spanish used to refer to something where gender cannot be clearly defined, such as an idea, situation or unknown object:

***Esto** no es justo.* This isn't fair.

*¿Qué es **eso**?* What's that?

REMEMBER

Use *por eso* to talk about cause and effect:

Estaba lloviendo. Por eso, nos quedamos en casa.
It was raining. Therefore, we stayed home.

Knowledge

Retrieval **GRAMMAR**

Answer the questions below. Cover the answers column with a piece of paper and write down as many answers as you can. Check and repeat.

Questions	Answers
1. What is the meaning of *usted* in Spanish?	You (formal)
2. Insert the correct subject pronoun in the sentence: _____ hablamos inglés.	*Nosotros/as* hablamos inglés
3. Which word would you use in a question? *quien / cuánto / que*	*Cuánto*
4. Rewrite the sentence using an indirect pronoun to replace the underlined phrase. *Escribo una carta <u>a mis padres</u>.*	*Les escribo una carta*
5. Name two indefinite pronouns.	Possible answers include: *ninguno, alguno, alguien, algo*
6. Translate this sentence into Spanish: I have three books. I have them at home.	*Tengo tres libros. Los tengo en casa*
7. Complete the sentence: *Me gusta esta novela. Estoy <u>la leyendo</u> / <u>leyéndola</u> ahora.*	*Me gusta esta novela. Estoy <u>leyéndola</u> ahora.*
8. How do you say 'Buy them!' in the *tú* form, when referring to two books, in Spanish?	*¡Cómpralos!*
9. What are the three singular indirect object pronouns?	*Me, te, le*
10. Translate this sentence into Spanish: I don't want those shoes, I want these ones.	*No quiero esos zapatos, quiero estos*
11. How do you say in Spanish: where?	*¿Dónde?*
12. Translate this question into Spanish: *Who do you live with?*	*¿Con quién vives?*

Previous questions

Use the questions below to check your knowledge from previous chapters.

Questions	Answers
1. How do you say in Spanish: I am very hungry?	*Tengo mucha hambre*
2. What is the opposite of *detrás*?	*Delante* (in front)
3. Say the Spanish words for four rooms inside a house.	*El salón, la cocina, el baño, el dormitorio*

Knowledge — GRAMMAR

The present indicative

The present tense of regular verbs

The present indicative

- The present indicative tense is used to describe actions that are taking place now or happening routinely.
  - *Escucho música todos los días.* I listen to music every day.
  - *Jugamos al baloncesto.* We play basketball.
  - *Mis padres escriben cartas a sus amigos.* My parents write letters to their friends.

Regular verbs

- Most verbs in the present tense follow a regular pattern. Remove the –*ar*, –*er* or –*ir* of the infinitive form of the verb and add the appropriate ending.

	-ar	-er	-ir
(yo)	trabaj**o**	com**o**	viv**o**
(tú)	trabaj**as**	com**es**	viv**es**
(él / ella / usted)	trabaj**a**	com**e**	viv**e**
(nosotros/as)	trabaj**amos**	com**emos**	viv**imos**
(vosotros/as)	trabaj**áis**	com**éis**	viv**ís**
(ellos / ellas / ustedes)	trabaj**an**	com**en**	viv**en**

Estamos muy felices cuando ganamos. We're very happy when we win.

Los niños aprenden idiomas fácilmente. Children learn languages easily.

Vosotros escribís muy bien en inglés. You write very well in English.

GRAMMAR TIP

The Spanish present indicative can be translated into English as present simple or present continuous.

Trabajan en una fábrica. They work / are working in a factory.

Verbs like *gustar*

- Some verbs in Spanish follow a different structure. They use the object as the subject of the action.

  Me gusta el fútbol. I like football. (literally 'Football pleases me.')

- Other verbs that work in this way are:
  - *encantar* = to love
  - *faltar* = to lack, be missing
  - *interesar* = to be interested in
  - *molestar* = to annoy, bother
  - *parecer* = to seem
  - *preocupar* = to worry
  - *quedar* = to remain, have left

- The indirect object pronoun (*me, te, le*) shows who is 'doing' the liking.

  Me interesa este tema. I'm interested in this topic.

  ¿Te preocupa algo? Are you worried about anything?

- If the object is plural, use the third person plural of the verb.

  Le quedan unos días aquí. She's got a few days left here.

  Me gustan las vacaciones. I like holidays.

Knowledge GRAMMAR

The present indicative

Radical-changing verbs

Stem-changing patterns

- Some verbs in the present indicative tense have stem changes in the 'I', 'you', 'he / she' and 'they' forms of the verb.
- **e changes to i**

pedir (to ask for)	
p**i**do	pedimos
p**i**des	pedís
p**i**de	p**i**den

- Other verbs that follow this pattern: *repetir* (to repeat), *seguir* (to follow, continue), *servir* (to serve), *sonreír* (to smile), *vestir* (to dress).
- **Pido** *consejos a mis padres.* I ask my parents for advice.
- **e changes to ie**

pensar (to think)	
p**ie**nso	pensamos
p**ie**nsas	pensáis
p**ie**nsa	p**ie**nsan

- Other verbs that follow this pattern: *comenzar* (to start), *empezar* (to start), *encender* (to turn on), *entender* (to understand), *querer* (to want), *perder* (to lose).
- **o changes to ue**

encontrar (to find)	
enc**ue**ntro	encontramos
enc**ue**ntras	encontráis
enc**ue**ntra	enc**ue**ntran

- Other verbs that follow this pattern: *costar* (to cost), *doler* (to hurt), *dormir* (to sleep), *morir* (to die), *poder* (to be able to), *probar* (to taste, try), *recordar* (to remember), *soñar* (to dream), *volver* (to return).
- *Las entradas* **cuestan** *cien euros.* The tickets cost a hundred euros.
- **u changes to ue**

jugar (to play)	
j**ue**go	jugamos
j**ue**gas	jugáis
j**ue**ga	j**ue**gan

- *¿J**ue**gas al tenis con él?* Do you play tennis with him?

> **REVISION TIP**
> Summarise everything you know about the present tense of regular and stem-changing verbs on a separate piece of paper.

The present tense of irregular verbs

- Some common verbs in Spanish have an irregular first person (*yo*). The rest of the conjugation follows the usual pattern. For example:
  - *conducir* = to drive → *conduzco*
  - *conocer* = to know → *conozco*
  - *hacer* = to do, make → *hago*
  - *poner* = to put → *pongo*
  - *saber* = to know → *sé*
  - *salir* = to go out → *salgo*

  Hago los deberes por la tarde, pero mis amigos los hacen por la mañana.
  I do my homework in the evening but my friends do it in the morning.

- There are several common verbs that are irregular in all persons in the present tense.

dar (to give)	decir (to say)	estar (to be)	ir (to go)
doy	digo	estoy	voy
das	dices	estás	vas
da	dice	está	va
damos	decimos	estamos	vamos
dais	decís	estáis	vais
dan	dicen	están	van

oir (to hear)	ser (to be)	tener (to have)	venir (to come)
oigo	soy	tengo	vengo
oyes	eres	tienes	vienes
oye	es	tiene	viene
oímos	somos	tenemos	venimos
oís	sois	tenéis	venís
oyen	son	tienen	vienen

REVISION TIP

Verbs that are irregular in one tense are not necessarily irregular in another. Learn with care the irregular verbs for each tense you study.

LINK

For the different uses of *ser* and *estar*, see page 154.

LINK

For a list of different expressions with *tener*, see page 155.

En el instituto At school

Por la mañana, **voy** al instituto con mi hermano. Él **tiene** ocho años, pero yo **tengo** quince. Primero, **estudio** matemáticas, luego **hago** deporte en el gimnasio. **Vuelvo** a casa a las cuatro y media, pero mi hermano no **puede** porque **tiene** una clase de judo. Los viernes **son** mis días favoritos porque **hago** deporte.

In the morning, I go to school with my brother. He is eight years old, but I am fifteen. First, I study Maths, then I do sports in the gym. I return home at half past four, but my brother can't because he has a judo class. Friday is my favourite day because I do sport.

REVISION TIP

Look at the bold present tense verbs in the text on the left. Notice how they are translated into English in the context of each sentence.

Knowledge

Retrieval

GRAMMAR

Answer the questions below. Cover the answers column with a piece of paper and write down as many answers as you can. Check and repeat.

#	Questions	Answers
1	Conjugate the verb *ir* (to go) in full, in the present tense.	Voy, vas, va, vamos, vais, van
2	What are the four types of stem-changing verbs?	E>i, e>ie, o>ue, u>ue
3	Translate this sentence into Spanish: They can study with me.	*Pueden estudiar conmigo*
4	What is the first person singular of the verb *saber* (to know) in the present tense?	*Sé*
5	Complete the missing forms of the verb *ser*: Soy, ___, es, somos, sois, ___	*Eres, son*
6	What does *salgo* mean in English?	I go out
7	Translate into Spanish: I want to go with my friends.	*Quiero ir con mis amigos*
8	List three verbs with the stem change e>ie.	Possible answers include: *pensar, empezar, perder, entender*
9	How do you say in Spanish: I don't drive?	*Yo no conduzco*
10	What is the 'I' form of *salir* (to go out) in the present tense?	*Salgo*
11	What are the endings for regular *-ir* verbs in the present tense?	-o, -es, -e, -imos, -ís, -en
12	What is the 'I' form of the verb *venir* (to come)?	*Vengo*

Previous questions

Use the questions below to check your knowledge from previous chapters.

#	Questions	Answers
1	When talking about sport, what does *una carrera* mean?	A race
2	Which word is the same in Spanish? identity / online / moda	Online
3	How do you say in Spanish: little boy?	*Niñito*

Knowledge GRAMMAR

The present continuous and reflexive verbs

The present continuous and present participles

The present continuous

- The present continuous tense is used to talk about an ongoing action in the present. It is formed by using the verb *estar* in the present tense and the present participle of the verb.

estar + present participle		
yo	estoy	
tú	estás	
él / ella / usted	está	cenando
nosotros/as	estamos	bebiendo
vosotros/as	estáis	conduciendo
ellos / ellas / ustedes	están	

Estoy viendo la televisión. I am watching TV.

REVISION TIP

There is little difference in meaning between the present tense and the present continuous tense, but it is important to learn both as they are so commonly used.

The present participle

- The present participle (or gerund) is formed by replacing the infinitive verb ending *-ar* with *-ando*, and the *-er* or *-ir* ending with *-iendo*: *jugar → jugando*, *beber → bebiendo*.

- Some verbs have an irregular present participle.
  - decir → diciendo
  - leer → leyendo
  - pedir → pidiendo

¿Qué estás diciendo? What are you saying?

Está leyendo un periódico. He / She is reading a newspaper.

- In English, present participles are commonly used as nouns, whereas in Spanish, the infinitive is used instead.

Fumar es malo para la salud. Smoking is bad for your health.

Estoy de exámenes *It's exam time*

Hoy **estoy pensando** en mis exámenes. **Estoy estudiando** mucho porque necesito **aprobarlos**. Esta tarde, tengo que **terminar** todos mis deberes. **Practicar** todos los días me ayudará a **mejorar** mucho. Mi padre **está diciendo** que estudiar con alguien es más práctico y divertido. Mañana, quiero ir a la biblioteca con mi amiga Sara.

Today I'm thinking about my exams. I'm studying a lot because I need to pass. This afternoon, I have to finish all my homework. Practicing every day will help me to improve a lot. My dad is saying that studying with someone is more practical and fun. Tomorrow, I want to go to the library with my friend Sara.

REVISION TIP

It is important to be aware of the many different ways infinitives and present participles are used. They can add complexity to your speaking and writing.

Knowledge **GRAMMAR**

The present continuous and reflexive verbs

Reflexive verbs

Reflexive verbs and pronouns

- Reflexive verbs indicate that the subject and the object of the action are the same. They are conjugated with reflexive pronouns, including: *me, te, se*.

Lavarse	To wash (yourself)
(yo) **me** lavo	I wash (myself)
(tú) **te** lavas	you wash (yourself)
(él / ella) **se** lava	he / she washes (himself)
(usted) **se** lava	you wash (yourself) (formal)

- Reflexive verbs are very common in Spanish and they are often used to talk about daily routine actions.

    Me levanto *temprano.* I get up early.

    Se viste *rápidamente.* He / She gets dressed quickly.

- Some verbs change meaning when used reflexively. Here are some examples:

Non-reflexive meaning		Reflexive meaning	
acordar	to agree on	acordarse	to remember
dormir	to sleep	dormirse	to fall asleep
ir	to go	irse	to leave
quedar	to meet up	quedarse	to stay
parecer	to seem	parecerse a	to look like
poner	to put	ponerse	to put on, become
vestir	to dress	vestirse	to get dressed

Parece triste. He seems sad.

Se parece a su madre. He looks like his mother.

- Reflexive verbs in their infinitive form have *se* attached at the end:

    *Es importante lavar**se** las manos.* It's important to wash your hands

- If there are two verbs in a construction, the reflexive pronoun is placed either before the first verb, or attached to the end of the second verb:

    Me *voy a poner un pantalón. / Voy a poner**me** un pantalón.*

    I'm going to put on a pair of trousers.

- A positive imperative attaches the reflexive pronoun to the end of it, often adding an accent to the verb.

    *¡Míra**te**!* Look at yourself!

Retrieval — GRAMMAR

Answer the questions below. Cover the answers column with a piece of paper and write down as many answers as you can. Check and repeat.

Questions / Answers

#	Question	Answer
1	Which tense is used in this sentence? *Estoy estudiando mucho.*	The present continuous tense
2	What is the present participle / gerund of the verb *leer*?	*Leyendo*
3	Conjugate the verb *estar* in full in the present tense.	*Estoy, estás, está, estamos, estáis, están*
4	Translate this sentence into Spanish: My brother gets up at 7 o'clock.	*Mi hermano se levanta a las siete*
5	What is the difference in meaning between *quedarse* and *quedar*?	*Quedarse* = to stay / *Quedar* = to meet up
6	What is the present participle / gerund of the verb *pedir*?	*Pidiendo*
7	Complete the sentence with the correct option: *Está llover / llueve / lloviendo mucho.*	*Está lloviendo mucho*
8	Name three verbs that change meaning when made reflexive.	Possible answers include: *irse* (to leave), *quedarse* (to stay), *parecerse a* (to look like), *ponerse* (to put on, become)
9	Translate this sentence into English: *¿Te acuerdas de esta canción?*	Do you remember this song?
10	Choose the correct option to complete the sentence and translate into English. *Nadando / Nadar es divertido.*	*Nadar es divertido* / Swimming is fun
11	Rewrite the sentence with the missing word: *Voy a cambiar de ropa.*	*Voy a cambiarme de ropa.* or *Me voy a cambiar de ropa.*
12	Translate this question into English: *¿Qué estás diciendo?*	What are you saying?

Previous questions

Use the questions below to check your knowledge from previous chapters.

#	Question	Answer
1	What date is *Nochebuena* celebrated in Spain?	Christmas Eve (24 December)
2	Which are the only two possessive adjectives that have a feminine form?	*Nuestra(s)* and *vuestra(s)*
3	What is the 'I' form of *salir* (to go out) in the present tense?	*Salgo*

Knowledge **GRAMMAR**

Modal and impersonal verbs

Modal verbs

Modal verbs and infinitives

- Modal verbs express necessity, ability, permission, or obligation. They are often followed by another verb in the infinitive form. Learn these modal verbs:

Deber (to have to / must)	*Querer* (to want)	*Poder* (to be able to, can)	*Saber* (to know)
debo	quiero	puedo	sé
debes	quieres	puedes	sabes
debe	quiere	puede	sabe
debemos	queremos	podemos	sabemos
debéis	queréis	podéis	sabéis
deben	quieren	pueden	saben

Debes estudiar *más.* You must study more.

Queremos viajar *a España.* We want to travel to Spain.

Puedo nadar *rápido.* I can swim fast.

Saben hablar *francés muy bien.* They know how to speak French very well.

- *Tener* can be used as a modal verb followed by *que* and an infinitive to express obligation or necessity.

Tienes que *comer más verdura.* You have to eat more vegetables.

> **REMEMBER**
> The conditional forms of *deber* and *poder* are very useful:
> *debería* (I should)
> *podría* (I could)

Un fin de semana ideal *An ideal weekend*

Este fin de semana **quiero** descansar un poco. El sábado **debemos** ir de compras, pero también **puedo** ir al cine con mis amigos. El domingo **debería** ir al parque porque hará buen tiempo. Luego, **debo** visitar a mis padres por la tarde. Hace tiempo que no los veo. Ellos **saben** comer bien. **Quiero** cenar en casa.

This weekend I want to rest a little. On Saturday we have to go shopping, but I can also go to the cinema with my friends. On Sunday, I should go to the park because the weather is going to be good. Afterwards, I must visit my parents in the afternoon. It's been a while since I last saw them. They know how to eat well. I want to have dinner at home.

> **REVISION TIP**
> Cover the Spanish text on the left. Find the seven modal verbs in the English text and think about how you would translate each one into Spanish.

Impersonal verbs

Using impersonal verbs

- Impersonal verbs do not have a specific subject. They don't refer to a particular person or thing so they are used in a more general way. They often appear in constructions with the third person singular form.

Hay

- *Hay* is the third person singular of the verb *haber*. It means 'there is / are'.

  Hay *muchas tiendas en este pueblo.* There are many shops in this town.

- The construction *hay que* + infinitive means 'one must' / 'it is necessary to' and is used to describe what must be done in a general sense.

  Hay que *reciclar.* One must / It is necessary to recycle.

Necessity and possibility

- These impersonal forms are used to talk about necessity and possibility.

  Es necesario *estudiar todos los días.* It is necessary to study every day.

  Es posible *aprender un nuevo idioma si practicas todos los días.*
  It is possible to learn a new language if you practise every day.

Weather-related verbs

- Verbs such as *hacer* (to do, make) and *llover* (to rain) are used in the third person singular to describe weather.

  Hoy **hace** *mucho sol. No llueve.* It is very sunny today. It's not raining.

Reflexive impersonal constructions

- The pronoun *se* and the third person of the verbs *necesitar* and *poder* are also commonly used together to express an impersonal 'you':

  Se necesita *una tarjeta para sacar dinero.*
  You need a card to withdraw money.

  Se puede *entrar el museo gratis los domingos.*
  You can enter the museum for free on Sundays.

> **REVISION TIP**
>
> Use each of the bold impersonal verbs on this page to say or write your own Spanish sentences.

Retrieval

GRAMMAR

Answer the questions below. Cover the answers column with a piece of paper and write down as many answers as you can. Check and repeat.

Questions | Answers

#	Question	Answer
1	Name three modal verbs in Spanish.	Possible answers include: *deber, poder, querer, saber, tener que*
2	What form of the verb follows the expression *hay que*?	The infinitive
3	Conjugate the verb *poder* in the present tense.	*Puedo, puedes, puede, podemos, podéis, pueden*
4	Translate this sentence into English: *Se puede entrar en el museo gratis*.	You can go in the museum for free
5	What do *debería* and *podría* mean in English?	I should, I could
6	Which expression does not have the same meaning as the other two: *debes / hay que / es posible*	*Es posible.* The other two expressions express necessity
7	Translate this sentence into Spanish: I must learn Spanish.	*Debo / Tengo que aprender español*
8	How do you say in Spanish: We want to play?	*Queremos jugar*
9	Complete the sentence with the correct verb: *Hoy es / está / hace mucho calor*.	*Hoy hace mucho calor*
10	What's the infinitive of the verb *hay* (there is / are)?	*Haber*
11	Translate this sentence into English: *No se puede hablar durante la película*.	You can't talk during the film
12	Conjugate the verb *saber* in the present tense.	*Sé, sabes, sabe, sabemos, sabéis, saben*

Previous questions

Use the questions below to check your knowledge from previous chapters.

Questions | Answers

#	Question	Answer
1	Write the present participle of the verbs *bailar, correr* and *escribir*.	*Bailando, corriendo, escribiendo*
2	What is the missing word in this sentence? *Tu teléfono está debajo ___ libro.* (Your phone is under the book.)	*Tu teléfono está debajo del libro*
3	Translate into Spanish: Where are our shoes?	*¿Dónde están nuestros zapatos?*

Knowledge GRAMMAR

The preterite tense

Preterite tense of regular verbs

The preterite

- The preterite tense is used to describe completed events in the past.

  *Ayer **compré** un coche.* Yesterday, I bought a car.

Regular verbs in the preterite tense

- To form the preterite tense of regular verbs, we remove the infinitive ending and add the correct endings for -*ar* verbs and -*er* or -*ir* verbs.

	-*ar* verbs	-*er* / -*ir* verbs
yo	trabaj**é**	com**í**
tú	trabaj**aste**	com**iste**
él / ella / usted	trabaj**ó**	com**ió**
nosotros	trabaj**amos**	com**imos**
vosotros	trabaj**asteis**	com**isteis**
ellos / ellas / ustedes	trabaj**aron**	com**ieron**

- Some verbs in the preterite tense have a spelling change in the first person singular only. This is to preserve the correct pronunciation of the word.

- -*zar* verbs change to -*cé*:

  empezar = to start   *yo empe**cé*** = I started

- -*gar* verbs change to -*gué*:

  jugar = to play   *yo ju**gué*** = I played

- -*car* verbs change to -*qué*:

  explicar = to explain   *yo expli**qué*** = I explained

- Some -*ir* verbs in the preterite tense undergo stem changes in the third person singular and plural forms.

	yo	*él / ella / usted*	*ellos / ellas / ustedes*
e changes to *i*	sentí	**sintió**	**sintieron**
o changes to *u*	dormí	**durmió**	**durmieron**
i changes to *y*	leí	**leyó**	**leyeron**

> **REVISION TIP**
>
> Practise using the same verbs and vocabulary in different time frames to prepare for speaking and writing tasks.

> **REMEMBER**
>
> The second person plural form (*nosotros/as*) of regular verbs is identical in the present indicative tense (*trabajamos*, *comimos*) and the preterite (*trabajamos*, *comimos*). You can only tell the difference through context.

> **REVISION TIP**
>
> Try chanting verbs in the preterite tense. This can help you focus on sounds and pronunciation, and will also help you remember them better, particularly the irregulars!

Knowledge — GRAMMAR

The preterite tense

Preterite tense of irregular verbs

Irregular verbs in the preterite tense

– Some common verbs have irregular forms in the preterite tense, with unique stem changes.

Verb	Stem change	Example
dar (to give)	di-	**Di** el mensaje al profesor. I gave the message to the teacher.
decir (to say)	dij-	**Dije** la verdad. I told the truth.
estar (to be)	estuv-	**Estuve** en la playa. I was at the beach.
hacer (to do)	hic-	**Hice** mis deberes. I did my homework. **Hizo** la cama. He made the bed.
ir (to go) / ser (to be)	fu-	**Fui** al cine. I went to the cinema.
poder (to be able to)	pud-	**Pude** llegar a tiempo. I was able to arrive on time.
poner (to put)	pus-	**Puse** el libro en la mesa. I put the book on the table.
querer (to want)	quis-	**Quise** visitar el museo. I wanted to visit the museum.
saber (to find out, know)	sup-	**Supe** la verdad. I found out the truth.
tener (to have)	tuv-	**Tuve** un examen difícil. I had a difficult exam.
traer (to bring)	traj-	**Traje** comida del restaurante. I brought food from the restaurant.
venir (to come)	vin-	**Vine** temprano. I came early.

> **REMEMBER**
> The verbs *ser* (to be) and *ir* (to go) are the same in the preterite tense (*fui, fuiste, fue…*), so you need to use context to work out the correct meaning.

> **GRAMMAR TIP**
> Several Spanish verbs are derived from *tener*, such as *mantener* and *contener*. These verbs follow the conjugation of *tener* in all tenses.

– Irregular verbs in the preterite do not have accents on their endings, unlike regular verbs.

Mi fin de semana *My weekend*

Tuve un fin de semana increíble en Italia. **Fui** con mi padre. ¡**Fue** muy divertido! Mi padre y yo **visitamos** sitios de interés y **sacamos** fotos. El sábado, él **volvió** al hotel a dormir, pero yo **di** un paseo y **conocí** un mercado tradicional. **Vi** muchas cosas que me **gustaron**. Le **compré** un regalo a mi madre. Ella se **quedó** en casa por trabajo.

I had an incredible weekend in Italy. I went with my dad. It was fun! My dad and I visited the sights and took photos. On Saturday, he went back to the hotel to sleep, but I went for a walk and I explored a traditional market. I saw lots of things I liked. I bought my mum a present. She stayed home because of work.

> **REVISION TIP**
> Look at the irregular preterite verbs in bold on the left. Which ones will you prioritise learning for your own speaking and writing?

Retrieval — GRAMMAR

Answer the questions below. Cover the answers column with a piece of paper and write down as many answers as you can. Check and repeat.

Questions | Answers

1. What are the regular preterite endings for *-ar* verbs? — -é, -aste, -ó, -amos, -asteis, -aron
2. What are the regular preterite endings for *-er* and *-ir* verbs? — -í, -iste, -ió, -imos, -isteis, -ieron
3. Using the verb *ver*, translate into Spanish: Did you watch the film? — ¿Viste la película?
4. Translate this sentence into English: *Ayer escribimos una carta.* — Yesterday we wrote a letter
5. What two meanings does *fui* have? — I went / I was
6. If *leí* is the past form for 'I read', how do you say 'he / she read' in Spanish? — Leyó
7. Translate this sentence into Spanish: They went to the party. — (Ellos/as) Fueron a la fiesta
8. Name three verbs that have irregular stems in the preterite and write the stem for each. — Possible answers include: tener (tuv-), poder (pud-), venir (vin-), poner (pus-), decir (dij-), hacer (hic-), estar (estuv-), ser / ir (fu-)
9. When is the preterite tense used? — When describing a completed event in the past
10. How do you say in Spanish: I wanted? — Yo quise
11. Spot the error in this sentence: *Ví a mis amigos en el parque* — Vi (I saw) should not have an accent on the *i*
12. Translate this sentence into English: *Puse el libro en la mesa.* — I put the book on the table

Previous questions

Use the questions below to check your knowledge from previous chapters.

Questions | Answers

1. How do you say in Spanish: no one? — Nadie
2. Answer the following question in Spanish and give a reason: *¿Cuál es tu fiesta favorita?* — Example: *Me gusta celebrar la Navidad con mi familia porque comemos comida rica*
3. What is the first person singular of the verb *saber* (to know) in the present tense? — Sé

Knowledge — GRAMMAR

The imperfect tenses

The imperfect and imperfect continuous tenses

The imperfect

- The imperfect tense is used to say what was happening in the past, or what used to happen regularly in the past. It is also used for describing situations, feelings, physical conditions and the time in the past.

  *Cuando **vivía** en Madrid, **trabajaba** en esa oficina.*

  When I lived in Madrid, I used to work in that office

- To form the imperfect tense, add the following endings to the stem of the verb:

	-ar	-er / -ir
yo	trabaj**aba**	com**ía**
tú	trabaj**abas**	com**ías**
él / ella / usted	trabaj**aba**	com**ía**
nosotros/as	trabaj**ábamos**	com**íamos**
vosotros/as	trabaj**abais**	com**íais**
ellos / ellas / ustedes	trabaj**aban**	com**ían**

REMEMBER

The *yo* ending is the same as the *él / ella / usted* ending in the imperfect tense (**-aba** and **-ía**). If needed, add a subject pronoun before the verb for clarity.

- Three common irregular verbs in the imperfect tense are *ser, ir* and *ver*.

	ser (to be)	*ir* (to go)	*ver* (to see)
yo	era	iba	veía
tú	eras	ibas	veías
él / ella / usted	era	iba	veía
nosotros/as	éramos	íbamos	veíamos
vosotros/as	erais	ibais	veíais
ellos / ellas / ustedes	eran	iban	veían

REVISION TIP

Make sure you know the imperfect verb *había* (there was/were, there used to be).

The imperfect continuous

- The imperfect continuous is used to describe actions that were ongoing in the past or happening at a specific moment in the past. It is formed by using the imperfect tense of *estar* + the present participle.

  *Yo **estaba hablando** con ella.* I was talking to her.

  *Nosotros **estábamos viajando** por Europa.* We were traveling through Europe.

LINK

See the present participles on page 137.

Preterite and imperfect tenses together

Using the preterite and the imperfect tenses

- The preterite and imperfect tenses both refer to the past. The preterite describes a complete action in the past (*Ayer comí pescado*), whereas the imperfect describes an action that took place in the past without a definite ending (*Ayer estaba comiendo pescado*).

- The preterite and imperfect tenses are often used together to provide context in a narrative. The imperfect sets the scene or provides background detail, while the preterite describes the action that interrupts or moves the story forward.

- In the example below, *estaba lloviendo* (imperfect) sets the scene (it was raining), and *salí* (preterite) indicates the action that took place (I left).

    Estaba lloviendo cuando **salí** de casa. It was raining when I left the house.

- To help you decide whether to use the preterite or imperfect tense, learn specific time expressions.

Examples of time phrases that refer to a completed action (preterite)	
ayer	yesterday
anoche	last night
la semana pasada	last week
el otro día	the other day

Examples of time phrases referring to a repeated continuous action in the past (imperfect or imperfect continuous)	
a veces	sometimes
cuando	when
siempre	always
todos los días	every day
todo el tiempo	all the time

Mi día libre *My day off*

Ayer, cuando **estaba comiendo** en un restaurante con mi amigo Raúl, **oímos** un ruido muy fuerte y **salimos** a la calle. ¡**Era** un desfile! **Estaba lloviendo** mucho, así que **nos fuimos** a casa. Allí, mientras **dormía**, mi tío **me llamó** por teléfono, pero **estaba** tan cansado que no **contesté**. En la casa de la playa, mi tío nos **visitaba** a veces y siempre **traía** dulces deliciosos.

Yesterday, when I was eating at a restaurant with my friend Raúl, we heard a very loud noise and we went outside. It was a parade! It was raining heavily, so we went home. There, while I was sleeping, my uncle called me, but I was so tired that I didn't answer. My uncle used to visit us frequently at the beach house and always used to bring delicious sweets.

> **REVISION TIP**
>
> Look at the verbs in bold in the text on the left. Decide if each verb is in the imperfect, imperfect continuous or the preterite.

Knowledge **147**

Knowledge — GRAMMAR

The present perfect tense

The present perfect tense and past participles

The present perfect
- The present perfect tense is used to talk about an action that took place in the past and is complete.
  He terminado *mi trabajo por hoy.* I have finished my work for today.
- The present perfect is formed by using the present tense of the verb *haber* (to have) as an auxiliary verb, followed by the past participle of the main verb.

haber + past participle		
yo	he	
tú	has	
él / ella / usted	ha	hablado
nosotros/as	hemos	comido
vosotros/as	habéis	vivido
ellos / ellas / ustedes	han	

LINK
Use the imperfect (not the present perfect) for repeated, habitual actions in the past. See page 146.

GRAMMAR TIP
Past participles can also function as adjectives. As adjectives, they agree with the noun they modify.
La ventana *está* **cerrada**. The window is closed.

The past participle
- The past participle is formed by adding to the verb stem *-ado* for *-ar* verbs and *-ido* for *-er* / *-ir* verbs.
  hablar → habl**ado**   comer → com**ido**   vivir → viv**ido**
- Some verbs have an irregular past participle.

Infinitive	Past participle
abrir (to open)	*abierto*
escribir (to write)	*escrito*
morir (to die)	*muerto*
poner (to put)	*puesto*

Infinitive	Past participle
resolver (to resolve)	*resuelto*
romper (to break)	*roto*
ver (to see)	*visto*
volver (to return)	*vuelto*

Has **roto** *la ventana.* You have broken the window.
Hemos **escrito** *un libro.* We have written a book.

- Negative constructions and object pronouns are placed before the verb *haber*.
  No lo he terminado. I haven't finished it.
- Time phrases like *antes*, *(dos) veces* and *hoy* are often used with the present perfect tense.
  Te ha llamado **dos veces.** He's called you twice.

REMEMBER
Remember that derived infinitives follow the same pattern as the main infinitive.
tener → *tenido* (had)
mantener → *mantenido* (to keep)

Retrieval — GRAMMAR

Answer the questions below. Cover the answers column with a piece of paper and write down as many answers as you can. Check and repeat.

Questions / Answers

#	Question	Answer
1	Translate this sentence into Spanish using the imperfect tense: There were many cars.	*Había muchos coches*
2	Conjugate the verb *soñar* (to dream) in the imperfect tense.	*Soñaba, soñabas, soñaba, soñábamos, soñabais, soñaban*
3	Translate this sentence into Spanish: Before, I used to live in France.	*Antes, vivía en Francia*
4	Translate this sentence into English: *He comido demasiado.*	*I've eaten too much*
5	Name the irregular verbs in the imperfect tense.	*Ser, ir, ver*
6	Conjugate *ir* in the imperfect tense.	*Iba, ibas, iba, íbamos, ibais, iban*
7	Change the verb in the imperfect tense into the imperfect continuous: *Llovía mucho en Bilbao.*	*Estaba lloviendo mucho en Bilbao*
8	Identify the imperfect tense verb and the preterite tense verb in this sentence: *Miraba por la ventana cuando vi a mi tía.*	*Miraba*- imperfect (I was looking) *Vi*- preterite (I saw)
9	Translate this sentence into Spanish: We have travelled to France.	*Hemos viajado a Francia*
10	What is the past participle of the verb *romper*?	*Roto*
11	What is the difference in meaning between these two sentences? *Fui a España. / He ido a España.*	*Fui a España.* I went to Spain *He ido a España.* I have been to Spain
12	Correct the word order in this sentence: *No he lo abierto.*	*No lo he abierto*

Previous questions

Now go back and use these questions to check your knowledge of previous topics.

#	Question	Answer
1	How do you say in Spanish: parade?	*El desfile*
2	Translate this sentence into English: *Es una gran ciudad.*	*It is a great city*
3	Write the plural form of *la acción*.	*Las acciones*

Knowledge **GRAMMAR**

The future tenses and the conditional

The immediate future and simple future tenses

The immediate future

- We use the immediate future to talk about what is going to happen.

  *Mi hermano **va a comprar** un coche nuevo.*

  My brother is going to buy a new car.

- The immediate future is formed using the correct form of the verb *ir* (to go) in the present tense + *a* + infinitive.

Pronoun	Ir	a	Infinitive
yo	voy	a	jugar comer hacer ir salir
tú	vas		
él / ella / usted	va		
nosotros/as	vamos		
vosotros/as	váis		
ellos / ellas / ustedes	van		

REMEMBER

The immediate future can translate in English as *going to* or *will*.

The simple future

- We use the simple future tense to say what will happen at some point in the future.

  *Algún día **viajarás** por todo el mundo.* One day you will travel around the world.

- To form the simple future, add the correct ending to the infinitive of the verb.

	-ar verbs	-er verbs	-ir verbs
yo	jugar**é**	comer**é**	pedir**é**
tú	jugar**ás**	comer**ás**	pedir**ás**
él / ella / usted	jugar**á**	comer**á**	pedir**á**

Some verbs have irregular stems in the future.

Infinitive	Stem
hacer (to do)	har-
poner (to put)	pondr-
poder (to be able to)	podr-
tener (to have)	tendr-

No **podré** ir a la fiesta. I will not be able to go to the party.

REVISION TIP

Use the future in your speaking and writing to impress the examiner. It is relatively easy to remember because the endings are always the same for all regular and irregular verbs.

REMEMBER

The verb *haber* (there is / are) is irregular in the present (*hay*) and future tense (*habrá*).

The conditional

The conditional

- The conditional is used to express what 'would', 'could' or 'should' happen or what someone 'would', 'could' or 'should' do.

   *Dijo que me **llamaría**.* He said he would call me.

   *¿**Podrías** ayudarme?* Could you help me?

- The conditional uses the same stem as the future tense, but with different endings.

	-ar	-er	-ir
yo	jugar**ía**	comer**ía**	pedir**ía**
tú	jugar**ías**	comer**ías**	pedir**ías**
él / ella / usted	jugar**ía**	comer**ía**	pedir**ía**

The conditional shares the same irregular verbs as the future tense.

*¿**Podrías** ayudarme con la tarea?* Could you help me with the homework?

Infinitive	Stem
hacer (to do)	har-
poner (to put)	pondr-
poder (to be able to)	podr-
tener (to have)	tendr-

REMEMBER

Even though *quisiera* is a subjunctive form, it is often translated as 'would like'.

***Quisiera** una ensalada.* I would like a salad.

LINK

The conditional endings are the same as the endings for the imperfect tense. See page 146.

GRAMMAR TIP

The conditional stem of the verb *haber* is *habr-*.

*No **habría** suficiente tiempo.* There wouldn't be enough time.

Vamos a México!   Let's go to Mexico!

El verano próximo voy a viajar a México y voy a visitar diferentes ciudades. No sé si **debería** ir en tren o en autobús. Comeré fajitas y **podría** probar tamales. No sé si tendré tiempo de ver todos los monumentos, pero no volvería sin visitar el de Frida Kahlo, porque sería una experiencia bonita.

Next summer, I'm going to travel to Mexico and visit different cities. I don't know if I should go by train or by bus. I will eat fajitas and I could try tamales. I don't know if I will have time to see all the monuments, but I wouldn't return without visiting the one of Frida Kahlo, because it would be a beautiful experience.

REVISION TIP

Two particularly useful verbs to learn in the conditional are *poder* (*podría* – I could) and *deber* (*debería* – I should).

Knowledge

Retrieval

GRAMMAR

Answer the questions below. Cover the answers column with a piece of paper and write down as many answers as you can. Check and repeat.

	Questions	Answers
1	What is difference in meaning between these two sentences? *Vamos a cenar a las ocho.* *Cenaremos a las ocho.*	*Vamos a cenar a las ocho.* We are going to have dinner at 8 o'clock *Cenaremos a las ocho.* We will have dinner at 8 o'clock
2	What is the missing word in this sentence? I am going to play football: *Voy jugar al fútbol.*	*Voy <u>a</u> jugar al fútbol*
3	Translate into Spanish: They are going to relax tonight.	*Van a descansar esta noche*
4	What are the endings of the simple future tense for *yo*, *tú* and *él / ella / usted*?	*é, ás, á*
5	Name three verbs with an irregular stem in the future tense and the conditional.	Possible answers include: *tener, poder, poner, hacer*
6	Translate into English: *En julio hará sol todos los días.*	In July, it will be sunny every day
7	Translate into Spanish: Yesterday, I had Maths.	*Ayer tuve matemáticas*
8	What is the conditional form of *hay*?	*Habría*
9	What is the irregular stem of *hacer* in the future tense and the conditional?	*Har*
10	Complete the sentence with the correct form of the conditional: *Me gusta / Me gustaría / Me gustaba venir a la fiesta pero no puedo.*	<u>*Me gustaría*</u> *venir a la fiesta pero no puedo*
11	How do you say in Spanish: I should?	*Debería*
12	Which of the following verb forms is in the conditional? *podría / hacía / será*	*Podría*

Previous questions

Use the questions below to check your knowledge from previous chapters.

	Questions	Answers
1	How do you say in Spanish: we are going to train?	*Vamos a entrenar*
2	Translate *modelo a seguir* into English.	Role model (literally: a model to follow)
3	What does *malísimo* mean in English?	Very bad

Knowledge GRAMMAR

The imperative

The imperative

Using the positive imperative

- The positive imperative is used to give commands, instructions or advice.

  ¡**Come** mucha verdura! Eat a lot of vegetables!

  ¡**Escribe** con bolígrafo negro! Write with a black pen!

- For the *tú* form of the imperative, use the third person of the present tense.

  ¡**Escucha** a tu madre! Listen to your mother!

  Cierra la puerta. Close the door.

- Several common verbs have irregular forms in the *tú* form of the imperative.

Verb	Imperative
decir	¡Di! (say / tell)
hacer	¡Haz! (do / make)
ir	¡Ve! (go)
poner	¡Pon! (put)
salir	¡Sal! (leave)
ser	¡Sé! (be)
tener	¡Ten! (have)
venir	¡Ven! (come)

> **REVISION TIP**
>
> Try giving some instructions in Spanish using different imperatives forms. For example: ¡**Haz** tu trabajo en silencio!
> Do your work in silence!

- The following pronouns can be attached to the end of positive commands:
  - Direct object pronouns: *me, te, lo, la, los, las*
  - Indirect object pronouns: *me, te, le, les*
  - Reflexive pronouns: *me, te, se*

  ¡Haz**lo**! Do it!

  ¡Di**me**! Tell me!

- If the verb has two or more syllables, an accent is usually added to maintain the original stress: ¡**Dí**melo! Say it to me!

Un viaje a la Habana *A visit to Havana*

Si vas a la capital de Cuba este verano, **explora** la ciudad y **visita** los lugares más interesantes. **Prueba** la comida típica y **habla** con la gente local. **Compra** algunos recuerdos y **saca** muchas fotos. ¡**Disfruta** del viaje y **pásatelo** bien!

If you go to the capital of Cuba this summer, explore the city and visit the most interesting places. Try the local food and talk to the local people. Buy some souvenirs and take lots of photos. Enjoy the trip and have a good time!

Knowledge **GRAMMAR**

Using *ser*, *estar* and *tener*

Ser and *estar*

Using *ser* and *estar*

- *Ser* and *estar* both mean 'to be', but they are used in different ways.
- *Ser* describes who or what someone is:

    Soy *estudiante.* I am a student.

    Ella **es** *profesora.* She is a teacher.

- *Ser* also describes characteristics that are unlikely to change:

    Mi pueblo **es** *pequeño.* My town is small.

    Juan y Pedro **son** *altos.* Juan and Pedro are tall.

- *Estar* describes location:

    Mis abuelos **están** *en España.* My grandparents are in Spain.

    ¿Dónde **está** *el baño?* Where is the bathroom?

- *Estar* also describes temporary conditions and emotions:

    Estoy *cansado hoy.* I am tired today.

    El café **está** *frío.* The coffee is cold.

- Sometimes, using *ser* or *estar* with the same adjective changes the meaning:
    - *ser aburrido* = to be boring
    - *estar aburrido* = to be bored
    - *ser listo* = to be clever
    - *estar listo* = to be ready
    - *ser rico* = to be rich
    - *estar rico* = to be tasty
- Both *ser* and *estar* have irregular preterite forms.

    Pedro **estuvo** *comiendo pescado.* Pedro was eating fish.

    Mi madre **fue** *profesora en España.* My mother was a teacher in Spain.

> **LINK**
> Remember that *estar* is also used before a present participle to describe an ongoing action. See page 137.

> **LINK**
> See the preterite tense on pages 143 and 144.

Expressions with *tener*

Idiomatic expressions with *tener*

Tener is an extremely useful verb in Spanish. It is used in many idiomatic expressions where in English you would use 'to be'.

Spanish	English
tener … años	to be … years old
tener hambre	to be hungry
tener sed	to be thirsty
tener frío	to be cold (referring to people)
tener calor	to be hot
tener sueño	to be sleepy
tener miedo (de)	to be afraid of
tener razón	to be right
tener suerte	to be lucky
tener éxito	to be successful
tener ganas de + infinitive	to feel like (doing something)
tener cuidado	to be careful
tener lugar	to take place
tener sentido	to make sense
tener confianza en	to have trust in

> **LINK**
>
> *Tener que* + infinitive means 'to have to'. See page 140.
>
> **Tengo que** *estudiar*. I have to study.

Tengo mucha suerte *de vivir aquí*. I am very lucky to live here.

Mi hermana **tiene** *doce* **años**. My sister is 12 years old.

Si no hay comida, Julia **tendrá hambre**. If there is no food, Julia will be hungry.

Knowledge 155

Retrieval — GRAMMAR

Answer the questions below. Cover the answers column with a piece of paper and write down as many answers as you can. Check and repeat.

Questions / Answers

#	Question	Answer
1	Name two uses of *estar*.	*Estar* is used for temporary states and locations
2	Translate this question into Spanish: Where are my glasses?	¿Dónde están mis gafas?
3	Complete the sentence with the correct option. *Hoy yo soy / estoy / tengo un poco triste.*	Hoy <u>estoy</u> un poco triste (temporary emotion)
4	What is the difference between *ser rico* and *estar rico*?	*Ser rico* = to be rich *Estar rico* = to be tasty
5	Translate this sentence into Spanish: My brother is very tall.	Mi hermano es muy alto
6	Complete the sentence with the correct option: *Ella es / está / tiene en su dormitorio.*	Ella <u>está</u> en su dormitorio (location)
7	What does *tener razón* mean in English?	To be right
8	Translate this sentence into Spanish: I am successful.	Tengo éxito
9	What is the difference between *tener frío* and *estar frío*?	*Tener frío* is used to describe people feeling cold *Estar frío* is used to describe objects being cold
10	What is the imperative of *hablar* in the *tú* form?	Habla
11	Translate this sentence into English: *¡Dame una sorpresa!*	Give me a surprise!
12	What is the imperative of *hablar* in the *tú* form?	¡Habla!

Previous questions

Now go back and use these questions to check your knowledge of previous topics.

#	Question	Answer
1	What is the opposite of *detrás*?	Delante
2	What does *pocas oportunidades* mean?	Few opportunities
3	What are *fuegos artificiales*?	Fireworks

Knowledge GRAMMAR

Negatives and prepositions

Negatives

Negative expressions

- In Spanish, the negative is usually placed before the verb. *No* is the most basic form of negation, but there are a range of other negative expressions that can be used, often in combination.

  ***No** puedo salir esta tarde.* I can't go out this afternoon.

  *Mis amigos **no** quieren ir a la universidad.* My friends don't want to go to university.

- Other negative expressions that are used commonly in Spanish are the following:
  - *nada* = nothing
  - *nadie* = no one
  - *ninguno/a/s* = no, none, not any
  - *nunca* = never

Double negatives

- Unlike in English, the double negative is commonly used in Spanish.

  ***No** tengo **ningún** libro.* I don't have any book.

  ***No** hicimos **nada**.* We didn't do anything.

- *Nunca*, *nadie* and *nada* can either be placed before the verb (with *no* omitted), or *no* can go before the verb, with *nunca*, *nadie*, *nadie* and *nada* after it.

  ***Nunca** he estado en México. / **No** he estado **nunca** en México.*

  I have never been to Mexico.

  ***Nada** es más importante que la salud.*

  Nothing is more important than your health.

  ***No** quiero **nada**.* I don't want anything.

  ***Nadie** vino a la fiesta. / **No** vino **nadie** a la fiesta.* No one came to the party.

> **GRAMMAR TIP**
>
> You can even have triple negatives in Spanish:
>
> ***No** dije **nada** a **nadie**.*
> I didn't say anything to anyone.

Mis primos *My cousins*

Mañana es la boda de mi hermana mayor y mis primos van a estar. **Nadie** ha hablado con ellos durante mucho tiempo. **No** tenemos mucho en común. **Nunca** nos gustaron las mismas cosas y **no** hacen **nada** interesante en su tiempo libre. Sin embargo, cuando estamos en familia, nos reímos mucho. Voy a hacer un esfuerzo para conocerlos mejor.

Tomorrow is my older sister's wedding, and my cousins are going to be there. No one has spoken to them for a while. We don't have much in common. We've never liked the same things, and they don't do anything interesting in their free time. However, when we're with family, we laugh a lot. I'm going to make an effort to get to know them better.

> **REVISION TIP**
>
> Take care when reading and listening to notice any negatives.

Knowledge GRAMMAR

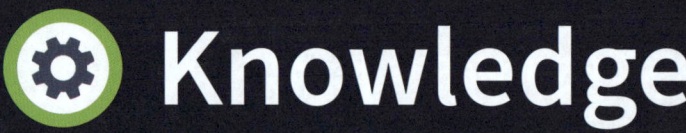

Negatives and prepositions

Verbs with prepositions

Verbs followed by different prepositions

In Spanish, some verbs are followed by specific prepositions, then a noun, or an infinitive.

*Voy a **aprender a cocinar**.* I am going to learn to cook.

Verbs followed by *a*

aprender a	to learn to	***Estoy aprendiendo a** nadar.* I am learning to swim.
ayudar a	to help to	*¿**Me ayudas a** preparar la cena?* Can you help me make dinner?
empezar a	to start to	***Voy a empezar a** aprender italiano.* I am going to start learning Italian.

The structure *volver a* + infinitive means 'to do something again'.

***Vuelvo a llamarte** más tarde.* I will call you again later.

Verbs followed by *de*

acordarse de	to remember	***Me acuerdo de** ti.* I remember you.
dejar de	to stop	***Dejé de** fumar.* I stopped smoking.
depender de	to depend on	*Todo **depende de** tu decisión.* Everything depends on your decision.
pensar de + noun	to think about	*¿Qué **piensas de** este libro?* What do you think about this book?

Verbs followed by *en*

creer en	to believe in	***Creo en** la importancia de la educación.* I believe in the importance of education.
entrar en	to enter (into)	***Entré en** el supermercado para comprar pan.* I entered the supermarket to buy bread.
participar en	to participate in	*Mi hermana **participó en** el concierto.* My sister participated in the concert.
pensar en	to think about	***Pienso en** mis vacaciones.* I am thinking about my holidays.

> **GRAMMAR TIP**
>
> When using the verb *empezar* in the immediate future tense, there is a double *a* construction:
>
> *Voy **a** empezar **a** estudiar.* I am going to start studying.

> **REMEMBER**
>
> *Pensar* can be used with these three structures: *pensar en*, *pensar de* and *pensar* + infinitive.
>
> *Siempre **pienso en** volver a Malabo.* I always think about returning to Malabo.
>
> *¿Qué **pensáis de** mi?* What do you think of me?
>
> *El jueves pasado **pensé comprar** otra casa.* Last Thursday I thought of buying another house.

> **REMEMBER**
>
> Don't translate prepositions from English to Spanish as they often don't match. For example, 'to dream of' is *soñar con* and 'to speak to' is *hablar con*.

The personal *a*, uses of *de*, *para*, *por* and *sin*

The personal *a*

- When a verb refers to a specific person, the direct object must be preceded by the preposition **a**.

  *No conozco **a** tu hermana.* I don't know your sister.

Uses of *de*

- *De* is used to talk about:

  Possession: *El coche **de** Juan.* Juan's car.

  Origin: *Soy **de** España.* I am from Spain.

  Material: *La mesa es **de** plástico.* The table is made of plastic.

- Remember, when forming questions that involve a preposition in Spanish, the preposition is usually placed before the question word, unlike in English.

  *¿**De** qué hablas?* What are you talking about?

Using *para* and *por*

- *Para* and *por* often cause confusion. *Para* is used to talk about:

  Purpose: *Estudio **para** aprender.* I study in order to learn.

  Destination: *Este regalo es **para** ti.* This gift is for you.

- *Por* is used to talk about:

  Movement: *Caminé **por** el parque.* I walked through the park.

  Duration of time: *Viví en España **por** dos años.* I lived in Spain for two years.

  Means: *Te llamé **por** teléfono.* I called you on the phone.

  Exchange: *Te doy cinco euros **por** el libro.* I'll give you five euros for the book.

  Cause: *Lo hice por amor.* I did it out of love.

> **REMEMBER**
>
> To thank someone for something, you must use *por*:
>
> *Gracias **por** tu ayuda.* Thanks for your help.

Using *sin*

- *Sin* means 'without'.

  *Salió **sin** decir adiós.* He left without saying goodbye.

Knowledge 159

Retrieval

GRAMMAR

Answer the questions below. Cover the answers column with a piece of paper and write down as many answers as you can. Check and repeat.

#	Questions	Answers
1	Make this sentence negative: *Alguien vive en esa casa.*	*Nadie vive en esa casa*
2	Translate this sentence into English: *Estoy pensando en comprar un coche.*	I am thinking about buying a car
3	What preposition follows the verb *aprender* (to learn)?	*A*
4	Translate this sentence into Spanish: I've never been to Colombia.	*Nunca he estado en Colombia / No he estado nunca en Colombia*
5	Translate this sentence into English: *¿Te acuerdas de mi nombre?*	Do you remember my name?
6	When is the personal *a* used in Spanish?	It is used before a direct object referring to a person
7	Translate this sentence into Spanish: I see my friend.	*Veo a mi amigo/a*
8	What preposition follows the verb *depender*?	*De*
9	Rewrite the sentence in order: *Raúl / nunca / no / lee*	*Raúl no lee nunca*
10	Choose the correct word to complete the sentence: *Necesito una maleta nueva por / de / para mis vacaciones.*	*Necesito una maleta nueva <u>para</u> mis vacaciones*
11	Fill in the gaps with either *por* or *para* to complete the sentence: *Gracias ____ tu ayuda.*	*Gracias <u>por</u> tu ayuda*
12	Translate this sentence into English: *Mi hermano no quiere hacer nada mañana.*	My brother doesn't want to do anything tomorrow

Previous questions

Use the questions below to check your knowledge from previous chapters.

#	Questions	Answers
1	What is the opposite of each of these two prepositions? *lejos / delante*	*Cerca* (near to); *detrás* (behind)
2	How do you say in Spanish: owner?	*Dueño*
3	What is the difference in meaning between *parecer* and *parecerse*?	*Parecer* = to seem, *parecerse* = to look like

Knowledge  GRAMMAR

Word formation

Recognising suffixes

You are expected to be able to recognise how certain suffixes can change the meaning of core vocabulary from AQA's set word list. These grammar rules are only required for the reading exam.

Adding -ito, -ita

- The suffix -ito or -ta can be added to a Spanish noun after removing the final -o/-a. Doing this changes the meaning of a word to 'little'. It can also imply endearment.
    - *regalo* (present) → *regal**ito*** (a little present)
    - *abuela* (grandmother) → *abuel**ita*** (dear granny)

Adding -ísimo, -ísima

- The suffix -ísimo or -ísima can be added to a Spanish adjective after removing the final -o/-a. Doing this intensifies its meaning by adding 'very' or 'extremely':
    - *raro* (strange) → *rar**ísimo*** (very strange)
    - *guapa* (pretty) → *guap**ísima*** (very pretty)

Adding -mente

- An adverb can be created by adding -mente to an adjective in the singular feminine form. The English equivalent of this suffix is '-ly'.
    - *alegre* (cheerful) → *alegre**mente*** (cheerfully)
    - *perfecta* (perfect) → *perfecta**mente*** (perfectly)

Adding -idad

- A noun can be created by adding -idad to an adjective stem. The English equivalent of this suffix is '-(i)ty'.
    - *activo* (active) → *activ**idad*** (activity)
    - *común* (common) → *comun**idad*** (community)

Adding -able

- An adjective can be created by adding -able to a verb stem. The English equivalent of this suffix is '-able'.
    - *agradar* (to please) → *agrad**able*** (pleasant)
    - *evitar* (to avoid) → *evit**able*** (avoidable)

> **REMEMBER**
>
> The first *i* in this suffix always has a written accent (tilde). If an adjective has an accent mark, it loses it:
> *fácil* (easy) ⊠ *facilísimo* (very easy)

> **EXAM TIP**
>
> Remember, you only need to be able to work out the meanings of words using these suffixes in the reading paper. They won't be required in any other paper.

Knowledge EXAM

Paper 1 Listening

What to expect in the Listening exam

This exam knowledge section will help you understand the structure of the Listening exam and how to tackle some of the types of questions that may come up.

Try covering up the tips and having a go at the tasks before checking the answers in the transcripts.

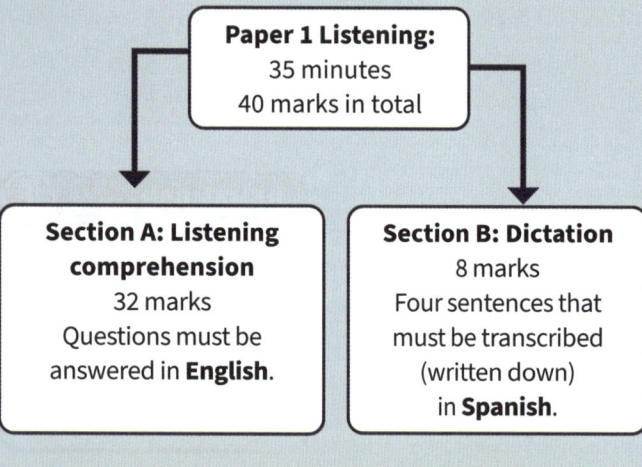

Paper 1 Listening	Timings	Marks
Reading through the paper	5 minutes	–
Section A: Listening comprehension	33 minutes	32
Section B: Dictation		8
Checking your answers	2 minutes	–

EXAM TIP

Use the 5 minutes' reading time at the start to read through **Section A** to familiarise yourself with the topics, instructions and question types.

Section A: Listening comprehension

In Section A:
- You might hear a range of audio items, such as a conversation, an interview, an advert, a news story or a podcast.
- Most of the questions will be multiple choice – you might have to write the correct letter or letters from the answer options provided.
- Some of the questions will require you to complete sentences or answer questions in English to show your understanding.
- Each item will be heard **twice**, with pauses built in for you to read and then answer each question. There will be a bleep before each question starts.

EXAM TIP

You can make notes at any time, for example, jotting down any key words in Spanish that you might expect to hear in a particular question.

Sample listening comprehension questions

Listen to this example of a multiple-choice question.

Plans for the weekend

Listen to two friends talking about their weekend plans.

What is their opinion on the following activities?

Write **P** for a positive opinion.

    N for a negative opinion.

    P + N for a positive and negative opinion.

1	Going cycling		[1 mark]
2	Attending a concert		[1 mark]
3	Playing football		[1 mark]
4	Painting		[1 mark]

EXAM TIP

Write your answers neatly in the boxes provided. Do not leave any answers blank. If you are not sure of the answer, make an intelligent guess.

Here is a copy of the transcript for this question:

1. Mis padres dicen que montar en bicicleta no es una buena idea porque las carreteras en mi pueblo son peligrosas. Yo no estoy de acuerdo con ellos. ¡Es un deporte genial!

2. Mi primo me ha invitado mañana a un concierto de música al aire libre. No iré. Voy a quedarme en casa porque mañana va a llover todo el día.

3. No me importa si nuestro equipo de fútbol pierde el partido. Siempre lo paso bien jugando al fútbol con mis amigos los fines de semana.

4. Normalmente me encanta pintar paisajes porque es relajante, aunque a veces cuando intento pintar algo difícil, me pone de muy mal humor.

Don't assume that a 'not' statement means the opinion is negative. Here, it is only the parents who are expressing the negative opinion.

Watch out – *quedarme en casa* means 'to stay at home'.

The word *siempre* (always) suggests that the statement that follows will provide the answer.

The word *aunque* (although / even though) is a clue that this answer contains both positive and negative statements.

EXAM TIP

There will be a mixture of low, medium and high demand questions appearing at different points throughout the paper so don't panic if you get stuck on one question as the next one might be easier.

Knowledge 163

Knowledge EXAM

Paper 1 Listening

Sample listening comprehension questions

Listen to this example comprehension question – there are **two** questions about this extract rather than separate audio items for each.

> **A podcast**
>
> You hear this podcast from María, a young Spanish actress. Answer the questions in English. **Answer both parts of question 5**.
>
> 5.1 How did María become so successful? [1 mark]
>
> ....
>
> 5.2 What does she like about being famous? [1 mark]
>
> ....

The marks for each question are shown in brackets. There is one mark for each piece of information required. You don't need to write full sentences to get the mark, but make sure you provide all the relevant detail.

Here is a copy of the transcript for this question:

> La gente dice que he tenido éxito porque soy hija de un director de cine, pero en realidad, esto está lejos de la verdad. He tenido que trabajar muy duro para ganar tantos premios.
>
> La verdad es que es difícil ser famosa, pero me gusta poder apoyar a las organizaciones que están a favor de los derechos de los animales.

Listen to the **whole** of the first section carefully. The answer to the first question is near the end of this section. Ignore the first item mentioned that is **not** a reason for her fame (her film director father).

The clue here is the phrase 'I like to …' The key information (supporting animal rights' organisations) follows this.

EXAM TIP

Once you have had a go at a practice listening task, look at the transcript and translate anything you missed. You can use an online dictionary or translation tool to help you.

Section B

In Section B:

- You will hear four short sentences dictated to you and you must write them down in Spanish.
- The sentences are marked as a whole – there are four marks for communication and four marks for accuracy.
- You will hear each sentence three times: first as a full sentence, then in short sections and finally as a full sentence again.

> **REVISION TIP**
>
> Cover the transcript at the bottom of this page and try doing the sample dictation task before checking the answers.

Sample dictation sentences

Listen to these example dictation sentences. In the answer booklet, you will have two blank lines to write each sentence.

> Listen carefully and using your knowledge of **Spanish** sounds, write down in Spanish exactly what you hear for each sentence.
>
> You will hear each sentence **three** times: the first time as a full sentence, the second time in short sections and the third time again as a full sentence.
>
> Use your knowledge of Spanish sounds and grammar to make sure that what you have written makes sense. Check carefully that your spelling is accurate.
>
> **[8 marks]**

Sentence 1	Voy / a casa / ahora.
Sentence 2	Quiero / trabajar / de médico.
Sentence 3	Llevo / una dieta **saludable**.
Sentence 4	Tengo que pagar / la **factura** / de la luz.

← The sentences will gradually increase in difficulty.

← There will always be two words that are not on AQA's set vocabulary list that will be unfamiliar to you. You will need to use your knowledge of Spanish sounds and grammar to write what you hear.

> **EXAM TIP**
>
> Use the two minutes' checking time at the end of the paper to make sure that what you have written makes sense, is grammatically accurate and is spelled correctly.

Knowledge **165**

Retrieval  EXAM

Answer the questions below. Cover the answers column with a piece of paper and write down as many answers as you can. Check and repeat.

Questions | Answers

#	Question	Answer
1	What is the difference between the types of question in Section A and Section B for Paper 1: Listening?	Section A contains comprehension questions and Section B is the dictation task
2	How many marks are there for Section A of Paper 1: Listening?	32 marks
3	How many marks are there for Section B of Paper 1: Listening?	8 marks
4	How long do you have to read through the Listening paper before the test begins?	5 minutes
5	How many times will you hear each item in Section A of Paper 1: Listening?	Twice
6	How many times will you hear each dictation sentence in Section B of Paper 1: Listening?	Three times
7	Does the Listening paper only contain vocabulary from AQA's set vocabulary list?	No – there will be two words in Section B that are not on the set vocabulary list
8	Are you allowed to make notes during the Listening paper?	Yes – you can make notes at any time
9	How will you know that the next question in the Listening paper is about to start?	You will hear a bleep
10	What should you do if you are unsure of an answer in the Listening paper?	Make an intelligent guess – do not leave any blank answers
11	What would be a good way to use the two minutes' checking time at the end of the Listening paper?	To check the grammar, spelling and sense of the sentences in Section B

Previous questions

Use the questions below to check your knowledge from previous chapters.

Questions | Answers

#	Question	Answer
1	Choose the correct word to complete the sentence. *Tengo / He / Soy usado mi móvil esta mañana.*	*He usado mi móvil esta mañana*
2	Name at least four body parts in Spanish.	Possible answers include: *la cabeza, el corazón, el diente, la mano, el ojo, el pie*
3	What is the plural form of *feliz* (happy)?	*Felices*

Practice EXAM

Paper 1 Listening

Section A: Listening comprehension

Careers advice

You listen to two students talking about their school. Write the correct letter in each box.

1. What does Marta say about her maths teacher?

A	He is very strict in class.
B	He explains things carefully.
C	He has always been Marta's maths teacher.

   [1 mark]

2. What does Luis say about the food in his new school?

A	He likes the fruit most.
B	It is better than the food in his old school.
C	It is quite expensive.

   [1 mark]

Celebrity news

Listen to this news report. What is reported?

Write the correct letter in each box.

Answer both parts of question 3.

3.1 What has been reported about the singer Sofía Reyes? [1 mark]

A	Her concert this Saturday has sold out.
B	She has lost her voice.
C	She has announced a world tour.

3.2 What is Sofía's message to her fans? [1 mark]

A	They should arrive early.
B	She is grateful for their loyalty.
C	They should keep hold of their tickets.

Answer both parts of question 4.

4.1 What does a recent study reveal about celebrities? [1 mark]

A	The lack of trust they have of others.
B	The abuse they receive online.
C	The large salaries they earn.

4.2 What does the majority of famous people suffer from? [1 mark]

A	a lack of privacy
B	stress
C	a fear of failure

Practice 167

Practice EXAM

Paper 1 Listening

Environmental actions

Listen to Pablo talking about how he helps the environment.

Answer the questions in **English**.

5. What did Pablo and his friends do last Sunday at the park? [1 mark]

   ....

6. How did Pablo feel afterwards? [1 mark]

   ....

7. What does Pablo feel people should do to improve the environment? [1 mark]

   ....

8. What is Pablo going to do tomorrow? [1 mark]

   ....

Exam timetable

Listen to a teacher give information about three upcoming exams. Which subject is each exam in and on what date will it take place?

Write the correct **number** for the subject.

Write the correct **letter** for the date.

Subject

1	Art
2	Biology
3	English
4	History
5	French
6	Music

Date

A	5 May
B	15 May
C	20 May
D	3 June
E	13 June
F	25 June

	Subject	Date	
9.	☐	☐	[2 marks]
10.	☐	☐	[2 marks]
11.	☐	☐	[2 marks]

New technology

Listen to Marcos talking to his friend about technology.

Complete the sentences in **English**.

Write **one** word in each space.

Answer both parts of question 12.

Example

Today, Esteban is going to buy a new ......computer...... because he needs it for ......homework.......

12.1 His friend wants a .... because he says it is difficult to

.... on his tablet. **[2 marks]**

12.2 They are .... that in the future they are going to work as

.... **[2 marks]**

Section B: Dictation

You will now hear 4 short sentences. Listen carefully and using your knowledge of **Spanish** sounds, write down exactly what you hear for each sentence. **[8 marks]**

Sentence 1

....

....

Sentence 2

....

....

Sentence 3

....

....

Sentence 4

....

....

> **EXAM TIP**
>
> You will hear each sentence **three** times: the first time in full, the second in short sections, and the third time again as a full sentence.

Practice **169**

Knowledge EXAM

Paper 2 Speaking

What to expect in the Speaking exam

This exam knowledge section will help you understand the structure of the Speaking exam and how to tackle each task.

Paper 2 Speaking:
7–9 minutes
(+15 minutes' supervised preparation time) 50 marks in total
All parts of the test must be completed in **Spanish**.
There will be a task from each theme of the specification.

Part 1: Role-play
10 marks
Five prompts for a conversation in Spanish with your teacher.

Part 2: Reading aloud task and four questions
15 marks
40 words to read aloud.
Four questions related to the topic of the text.

Part 3: Photo card task and conversation
25 marks
Talk about the content of two photographs.
Unprepared conversation questions related to any topic within the photo card theme.

Paper 2 Speaking	Timings	Marks
Supervised preparation time	15 minutes	–
Part 1: Role-play	1–1.5 minutes	10
Part 2: Reading aloud task and four questions	2–2.5 minutes	15
Part 3: Photo card task and conversation	1 minute responding to the photos 3–4 minutes unprepared conversation	25

EXAM TIP

During the 15 minutes' supervised preparation time, you will have time to look at the role play card, reading aloud task and photo card. You are allowed to make notes in Spanish on the answer sheet provided by your teacher to refer to during the test.

Part 1 – Role-play

For the role-play:
- The scenario will be a conversation with a friend so remember to use the *tú* form when asking questions.
- The five role-play prompts are in English and will direct you about what to say in Spanish.
- You will need to ask one question. This will be shown with a '?' symbol next to the prompt.
- You only need to give **one** detail for the other prompts, but you must use a full sentence.

REVISION TIP

Cover the role play notes at the bottom of page 171 and record yourself responding to the task before checking the sample answers.

Sample role-play card

Prepare the following role-play task. Then listen to the teacher's prompts and respond.

> You are talking to your Argentinian friend.
> The teacher will play the part of your friend and will speak first.
> You should address your friend as *tú*.
> When you see this -?- you will have to ask a question.
>
> **In order to score full marks, you must include a verb in your response to each task.**
>
> 1. Say what your favourite place in your town is. (Give **one** detail.)
> 2. Give **one** opinion about public transport in your area.
> 3. Mention **one** problem with the environment where you live.
> 4. Say what you do to help the environment. (Give **one** detail.)
> ?5. Ask your friend a question about his/her town.

EXAM TIP

For the role-play task, there are two marks per prompt. Say only what is required for each prompt and no more.

You could start by saying *Mi lugar favorito es el / la…*

A correct answer here only requires an opinion verb *(me gusta mucho, no me gusta nada)*.

The verb *hay* (there is / are) is very useful in role play tasks.

An easy way to ask a question is to say *¿Te gusta…?* or *¿Qué piensas de…?*

Start your answer with a present tense verb and add one thing you do, for example: *Reciclo…*

Sample role-play card notes and script

Here is a sample of some notes that have been written for the role-play task:

> 1. Mi lugar favorito es el parque.
> 2. Es muy rápido.
> 3. Hay mucha basura.
> 4. Reciclo papel.
> 5. ¿Te gusta tu pueblo?

EXAM TIP

Use around five minutes of the supervised preparation time to write down what you want to say for each prompt on the answer sheet provided. Keep it simple and use Spanish you know.

Here is a sample teacher's script for this task:

> Introductory text: Estás hablando con tu amigo/a argentino/a. Yo soy tu amigo/a argentino/a.
>
> 1. ¿Cuál es tu lugar favorito en tu pueblo?
> 2. ¿Qué piensas del transporte público donde vives?
> 3. ¿Hay algún problema con el medio ambiente en tu zona?
> 4. ¿Qué haces para ayudar al medio ambiente?
> 5. Allow the candidate to ask you a question and give an appropriate response, e.g. Sí, es muy bonito.

Scan the QR code to listen to the sample role-play in full.

Knowledge

Knowledge EXAM

Paper 2 Speaking

Part 2 – Reading aloud task and four questions

For the reading aloud task:

- You should read out the sentences in Spanish using your best pronunciation and intonation.
- The sentences will include some of the phonics that are required by the AQA specification.
- Your teacher will then ask you four questions related to the topic of the text. You should answer all four questions as fully as you can.
- There are five marks for the reading aloud task and ten marks for the short conversation afterwards.

LINK

Make sure you can recognise and say all the sounds required for this part of the text. A full list is provided on page 197.

EXAM TIP

Your last attempt at the reading aloud task will be the one that is marked so you can stop and start again if you need to, as long as you don't go over the allotted time for the task.

Sample reading aloud task

Read aloud the following text in Spanish.

> Mi primo lleva una vida muy sana.
>
> Es vegetariano, y evita el azúcar.
>
> Además, corre en el parque tres veces a la semana.
>
> No fuma y duerme ocho horas todos los días.
>
> Creo que tiene poco estrés.

You could write this phonetically as 'beh-he-ta-ri- ah-no'.

A vowel with an accent above it is pronounced with a stronger emphasis than the rest of the word.

EXAM TIP

Use a couple of minutes of the supervised preparation time to read through the text in your head. Notice any words that you find tricky to say and practise them quietly. You could also write them down phonetically on the answer sheet provided.

 Scan the QR code to listen to the sentences being read aloud and practise repeating them to improve your pronunciation.

172 Paper 2 Speaking

Sample four questions

A short conversation follows the reading aloud task. You will not be able to prepare the answers to the questions ahead of time but you could use some of the preparation time to anticipate the kind of questions you might be asked.

> You will then be asked four questions **in Spanish** that relate to the topic of the **Environment and where people live**.
>
> In order to score the highest marks, you must try to **answer all four questions as fully as you can**.

Here is an example of the kind of questions you might anticipate on environment and where people live:

- What is your favourite food?
- Do you have a healthy diet?
- Why is fast food so popular?
- What do you do to keep fit?
- Do you do any sports?
- What causes you stress?
- What is your opinion about drugs?

REVISION TIP

Try recording your answers to these questions in Spanish.

Here are four questions in Spanish that you could be asked:

1. ¿Cuál es tu comida favorita?
2. ¿Tienes una dieta sana?
3. ¿Qué haces para estar en forma?
4. ¿Tienes estrés?

EXAM TIP

An extended response to each question would contain at least **three** bits of information, each with a suitable verb.

An example of a fully developed answer to question 1 would be: *Mi comida favorita es el pescado blanco, porque es muy sano y no tiene grasa.*

Part 3 – Photo card task and conversation

For the photo card task:
- You must talk about the content of two photos for about 1 minute and say at least one thing about each photo.
- After you have described the photos, your teacher will then ask you questions related to any of the topics within the theme of the photo card.
- You should try to develop your answers to the conversation questions during the 3–4 minutes that this part of the test lasts.
- There are five marks for the photo descriptions and twenty marks for the unprepared conversation.

Knowledge

Knowledge

EXAM

Paper 2 Speaking

Sample photo card task

During your preparation time, look at the two photos. You may make as many notes as you wish on an Additional Answer Sheet and use these notes during the test.

Your teacher will ask you to talk about the content of these photos. The recommended time is approximately **one minute**. **You must say at least one thing about each photo**.

After you have spoken about the content of the photos, your teacher will then ask you questions related to **any** of the topics within the theme of **Customs, festivals and celebrations**.

Photo 1

Photo 2

> **EXAM TIP**
>
> The photos in the paper will be black and white but that doesn't mean you can't mention colours in your description if you want to.

> **REVISION TIP**
>
> Have a go at this photo card task before you check the sample description on page 175.

Here is a sample description that a student might make about the photos:

> **En la primera foto hay** un mercado en la calle. **Creo que es** un mercado de Navidad. Hace frío, **sin embargo**, hay un ambiente agradable. **En mi opinión**, los puestos son bonitos y grandes. Hay un castillo. **A la derecha**, hay dos señoras.
>
> En la segunda foto, hay una celebración importante. **Pienso que** es la fiesta de cumpleaños de la chica en el centro de la foto. Tiene el pelo rizado y los ojos marrones. **También veo** a un chico. La fiesta de cumpleaños tiene lugar al aire libre.

> **EXAM TIP**
>
> Learn some standard phrases like the ones in bold here, that you can use or adapt to describe any photo.

After the photo description, you will be asked questions related to any topics within the theme of that card. Spend a minute of your preparation time thinking about what these questions might cover.

Here are some possible question starters:

- *Háblame de…*
- *Describe tu…*
- *¿Prefieres … o …?*
- *¿Qué piensas sobre…?*

> **EXAM TIP**
>
> Listen carefully to each question that you are asked to understand how to respond. You can often adapt the verb in the question to give your answer. For example:
>
> *¿Qué **piensas** sobre…? **Pienso** que es…*

> **EXAM TIP**
>
> To get the best marks, make sure you develop each response, with at least **two** bits of information, including a suitable verb. Use a variety of vocabulary and structures. For example:
>
> *¿Cuál es tu celebración favorita?*
> *Me gusta mucho la Navidad porque es divertida y hay muchos regalos. Además, comemos comida muy rica.*

Knowledge

Retrieval — EXAM

Answer the questions below. Cover the answers column with a piece of paper and write down as many answers as you can. Check and repeat.

Questions | Answers

#	Question	Answer
1	What do the three different parts of the Speaking paper consist of?	Role-play task, reading aloud and short conversation, photo card discussion
2	How long will you have to prepare the exam materials before the Speaking paper starts?	15 minutes' supervised preparation time
3	Which part of the Speaking paper carries the most marks?	The photo card discussion: 25 marks (five marks for the photo descriptions and 20 marks for the unprepared conversation)
4	Is this statement true or false: You should give as much information as possible for each role-play prompt?	False. You should say only what is required for each prompt and no more
5	In which part of the Speaking paper will you have to ask a question?	In the role-play
6	How many questions will you be asked after the reading aloud task?	Four
7	How many photos will you have to talk about during the photo card discussion?	Two
8	Is this statement true or false: You must use a verb in every answer for the Speaking paper?	True. To get the best marks you will need to use full sentences throughout, including suitable verbs
9	What should an extended answer in the Speaking paper include?	Two bits of information, with suitable verbs
10	Can you refer to your notes during the Speaking paper?	Yes. You can look at your notes on the additional answer sheet at any time

Previous questions

Use the questions below to check your knowledge from previous chapters.

Questions | Answers

#	Question	Answer
1	Change the verb in this sentence to the perfect tense: *Mandé un mensaje a mi amigo.*	*He mandado un mensaje a mi amigo*
2	What is the difference between the types of question in Section A and Section B for Paper 1: Listening?	Section A contains comprehension questions and Section B is the dictation task
3	What would be a good way to use the two minutes' checking time at the end of the Listening paper?	To check the grammar, spelling and sense of the sentences in Section B

 # Practice **EXAM**

Paper 2 Speaking

Part 1: Role-play

Prepare the following role-play task. Then listen to the teacher's prompts and respond.

You are talking to your Spanish friend.

The teacher will play the part of your friend and will speak first.

You should address your friend as *tú*.

When you see this - **?** - you will have to ask a question.

> **In order to score full marks, you must include a verb in your response to each task.**
>
> 1. Say what your favourite subject is.
> 2. Say **one** thing about the facilities in your school.
> 3. Describe your school uniform. (Give **one** detail.)
> 4. Say what your ideal job is. (Give **one** detail.)
> ? 5. Ask your friend a question about their school.

Part 2: Reading aloud task

Read aloud the following text in **Spanish**.

> Nuestras clases comienzan a las nueve y diez.
>
> Me gusta la religión porque es interesante.
>
> Algunos ejercicios de matemáticas son difíciles.
>
> A veces en el recreo jugamos al fútbol.
>
> Llevamos uniforme, pero no es muy cómodo.

EXAM TIP

Use the punctuation to add pauses to give you time to think about what you are going to say next.

Then listen and respond to the four questions on the topic of **Education and work**.

In order to score the highest marks, you must try to **answer all four questions as fully as you can**.

Practice 177

Practice EXAM

Paper 2 Speaking

Part 3: Photo card task

- Prepare a description of these two photos. You may make as many notes as you wish and use these notes during the test.
- Then record yourself describing the content of both photos for approximately **one minute**. **You must say at least one thing about each photo**.
- After you have spoken about the content of the photos, you will be asked questions related to **any** of the topics within the theme of **Communication and the world around us**. Listen to and respond to the example questions.

EXAM TIP

Make sure you have enough time to say **at least** one thing about each photo, as you must talk about both.

Photo 1

Photo 2

Paper 3 Reading

What to expect in the Reading exam

This exam knowledge section will help you understand the structure of the Reading exam and how to tackle some of the types of questions that may come up.

Try covering up the tips and having a go at the tasks before checking the answers.

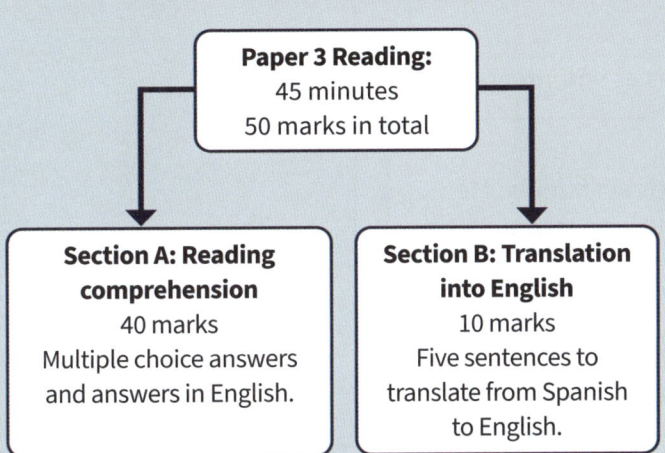

Paper 3 Reading	Timings	Marks
Section A: Reading comprehension	Approximately 34 minutes	40
Section B: Translation into English	Approximately 9 minutes	10
Checking your answers	Approximately 2 minutes	–

EXAM TIP

Leave a few minutes to check your translations and review any comprehension answers you were not sure about. Do not leave any answers blank.

Section A

In Section A:
- You will read a variety of different text types in Spanish, such as adverts, headlines, articles, emails and website content.
- The texts will vary in length, from short sentences up to about 100 words.
- Most of the questions will be multiple choice – you might have to write the correct letter or letters from the answer options provided.
- Some of the questions will require you to answer questions in English to show your understanding.
- There will be a few words that are not on AQA's set vocabulary list that you will need to work out from the context. There might also be some cognates (Spanish words that look very similar to English and that have the same meaning).

Knowledge

EXAM

Paper 3 Reading

Sample reading comprehension questions

Read the sample reading comprehension questions and annotations.

Volunteering abroad

You read this online forum.

Three young people talk about their recent experiences as volunteers.

Aurelio
Viajé a Bolivia donde ayudé en una escuela para niños sin familia. Me gustó mucho y el alojamiento fue gratis. Disfruté de la vida tranquila sin presión.

Beatriz
Pasé varios meses en un pueblo en el sur de Portugal enseñando deportes a los alumnos en un instituto allí. Me molestó el estilo de vida: ¡nadie tenía **prisa*** nunca!

Cristóbal
En Chile trabajé para una organización que ayudaba a las personas sin un lugar para vivir. No me pagaron, pero me encantó. Fue una experiencia única e importante. Estoy seguro de que volveré a hacerlo.

*****prisa** = rush

> If you see an unfamiliar word marked with * in a sentence, it means that the English meaning is provided below the text.

Who mentions the following information?

Write   **A** for Aurelio
       B for Beatriz
       C for Cristóbal

Write the correct letter in each box.

1. Enjoying the relaxed lifestyle.   ☐ [1 mark]
2. Doing it again in the future.   ☐ [1 mark]
3. Helping the homeless.   ☐ [1 mark]
4. Teaching in a school.   ☐ [1 mark]
5. Not paying for accommodation.   ☐ [1 mark]

> Aurelio mentions enjoying a quiet life without pressure. Be careful! Beatriz found the relaxed lifestyle annoying.

> The structure *volver a* + infinitive means 'to do something again.'

> *Sin lugar para vivir* means they are homeless.

> Both Aurelio and Beatriz mention school, but *enseñar* means 'to teach'.

> Aurelio refers to *alojamiento gratis* (free accommodation).

A positive role model

You see an article online by Pilar, a teenager who follows a famous sportsperson.

> La historia del jugador de fútbol Lamine Yamal es muy interesante. Cuando tenía solo 15 años, ==fue el jugador más joven en jugar un partido con el FC Barcelona y poco después el jugador más joven en ganar una copa internacional.== Pienso que Lamine es un buen ==modelo a seguir porque tiene una actitud positiva y estudia mucho.==
>
> Lamine tiene millones de seguidores en las redes sociales. Lamine es tan famoso que cuando anda por la calle, ==necesita a alguien como **guardaespaldas** para protegerlo.==

Pilar mentions that Lamine was the youngest player to play for Barcelona and to win an international trophy.

Look for the expression modelo a seguir. *Lamine has a positive attitude and he studies a lot.*

You need to work out the most likely meaning of guardaespaldas *from the context.* Alguien … para protegerlo *means 'someone … to protect him' so we know the answer is a person (a bodyguard).*

6. What **two** records does Lamine Yamal hold? **[2 marks]**

   ....

   ....

7. According to Pilar, why is Lamine Yamal considered a good role model? Mention **two** reasons. **[2 marks]**

   ....

   ....

8. Read the last sentence again. What is a **guardaespaldas**? **[1 mark]**

   Write the correct letter in the box.

A	a pet animal
B	an item of clothing
C	a person

   ☐

EXAMTIP

Don't panic if you get stuck on a question – make an intelligent guess and move on to the next question, which might be easier.

EXAMTIP

You are not expected to know that *guardaespaldas* means 'bodyguard' as this word is not on AQA's set vocabulary list. This is an example of a question where you have to infer what the noun might mean from context.

Knowledge

Knowledge — EXAM

Paper 3 Reading

Section B: Translation into English

In Section B:
- You will translate five sentences from Spanish to English.
- The sentences will include different tenses and grammatical structures.
- All of the vocabulary will be taken from AQA's set vocabulary list, covering a range of different topics.

EXAM TIP
Each sentence is broken into two parts for marking, with one mark for each clause.

Sample translation into English

Read the sample sentences for translation into English and the annotations. Try translating the sentences before you look at the answers on the next page.

EXAM TIP
Start by identifying the verbs and tenses, then look out for cognates.

Translate these sentences into **English**.

Mi piso **no** es muy cómodo. **[2 marks]**
— Don't forget to include 'not' or 'isn't'.

A veces veo **programas de telerrealidad**. **[2 marks]**
— Make sure you change the word order of *programas de telerrealidad* in English.

El domingo **pasado**, fui a la plaza de toros. **[2 marks]**
— The word *pasado* tells you the sentence is in the past tense.

Quiero aprobar todos mis exámenes este verano. **[2 marks]**
— *Querer* + infinitive means 'to want to do something'.

Mi amigo **va a nadar** en el río. **[2 marks]**
— *Ir a* + infinitive is translated as 'going to do something'.

Sample translation answers

Each sentence is divided into two for marking. Here is an example of how the sentences are divided and the answers that would be accepted.

Spanish	English translation	Alternative translation	Mark
Mi piso	My flat	My apartment	1
no es muy cómodo.	is not very comfortable.		1
A veces veo	Sometimes I watch		1
programas de telerrealidad.	reality TV programmes.	reality shows on TV.	1
El domingo pasado	Last Sunday		1
fui a la plaza de toros.	I went to the bullring.		1
Quiero aprobar	I want to pass		1
todos mis exámenes este verano.	all my exams this summer.	all of my exams this summer.	1
Mi amigo va a	My friend is going to		1
nadar en el río.	swim in the river.	go swimming in the river.	1

EXAM TIP

There is often more than one way to translate a sentence correctly and the mark scheme allows for this.

Retrieval EXAM

Answer the questions below. Cover the answers column with a piece of paper and write down as many answers as you can. Check and repeat.

Questions / Answers

#	Question	Answer
1	What is the difference between the types of question in Section A and Section B for Paper 3: Reading?	Section A contains comprehension questions and Section B is the translation into English
2	How many marks are there for Section A in Paper 3: Reading?	40 marks
3	How many marks are there for Section B in Paper 3: Reading?	10 marks
4	How long does the Reading paper last?	45 minutes
5	What language should you use to write your answers in the Reading paper?	English
6	What is the length of the longest text you will have to read in the Reading paper?	Approximately 100 words
7	Is this statement about the Reading paper true or false: Section A will only contain vocabulary from AQA's set vocabulary list?	False – there will be some words in Section A that are not on the set vocabulary list (cognates and words you have to work out from the context)
8	Is this statement about the Reading paper true or false: there may be more than one possible correct answer for the translation sentences in Section B?	True
9	In the Reading paper, if you see a word marked with* in a text, what does it mean?	It means that the English meaning is provided below the text
10	If you have a few minutes at the end of the Reading paper, what should you do?	Check your answers

Previous questions

Now go back and use these questions to check your knowledge of previous topics.

Questions / Answers

#	Question	Answer
1	How long do you have to read through the Listening paper before the test begin?	5 minutes
2	Complete the sentence with the correct preposition: *Estoy pensando __ hacer mis deberes.*	*Estoy pensando <u>en</u> hacer mis deberes*
3	What is the conditional form of *hay*?	*Habría*

Paper 3 Reading

Section A: Reading comprehension

School facilities

Read what these students say about their school.

Manuel	En el recreo, voy a la biblioteca.
Marina	Las clases de informática son las mejores.
Rubén	Tenemos una piscina. ¡Qué suerte!
Sonia	Me gusta hablar con mis amigas en el patio.

What school facility does each teenager mention?

Write the correct letter in each box.

1. Manuel ☐ **[1 point]**
2. Marina ☐ **[1 point]**
3. Rubén ☐ **[1 point]**
4. Sonia ☐ **[1 point]**

A	Art studio
B	ICT rooms
C	Library
D	Theatre
E	Swimming pool
F	Playground

Holidays. What does Gloria say about her holidays?

Write   **P** for something she did **in the past**
        N for something she is doing **now**
        F for something she will be doing **in the future**

Write the correct letter in each box.

Me encanta viajar. Cuando era joven, me gustaba mucho ir a la costa con mi familia. Hacía sol todos los días y pasamos mucho tiempo en la playa jugando. El próximo noviembre, voy a ir a una casa en la montaña. ¡Será muy diferente!

Ahora, estoy de vacaciones en una ciudad histórica. Me encanta sacar fotos de los monumentos aquí, y la comida es deliciosa. La semana que viene, voy a hacer una excursión en barco para ver la ciudad desde el agua. ¡Va a ser estupendo!

En el pasado no me interesaba la idea de montar una tienda en el campo, pero el próximo año lo haré por primera vez con algunos amigos.

EXAM TIP

Look carefully at the time phrases and tenses in the text.

5. A beach holiday   ☐ **[1 mark]**
6. A mountain retreat   ☐ **[1 mark]**
7. A city break   ☐ **[1 mark]**
8. A boat trip   ☐ **[1 mark]**
9. A camping holiday   ☐ **[1 mark]**

Practice EXAM

Paper 3 Reading

Newspaper headlines. You read some headlines in a Spanish newspaper.

A	Los jóvenes pasan demasiado tiempo con el móvil, según un estudio.
B	Una nueva biblioteca abre en el centro del pueblo.
C	El equipo nacional español espera ganar otra copa.
D	Las tiendas bajan los precios después de Navidad.
E	Los colegios prohíben el uso de plástico en la cantina.

EXAM TIP
Try reading the questions **before** you read the Spanish headlines so you know exactly what you are looking for.

Which headline matches each description?

Write the correct letter in each box.

10. News about a sports team. ☐ [1 mark]

11. News about the January sales. ☐ [1 mark]

12. News about a new facility opening in town. ☐ [1 mark]

Online life

Read this article about technology.

> Los ordenadores no son tan populares como antes. Ahora la gente prefiere usar sus móviles aun para trabajar.
>
> Las redes sociales juegan un papel importante en la vida, pero también presentan muchos riesgos en nuestra sociedad. Sabemos que muchos jóvenes comparten demasiados detalles personales online.
>
> Sin embargo, gracias a Internet, es fácil encontrar información y aprender cosas nuevas. Mucha gente ya usa un **altavoz** inteligente que te da información útil.

Using the information from the text, complete the sentences in English.
Write **one** word in each space.

Example: Computers are not as ......*popular*...... as before.

13. People now prefer using their .... even for work. **[1 mark]**

14. Social media pose many .... in our society. **[1 mark]**

15. Many young people share too many personal .... online. **[1 mark]**

16. The internet makes it easy to look for information and .... new things. **[1 mark]**

17. Read the last sentence again. What is an **altavoz**? Write the correct letter in the box.

A	Something you type on
B	Something you listen to
C	Something you wear

☐ **[1 mark]**

Free time

Three young people are chatting online about their hobbies and free time.

> **Carlos**
> Siempre he sido muy activo. Juego al fútbol en un equipo local los fines de semana. Dejé de jugar al baloncesto, pero ahora monto en bici con mis amigos.
>
> **Lucía**
> En mi tiempo libre prefiero actividades más tranquilas. Puedo pasar horas con un buen libro, pero cuando quiero hacer ejercicio, siempre doy un paseo.
>
> **Raúl**
> El arte me interesa mucho. Me encanta pintar en mi dormitorio. Prefiero hacerlo por la noche así que voy a la cama tarde.

Answer the following questions in **English**.

18. What sport does Carlos no longer do?

.... **[1 mark]**

19. What does Lucía do when she wants to exercise?

.... **[1 mark]**

20. What two things does Raúl do in the evenings?

.... **[2 marks]**

Section B: Translation into English

21. Translate these sentences into **English**.

El cambio climático es un problema muy grave.

....

.... **[2 marks]**

Mi hermana es muy simpática, aunque a veces discutimos.

....

.... **[2 marks]**

Voy a ver una entrevista con mi actriz alemana favorita.

....

.... **[2 marks]**

No me llevo bien con mis primos. Nunca me apoyan.

....

.... **[2 marks]**

El año pasado lo pasé genial cuando visité esa isla española.

....

.... **[2 marks]**

Knowledge  EXAM

Paper 4 Writing

What to expect in the Writing exam

This exam knowledge section will help you understand the structure of the Writing exam and how to tackle each task.

Have a go at each task before checking the sample answers.

Paper 4 Writing:
1 hour 10 minutes
50 marks in total
Questions must be answered in **Spanish.**

↓

Section A
Question 1: Photo description
10 marks
Write five sentences to describe a photo
Question 2: 50-word answer
10 marks
Write approximately 50 words in Spanish
Question 3: Grammar gap-fill
5 marks
Five gapped sentences with a choice of three missing words each
Question 4: Translation into Spanish
10 marks
Five sentences to translate from English to Spanish

↓

Section B
Question 5: 90-word answer
15 marks
Answer **one** of the two question options
Write approximately 90 words in Spanish

Paper 4	Timings	Marks
Section A: Questions 1-4	Approximately 45 minutes	35
Section B: 90-word answer	Approximately 20 minutes	15
Checking your answers	5 minutes	–

EXAM TIP

Remember you only need to write **one** answer for Section B. Take a minute to read the two question options for each section carefully to choose the topic you feel most confident to write about.

Section A

Question 1:

- You must only describe what is in the photo, using five short sentences.
- You can repeat structures more than once. For example *hay* with different nouns.
- Use a suitable verb in each sentence. You are allowed to use verbs in the 'I' or 'we' forms.
- You can also use *aquí está / allí está* with nouns to avoid using a verb.

EXAM TIP

Each sentence is marked individually and is worth 2 marks for a clearly communicated message.

LINK

To practise written photo descriptions, go to pages 55, 114 and 194.

188 Paper 4 Writing

Question 2:
- You must write something about each of the five bullet point prompts.
- You should write about 50 words.
- There are 5 marks for communication and 5 marks for variety of language and accuracy.
- You could get full marks using only the present tense.

Question 3:
- You must complete five sentences by writing the correct word in each gap.
- There will be a choice of three words to complete each gapped sentence.
- You must use your knowledge of grammar to choose the correct answer.
- The words you write in the gap must be totally correct, including any accents.

Question 4:
- You will translate five sentences from English to Spanish.
- The sentences will include different tenses and grammatical structures.
- All of the vocabulary will be taken from AQA's set vocabulary list, covering a range of different topics.

EXAM TIP

All five translation sentences will be marked as one set, with five marks for getting the meaning across and five marks for vocabulary knowledge and grammatical accuracy overall.

EXAM TIP

You don't need to write the same amount on each bullet point.

LINK

To practise 50-word tasks, go to pages 79 and 194.

EXAM TIP

Make sure you copy the word you choose correctly, avoiding spelling mistakes.

LINK

To practise grammar gap-fills, go to pages 55, 79, 114 and 195.

Knowledge  EXAM

Paper 4 Writing

Sample translation into Spanish

Read the sample sentences for translation into Spanish and the annotations.

Cover the bottom half of this page and try translating the sentences before you check the sample answers.

EXAM TIP
Think about translating chunks of language or phrases in context rather than individual words.

Translate the following sentences into **Spanish**.
[10 marks]

- **I play tennis** every day.
- **I like** wearing my uniform.
- I prefer to eat **healthy food**.
- Yesterday, **I visited** the library.
- **They must improve** public transport in the city.

- Remember to include *al* (*juego al tenis*).
- Use the structure *gustar* + infinitive.
- Use the modal verb *deber* here, followed by an infinitive.
- Remember Spanish word order (*comida sana*).
- This requires the verb *visitar* in the past tense.

Sample translation answers

Here are possible translations for each of the sentences:

Juego al tenis todos los días.
Me gusta llevar mi uniforme.
Prefiero comer comida sana.
Ayer, visité la biblioteca.
Deben mejorar el transporte público en la ciudad.

EXAM TIP
There is often more than one correct way to translate something into Spanish.

Five marks are awarded for getting the meaning across. The mark scheme for this is applied by breaking the sentences down into fifteen elements (around three for each sentence) and awarding a tick for each. If you get 13–15 ticks, you are awarded the full five marks.

A further five marks are awarded for knowledge of vocabulary and grammar. This mark is based on all five sentences as a whole. Your vocabulary and grammar don't have to be perfect to be awarded the full five marks, but there should only be minor errors.

Section B

In Section B:

- You will have a choice of tasks and should answer **either** question 5.1 **or** question 5.2.
- You must write something about each of the three bullet point prompts in your chosen task.
- You will need to use verbs in different time frames and give opinions.
- You should aim to write about 90 words.
- There are 10 marks for communication and development of ideas.
- There are 5 marks for variety of language and grammatical complexity.

EXAM TIP

You don't need to spend time in the exam counting every word you write as everything you write will be marked. Aim to answer the question fully, to the best of your ability, in the time you have allocated to Section B.

Sample 90-word task

You are writing an article about holidays and travel.

Write approximately 90 words in Spanish.

You must write something about each bullet point.

> Mention:
> - your favourite place to visit
> - what activities you did during your last holidays
> - where you are going to go next year. **[15 marks]**

EXAM TIP

Answer each bullet point separately, in the order they appear. Use different vocabulary for each point, to avoid repeating yourself.

REVISION TIP

Try writing your own response to this task before looking at the sample answer on the next page.

Knowledge 191

Knowledge — EXAM

Paper 4 Writing

Sample 90-word answer

Read the sample answer to the 90-word task and the annotations on it. This answer would score the full 15 marks.

EXAM TIP

You don't have to just use Spanish words that are on AQA's set vocabulary list for your answer, but make sure your writing is as accurate as possible.

- This answer uses a fine range of nouns, adjectives and verbs in the present tense.
- As you're writing about your last holidays, start it with a past time expression (*el año pasado...*)

> Me encanta ir de vacaciones a Cornwall. Me gusta mucho el ambiente tranquilo allí. Es una oportunidad para descansar y descubrir lugares nuevos. Ir al extranjero es divertido, sin embargo **disfruto visitando ciudades en mi país**.
> **El año pasado** **fui** a Italia con mi familia. **Visitamos** Roma, donde **vimos** monumentos increíbles y **comimos** comida deliciosa. Además, **compré** ropa y **saqué** muchas fotos.
> El próximo año quiero ir a Grecia. Me interesa mucho la historia, así que visitaré Atenas y sus templos. También **me gustaría** probar la comida griega y tomar el sol en la playa.

- Using *disfrutar* (to enjoy) is an impressive way to share an opinion.
- Make sure your past tense verbs are accurate or you cannot be credited for this bullet point.
- *Me gustaría* (I would like) is a relatively simple way of including a future tense expression and an opinion at the same time.

Here is a translation of the answer:

> I love going on holiday to Cornwall. I really like the peaceful atmosphere there. It's an opportunity to relax and discover new places. Going abroad is fun; however, I enjoy visiting cities in my own country.
>
> Last year, I went to Italy with my family. We visited Rome, where we saw incredible monuments and ate delicious food. Additionally, I bought clothes and took lots of photos.
>
> Next year, I want to go to Greece. I'm very interested in history, so I will visit Athens and its temples. I would also like to try Greek food and sunbathe on the beach.

Retrieval — EXAM

Answer the questions below. Cover the answers column with a piece of paper and write down as many answers as you can. Check and repeat.

Questions / Answers

#	Questions	Answers
1	What four types of question appear in Section A of the Writing paper?	Photo description, 50-word answer, grammar gap-fill and translation into French
2	What does Section B of the Writing paper consist of?	A 90-word answer
3	Do you have to answer every question in the Writing paper?	No – there is a choice of two question options for sections B
4	How long does the Writing paper last?	1 hour 10 minutes
5	Is this statement true or false: There is only one correct way to translate the sentences in question 4 of the Writing paper?	False – there may be more than one way to correctly translate certain words or phrases
6	How many bullet point prompts will there be for the 50-word task?	Five
7	How many bullet point prompts will there be for the 90-word task?	Three
8	Is this statement true or false: You can get full marks without responding to all the bullet points in the Writing paper?	False
9	Will you lose marks for writing fewer words or more words than recommended in the Writing paper?	No. However, very short answers may not contain enough content and over-long answers may contain more mistakes
10	How many time frames are required in the 90-word task?	Three (past, present and future)

Previous questions

Now go back and use these questions to check your knowledge of previous topics.

#	Questions	Answers
1	If *tranquilo* means 'calm', how do you say 'calmly' in Spanish?	*Tranquilamente*
2	How long will you have to prepare the exam materials before the Speaking paper starts?	15 minutes' supervised preparation time
3	What language should you use to write your answers in the Reading paper?	English

Practice EXAM

Paper 4 Writing

Section A

1. You send this photo on WhatsApp to a friend in Chile.

What is in this photo?

Write **five** sentences in **Spanish**.

1.1 .... [2 marks]

1.2 .... [2 marks]

1.3 .... [2 marks]

1.4 .... [2 marks]

1.5 .... [2 marks]

2. Your Spanish friend wants to know about where you live.

Write approximately **50** words in **Spanish**.

You must write something about each bullet point.

Mention:

- location
- things to do there
- your favourite place
- your house
- your room

[10 marks]

EXAM TIP

Your sentences must refer to what you can see on the photo, **not** about what you can't see. For example, you can say 'There is a teacher' (*Hay un profesor*) but you can't say 'There isn't a dog' (*No hay un perro*).

EXAM TIP

Each sentence is marked separately and is worth two points. You must include a verb, but you do not have to use a different verb for each sentence.

REVISION TIP

The number of words is approximate. You can write a bit more to get your point across.

REVISION TIP

All bullet points must be mentioned, but you can write and develop a few more than the others. Different tenses are not needed on this task, but you can use them.

3. Using your knowledge of grammar, complete the following sentences in **Spanish**.

Choose the correct Spanish word from the three options in the grid.

Write the correct **word** in the space, as shown in the example below.

Example:

Nosotros .... *vamos* .... a la playa todos los veranos.

| vamos | voy | van |

REVISION TIP

This activity tests your knowledge of grammar. That is, verb endings, question words, adjective endings, etc. Make sure you revise your grammar ahead of your exams.

3.1 La película es muy ....

| interesante | interés | interesar |

[1 mark]

3.2 Mi hermano .... en casa hoy.

| está | hay | es |

[1 mark]

3.3 Llevo un pantalón .... a la fiesta.

| verdes | negra | azul |

[1 mark]

3.4 ¿............................... te gusta más, el té o el café?

| Dónde | Cuál | Cómo |

[1 mark]

3.5 Tengo .... estudiar para el examen.

| de | a | que |

[1 mark]

Practice
EXAM

Paper 4 Writing

4. Translate the following sentences into **Spanish**. **[10 marks]**

I have two sisters and a brother.

....

....

I don't like red meat.

....

....

She always speaks French in class.

....

....

I am going to be a lawyer in the future.

....

....

Yesterday, I bought presents for my father's birthday.

....

....

EXAM TIP

Your translations don't have to be perfect to gain full marks. Minor spelling mistakes or missing accents won't cost you points as long as the message is conveyed… but several minor errors will cost you points, so be as accurate as you can.

Section B

Answer **either** Question 5.1 **or** Question 5.2.
You must only answer **one** of these questions.

Either

Question 5.1

You are writing an article about free time. Write approximately **90** words in **Spanish**.
You must write something about each bullet point.

Describe:

- your favourite celebrity
- what you did online last week
- what you will do to relax this weekend. **[15 marks]**

EXAM TIP

Spend a few minutes planning your answer, noting down some ideas in Spanish before you start writing.

Or

Question 5.2

You are writing a blog post for the school website about daily routines.
Write approximately **90** words in **Spanish**.
You must write something about each bullet point.

Describe:

- how you spend time with your family
- what you did last week to keep fit
- how you are going to improve your diet. **[15 marks]**

Knowledge

Sound-spelling links

Here is a list of the sound-spelling links included within the specification. You need to learn these to be able to complete the dictation task (Paper 1: Listening) and the reading aloud task (Paper 2: Speaking).

Scan the QR code to listen to and practise the example words provided for each sound.

Sound	Examples
a	canta, la casa
o	come, bocadillo, raro
e	escribe, perro, es
i	invita, primo, isla
u	cumpleaños, concurso, nunca
ll	lluvia, calle, ella
ch	mucho, chico, fecha
ca	caramelo, campo, música
co	coche, comenzar, costar
cu	escuchar, cultura, discutir
cu + vowel	cuando, cuerpo, cuidado
ce	cerrado, cena, parecerse
ci	cien, ciudad, principio
z	zapato, hizo, azúcar
que	que, quería, porque
qui	quiere, aquí, equipo

Sound	Examples
ga	gato, negativo, llegar
go	gordo, juego, negocio
gu	guapo, gustar, alguno
ge	gente, genial, imagen
gi	gimnasio, página, colegio
gue	hamburguesa, jugué, pagué
gui	seguidor, alguien, guitarra
j	jamón, junio, jugar
ñ	niña, mañana, otoño
v	uva, vende, vivir
-r- -r	parque, árbol, tarde por, señor, autor
rr r- -r- (after n or l)	perro, barrio, correo recoger, riesgo, ruido sonrisa
silent h	hablas, ahora, prohibir

Notes

Notes

Great Clarendon Street, Oxford, OX2 6DP, United Kingdom

Oxford University Press is a department of the University of Oxford.
It furthers the University's objective of excellence in research, scholarship,
and education by publishing worldwide. Oxford is a registered trade mark
of Oxford University Press in the UK and in certain other countries.

© Oxford University Press 2025

Written by José Antonio García Sánchez and Tony Weston
The moral rights of the authors have been asserted

First published in 2025

All rights reserved. No part of this publication may be reproduced, stored
in a retrieval system, transmitted, used for text and data mining, or used
for training artificial intelligence, in any form or by any means, without
the prior permission in writing of Oxford University Press, or as expressly
permitted by law, by licence or under terms agreed with the appropriate
reprographics rights organization. Enquiries concerning reproduction
outside the scope of the above should be sent to the Rights Department,
Oxford University Press, at the address above.

You must not circulate this work in any other form and you must impose
this same condition on any acquirer

British Library Cataloguing in Publication Data
Data available

978-1-382-07025-6
978-1-382-07024-9 (eBook)

10 9 8 7 6 5 4 3 2 1

The manufacturing process conforms to the environmental regulations
of the country of origin.

Printed in the UK by Bell & Bain

The manufacturer's authorised representative in the EU for product
safety is Oxford University Press España S.A. of El Parque Empresarial
San Fernando de Henares, Avenida de Castilla, 2 – 28830 Madrid
(www.oup.es/en or product.safety@oup.com). OUP España S.A. also
acts as importer into Spain of produ cts made by the manufacturer.

Acknowledgements

The publisher would like to thank Sheena Newland and Eve Hedley for
sharing their expertise and feedback in the development of this resource.

The publisher and authors would like to thank the following for
permission to use photographs and other copyright material:

Photos: **p41(l)**: Rido / Shutterstock; **p41(r)**: wavebreakmedia /
Shutterstock; **p52(t)**: Stockbroker / MBI / Alamy Stock Photo; **p52(b)**:
Visuals Stock / Alamy Stock Photo; p55: Giuseppe Lombardo / Alamy
Stock Photo; **p76(t)**: DCPhoto / Alamy Stock Photo; **p76(b)**: Jozef Polc
/ Alamy Stock Photo; **p111(t)**: Gordon Scammell / Alamy Stock Photo;
p111(b): Anatoliy Gleb / Alamy Stock Photo; **p114**: Miljan Zivkovic /
Shutterstock; **p174(t)**: Kumar Sriskandan / Alamy Stock Photo; **p174(b)**:
Tony Tallec / Alamy Stock Photo; **p178(t)**: Goddard on the Go / Alamy
Stock Photo; **p178(b)**: Cum Okolo / Alamy Stock Photo; **p194**: Gregg Vignal
/ Alamy Stock Photo

Artwork by QBS Learning

Every effort has been made to contact copyright holders of material
reproduced in this book. Any omissions will be rectified in subsequent
printings if notice is given to the publisher.

Links to third party websites are provided by Oxford in good faith
and for information only. Oxford disclaims any responsibility for the
materials contained in any third party website referenced in this work.